THE LANDER LEGACY

The Life Story of Rabbi Dr. Bernard Lander

THE LANDER LEGACY

The Life Story of Rabbi Dr. Bernard Lander

Peter Weisz

KTAV Publishing House, Inc.
Jersey City, New Jersey

Cover photo by Gruber Photographers, New York, NY
Cover design by: Weisz Marketing Services, West Palm Beach, FL

Manufactured in the United States of America

Touro College and University System
43 West 23rd Street
New York, NY 10010
(212) 463-0400
www.touro.edu

KTAV Publishing House, Inc.
888 Newark Avenue
Jersey City, NJ 07306
Tel. (201) 963-9524
Fax. (201) 963-0102
www.ktav.com
bernie@ktav.com

Printed in the U.S.A.
First Printing November, 2012

ISBN 978-1-60280-228-5 (hardcover)

Library of Congress Cataloging-in-Publication Data

Weisz, Peter.
   The Lander legacy : the life story of Rabbi Dr. Bernard Lander / Peter Weisz.
      pages. cm
   Includes bibliographical references.
   ISBN 978-1-60280-228-5 (hardcover)
   1. Lander, Bernard. 2. Rabbis--New York (State)--New York--Biography. 3. Touro
College--History. I. Title.
   BM755.L33W45 2013
   296.8ʾ32092--dc23
   [B]
                                                                2012043630

Dedication

This book is lovingly dedicated to the people
who most embody the enduring Lander Legacy:

The children of Sarah and Rabbi Dr. Bernard Lander
(both of blessed memory):

Esther and Martin Greenfield, Hannah Lander, Debra and
Dr. Richard Waxman, Rabbi Doniel and Phyllis Lander and
their children and grandchildren,

as well as

The students, faculty, administration and staff of
Touro College and University System.

Special Thanks
and Acknowledgements

The author wishes to express his deep appreciation to the many individuals and institutions without whose indispensable assistance, this book could not have been produced. A sampling is listed below:

To **Dr. Mark Hasten and the Board of Trustees of Touro College and University System** for their ongoing support and their dedication to sharing Dr. Lander's extraordinary life story with the world.

To **Dr. Alan Kadish** for his numerous contributions.

To **Esther Greenfield, Hannah Lander, Debra Waxman**, and **Rabbi Doniel Lander** for sharing their cherished memories of their beloved father.

To **Dr. Nathan Lander** for his informative input regarding his brother.

To **Dr. Simcha Fishbane** for sharing his loving recollections.

To **Rabbi Moshe Krupka** for his valued guidance.

To **Dean Jerome Miller** of Touro College for his tireless editorial services and eagle-eyed review of my work.

To **Melvin Ness** for his much appreciated assistance.

To **Dr. Michael Shmidman** for his counsel, review and suggestions.

and

To **Max Rosenblum** who, for years, carried out nearly all of the critical research about Dr. Lander's life referenced in this book and without whose efforts this book could certainly not have been written.

Table of Contents

Introduction

In Psalm 15, King David inquires: "O Lord, who shall sojourn in your tent? Who shall dwell on your holy mountain?" He then provides a three-point response: "He who walks blamelessly and does what is right and speaks truth in his heart." There can be no better summation of my brother's life than these three precepts.

Yes, I refer to Rabbi Dr. Dov Berish ben Dovid Lander as my brother even though we were not related by blood. I am blessed with a blood brother, Naftali Hertz Hasten, with whom I enjoyed a business partnership for more than forty years. But Dr. Lander was also my brother—a brother of the heart. It was a relationship forged from our shared commitment to the value of education and its role in the survival and sustenance of the Jewish people.

It was Dr. Lander who invited me to serve on the Touro Board of Directors. After several months of deliberation I responded to his request with these words: נעשה ונשמע "I will do and I will take to heart". I am pleased to say that I have, with G-d's help, been able to fulfill this promise, just as Dr. Lander fulfilled all his promises to me. I left home for my first board meeting bearing the following message from my wife, Anna Ruth: "Tell them, the Kahal, (those assembled) that the Ribbono shel Olam (the almighty) loves Dr. Lander." She was most certainly right about that.

It is from that promise to my brother, Dr. Lander, that the inception of this book was created. The idea was to provide a literary chronicle of this man's extraordinary life. But over the years of research and authorship, something more emerged. What you will find in these pages is the saga of a single-minded, tenacious, passionate, and devout Jew. A man who regarded insurmountable obstacles as insignificant diversions. A man whose mission was at times delayed, but never deterred. I am confident that by reading this book you will be transformed and will come away with a deeper understanding of the book's title, the Lander Legacy.

That legacy may be summed up in a single word: triumph. Triumph over ignorance, triumph over evil, and triumph over those who sought to destroy the Jewish people. I witnessed this with my own eyes when my parents, my brother, and I were forced to flee in the face of the turmoil, brutality, and destruction of the Holocaust. It is no exaggeration to say that it is thanks to righteous individuals like my brother, Bernard Berish Lander, that we are surviving as a thriving people today.

My late mother, Hannah Hasten, ע"ה, who understood much about Jewish life during her 102 years on this earth, would often comment: "You have to remember to be Jewish." This point was also made by Dr. Lander time and again in various contexts. You must consciously remember that you are a Jew. You must remember from where you came. As Jews we submit to the will of the Almighty and embrace his Torah and its way of life. As Jews we are also commanded to care for the society around us. Dr. Lander taught us well to strengthen and perpetuate the Jewish heritage and to take responsibility for humanity.

This book is designed to help the reader recall the events of Dr. Lander's life. It is also intended to sharpen one's focus on the values and traditions that motivated and inspired him. If you knew Dr. Lander personally, I hope you find the accounts in this book to be accurate, enlightening, and edifying. If this book is your first introduction to Dr. Lander, then prepare to meet someone whose story can truly change your life. In either case, you are invited to forward your comments and feedback via email to: landerbook@peterweisz.com.

This book is filled with an abundance of compelling accounts drawn from the life of this singular and unparalleled individual. A man who was my friend, my teacher, my colleague, and my brother. It is my hope that you will be touched by his story in the same profound manner that his life inspired mine and the lives of so many others. In this way my promise to Dr. Lander will indeed be fulfilled. נעשה ונשמע, "We will do and we will take to heart." I am confident that upon reading this incredible saga each of us will be better prepared to contribute to and expand upon the great gift that has been bestowed upon our generation and generations to come. The gift known as the Lander Legacy.

Dr. Mark Hasten, Chairman
Touro College and University System Board of Trustees

Preface

I t was through Dr. Bernard Lander's vision and idealism that Touro College was founded. It will be through the achievements of countless students that his legacy will endure. With dedication to Dr. Lander's noble mission, I am privileged to lead this unique college and university system, and I am honored to reflect on the meaning of his legacy.

Dr. Lander was a man of action and of high achievement even before he founded Touro College. At the pinnacle of a distinguished academic, rabbinic, and government service career, Dr. Lander decided to pursue a grand dream: the founding of a new college. His brilliance, creativity, and energy enabled him to successfully surmount obstacles along the path to the eventual realization of a dream that many considered to be unattainable.

I first met Dr. Lander when I was a child. I recall that he was always planning and dreaming of the future. As Touro expanded, Dr. Lander's dreams came true. Today, the Touro College and University System has more than 19,000 students at 32 locations throughout the New York City metropolitan area, across the country and around the world. They pursue degree programs in a comprehensive and growing spectrum of academic disciplines.

Dr. Lander's founding principles will continue to mold Touro's development. His legacy will inspire Touro's innovation and leadership.

Dr. Lander's legacy not only continues in Touro's myriad successes. It is perpetuated in the lives of his children, in their aspirations, and the remarkable goals they achieve. All of Touro joins them in taking great pride in Dr. Lander's accomplishments.

The second half of the book, focusing on Dr. Lander's establishment of Touro, reveals his invincible determination to actualize his dream. From chapter to chapter, the reader learns how Dr. Lander continued to turn impediments into catalysts for even greater accomplishment. His life is a testament to the power of perseverance and how it can ultimately change the world.

What is to be the legacy of Dr. Bernard Lander? The significance of his life transcends the many schools he founded, including those that bear his name. Perhaps the essence of Dr. Lander's legacy is in his untiring leadership, his character, and his remarkable capacity for turning challenges into opportunities.

As Dr. Lander's achievements continue to be honored, may others find in the multifaceted richness of his life and legacy the inspiration to accomplish their life goals.

Dr. Alan Kadish
President and CEO
Touro College and University System

CHAPTER ONE

David and Goldie

There are three partners in man: The Holy One, blessed
be He, his father, and his mother.
— *Talmud, Kiddushin 30b*

T he great Hasidic sage known as the Kotzker Rebbe *(Rabbi Menachem Mendel Morgensztern)* once cleverly noted that "All that
is thought should not be said, all that is said should not be written, all that is written should not be published, and all that is published
should not be read." While this argument on the virtues of discretion
certainly carries weight, it also implies its own converse. There do, in
fact, exist thoughts that *should* be articulated, words that indeed ought
to be written, and stories that deserve to be told. The saga of Bernard
Lander's parents is unquestionably such a story.

As immigrants, David and Goldie Lander were part of a tradition
that fundamentally defined the American experience. Social historians
have noted that America's strength is in large part due to something
described as the "filter of immigration." With the exception of Native
Americans and most African-Americans, everyone who has ever lived in
the United States has either passed through this filter or descended from
someone who has. There exists in every American's family tree at least
one person who possessed the initiative to immigrate to America, leaving those with less moxie behind. What force drives one of two brothers
to leave his homeland for a better life while the other elects to stay put?
What internal impetus prompts some to flee their country's oppressive
conditions while others elect to hang back and endure—or perhaps try to
change—those conditions? Whatever the reason, or so the theory goes,
the result is that throughout its history, the United States has served as a
powerful magnet for the striver, the dreamer, the entrepreneur.

According to this idealized model, it is the complacent and the less ambitious who are filtered out during the immigration process. As their strong-willed and independent brethren pass through the filter and go on to populate the nation, their work ethic and cherished values are internalized and passed on to each succeeding generation, creating a vast culture of accomplishment. Bernard Lander's parents, along with the many Jews who immigrated to the United States from eastern Europe during the late nineteenth and early twentieth centuries, were prime exemplars of this group.

David Lander was raised in the scenic *shtetl* of Mikulince, situated in the Seret Valley of what is today the Tarnopol district of western Ukraine. Tucked into the crook of the Seret River, Mikulince was typical of the many villages that dotted the main highway between Warsaw and Odessa in the 1880s. The town's 2,500 Jews, along with its roughly 1,500 gentiles, were subjects of the House of Hapsburg, which ruled what became part of the Austro-Hungarian Empire after Poland was partitioned in 1772. By the time of David's birth in 1888, Galicia was the largest, and the most impoverished, province of the realm. Thanks to the European Enlightenment, initiated by Napoleon and that finally reached Eastern Europe in the 1860s, Jews were afforded religious and individual rights and were able to participate in local political organizations.

Jews had actually been living in Mikulince since at least the early 1600s (according to gravestone dates) under alternating periods of repression and tolerance. By the 1880s, all Jewish families, including the Landers, lived in the town's central commercial area while the Christian peasantry worked the fertile black-dirt fields in the surrounding countryside. Political and economic forces that swept across Eastern Europe shortly after David Lander's birth would soon lead to the family's uprooting and to its being set awash amidst the historic wave of immigration that came crashing upon American shores.

Before this exodus, however, the Lander's hometown was a microcosm of the greater Jewish world it inhabited. Like all similar shtetls, Mikulince was buffeted by religious forces from both the east and the west. The rise of grassroots populist Judaism, known as Hasidism, spread by disciples of the Baal Shem Tov, from Lithuania throughout Galicia, resulted in a network of learning and prayer centers throughout the region. Despite the

Austrian regime's efforts to suppress it, Hasidic dynasties that challenged the established rabbinic authority arose and were met by resistance by the more educated adherents of traditional Judaism. This cultural conflict between the *Hasidim* and *Mitnagdim* raged in nearby Tarnopol, occasionally erupting into violence. The Jews of the satellite community of Mikulince were forced to align themselves with one faction or the other.

But a strong wind from the west was also blowing. The Jewish response to modernity known as *Haskalah* was having an impact on the shtetl and upon families such as the Landers. Haskalah urged Jews to set aside their traditional trappings and assimilate into the mainstream, mostly German-speaking, popular culture. This ongoing three-way dynamic among the rabbinic traditional school, the populist Hasidic strain, and the Haskalah modernists, led to an endless series of reactions and counter-reactions that characterized the era. In terms of sheer numbers, it was Hasidism that dominated Galicia, with six out of every seven Jews claiming to be an adherent of one Rebbe or another—hundreds of whom held court in nearby towns and villages where they enjoyed the support of the majority of the local Jewish population. Such was the case in Mikulince at the time David Lander was born. But the internecine squabbling among these prevailing streams of Judaism would soon seem petty and trivial when compared to the clouds of conflict that were now amassing on the horizon.

While the Jews of the region supported themselves as small shop-keepers, selling buttons, shoelaces, grain, fabrics, and even carriages and new-fangled sewing machines, the newly enfranchised Christian population remained mostly on the farm, raising their crops and hauling them to market each week. There, the non-Jews would observe the increasing disparity between their own lives and those of the town's Jewish populace, who were beginning to prosper commercially. In fact, Jews dominated many industries by the late 1800s. They owned flour mills, saw mills, alcohol distilleries, small oil refineries, tanneries, brickyards, and textile plants. Most such enterprises were small, family-operated businesses.

As public education proliferated, Jews began entering the professions. Christians soon came into an increasing level of contact with Jewish professionals working as doctors, lawyers, teachers, and civil servants. The dissonance created by this economic disparity was profound, particularly in light of the church's teachings concerning the fate of Jews who were supposed to be condemned for their rejection (and, in the view of many, the murder) of the messiah. In order to remedy this perceived inequity, non-Jews began organizing themselves into various credit and agricultural unions in an effort to improve their general economic standing. This striving, coupled with rising nationalistic aspirations on the part of Galicia's Polish and Ukrainian populations, stimulated ferocious economic competition. The newly formed trade associations circumvented Jewish businesses and organized widespread anti-Jewish boycotts. One such boycott, announced in 1893 at a Catholic convention in Cracow, remained in place until the outbreak of World War One.

These increasingly powerful trade associations exerted pressure on the Galician authorities to enact legislation that served to cripple Jewish commerce. Political parties arose in the region whose basic platform was an advocacy of anti-Semitic legislation. As it would during the rise of Nazism, such initiatives gathered steam thanks to Europe's centuries-old tradition of anti-Jewish dogma as espoused by the church. Not surprisingly, the fragile economic situation of Galician Jewry worsened rapidly. Life for the Landers soon became unbearable.

Adding to the crushing poverty, brought on by confiscatory taxation and discrimination, Jews also faced increasing exposure to life-long conscription into the Emperor's army as the worldwide military build-up gained momentum. As was the case for many Jews, hopes of a better future were soon vanishing for the Lander family. Along with millions of other Galician Jews, the Landers sought to join their co-religionists fleeing Czarist Russia in their flight across the Atlantic. Between the event that triggered this massive Russian exodus from the "Pale of Settlement"—the assassination of Czar Alexander II in 1881—until the outbreak of war in 1914, fully one third of Eastern European Jewry, fleeing government-sanctioned pogroms and institutionalized poverty, abandoned their homelands and passed through the filter of immigration, landing in America. Nearly one quarter of a million of these, including the Lander family, came from Galicia.

David Lander was not the first member of his family to make the Atlantic crossing. In fact, as David explained to friends at the time, he was going to America to pray at the grave of his father, Nissan. David had a strong appreciation for his family roots. His father had often stressed that

David was descended from the *Noda B'Yehuda*, the respected eighteenth century chief rabbi of Prague, who was among the greatest Jewish spiritual leaders of the age. The great sage, whose real name was Yechezkel ben Yehuda Landau, came from a distinguished family who traced its lineage back to Rashi, the eleventh century French exegete considered among the most learned Torah and Talmud scholars in history. The name Landau was later altered to Lander, presumably to avoid military conscription.

David was only ten years old when his forty-three-year-old father (Bernard's grandfather) left Mikulince for New York City. Like many immigrants, Nissan planned to earn some money and then arrange to transport the rest of his family to America. Sadly, he was in the country for less than a year before falling ill and succumbing to food poisoning, just as the nineteenth century was coming to a close. Seven years later, Nissan's son, David, embarked on a mission to the new world to complete his fallen father's dream of delivering the family to America's shores. David set sail from Rotterdam, arriving at Ellis Island on August 13, 1907, one day after his nineteenth birthday. He was greeted by his sister, Nechama, who had arrived to New York one year earlier.

Like many immigrants, David Lander dreamed of making it rich in the "Goldene Medinah." David initially resided with his uncle, Wolf Wasser, an observant Jew, who lived amidst the crowded immigrant tenements that were emerging across New York City. Other transplanted relatives were not so intent on maintaining the strict lifestyle of Orthodox Judaism. These family members had established new, successful businesses in their adopted homeland and taunted David, labeling him a "green onion" for his refusal to work on Shabbos. Despite this obstacle, David found work in the textile trade and soon had accumulated enough cash to pay for his sister Rosie's passage to America in 1910. Rosie at first moved in with David, who was living in a small cold-water apartment. Eventually he was able to secure the immigration of his mother and two remaining sisters who arrived in 1912, completing the family's transplantation and the fulfillment of his father's dream.

It was not long after, that David Lander met Goldie Teitelbaum.

Bernard Lander's mother, Goldie, was born in 1892 and grew up in Sieniawa. She was the eldest of three daughters born to Dov Berish and Hannah Teitelbaum. The community of Sieniawa was amazingly similar to David Lander's hometown, some 200 miles to the northeast, as it was to the thousands of other shtetls that dotted the Galician heartland. Today Sieniawa sits in southeast Poland, about 120 miles due east of Krakow. Like David Lander's shtetl of Mikulince, Sieniawa at the time Goldie left, contained about 2,500 Jews living in the central district with another 1,500 non-Jews living in the surrounding countryside.

Goldie's stone house was one of the few that boasted electricity. The Teitelbaums were among the town's leading families and claimed descent from one of Hasidism's towering figures: Reb Moshe Teitelbaum, the founder of the Satmar and Sighet Hasidic dynasties. Known as "Yismach Moshe," Teitelbaum served as the Rav of Sieniawa until his 1841 death in Sighet. He was succeeded by Yechezkel Halberstam, dubbed the Shineveh Rebbe, who held that title until his death in 1898. Halberstam's dedication to fighting the forces of Haskalah, in Tarnopol and throughout the region, became the hallmark of his tenure. The Shineveh Rebbe was also a widely respected scholar and sage who attracted a following of thousands of Hasidic disciples. Goldie's parents were evidently among them since the Shineveh Rebbe officiated at their wedding.

It was the Shineveh Rebbe who was responsible for sending the first emissary of this Jewish community to America and thereby set the wheels in motion that would eventually account for Bernard Lander's presence in New York City. Goldie's mother, Hannah, had an older half-brother, Israel Koenigsberg, who set out for New York City in 1888 at the behest of the Shineveh Rebbe. His mission was to solicit financial support for the *Galicianer Kollel*, the organization that raised money to support Torah scholars from Galicia who were studying in Palestine. Possessing an indomitable spirit and an abiding inner passion, Israel Koenigsberg passed through the filter of immigration and soon found success in America. He served for more than forty years as the chairman of *Kollel Chibas Yerushalayim*, a charity that channeled needed funds to Galician scholars in the Holy Land.

Koenigsberg found commercial success as well, emerging as a prosperous meat merchant. He was one of the founders of a yeshiva and a respected Talmud Torah school. Koenigsberg, early on, helped to create the *Shineveh Shtiebel*, which soon became one of the three most important Hasidic synagogues in New York's Orthodox community. It was at this Shineveh Shtiebel, established by her Uncle Israel, that Goldie Teitelbaum would meet her future husband, David Lander.

Of all of Israel Koenigsberg's many accomplishments, the one that had the most profound impact upon the life of Bernard Lander was Israel's fathering of Benjamin, his first child born in America. Ben would go on to become a nationally known leader, founding the Young Israel movement, and serving as Bernard's influential mentor throughout the course of his life.

Like David Lander, Goldie Teitelbaum also lost her father at an early age. During a particularly cold December in 1898, Goldie's father, Dov Berish, attended the funeral of his spiritual leader, the Shineveh Rebbe, who had died at age eighty-four. In accord with hasidic custom, Dov Berish visited the unheated Mikvah (ritual bath) prior to the burial. He caught cold and was soon stricken with pneumonia. He died six weeks later, leaving behind six-year-old Goldie and her two sisters.

Eleven years later, in 1909, Goldie was delighted to open one of the letters she regularly received from her Uncle Israel, now well-established in New York City. Goldie enjoyed corresponding with her wealthy American relative. She would write of life in the shtetl, bringing him up to date on the latest births, deaths, and other community news. His letters back to her were filled with the wonders of the new world. Descriptions of street-cars, subways, and motion pictures were included among Uncle Israel's accounts of Jewish life in the most celebrated city in America. This particular letter held a special announcement. It extended an invitation to Goldie to attend the forthcoming wedding of Israel's son, Ben. Sixteen and quite precocious, Goldie wrote back to her uncle thanking him for the invitation but pointing out that "an invitation without a ticket was meaningless." Israel got the message and sent Goldie a second-class steamer ticket enabling her to attend her cousin Ben's wedding in New York City and thereby making her most cosmopolitan dream come true.

Until his death, Bernard Lander attributed his mother's immigration—not to mention his very own existence—as being the direct result of the blessing that the Shineveh Rebbe bestowed upon Israel Koenigsberg as he was preparing to leave for America more than 120 years ago. In sending him off, the Rebbe instructed the young man: "Dedicate yourself to the needs of the community, and your sojourn in America will be successful. Not just for you, but for those who will follow you."

Not surprisingly, Goldie did not return to Sieniawa after attending cousin Ben's wedding. During the following four years she worked as a saleslady in a predominantly Italian neighborhood and regularly attended Shabbos services behind the *mechitzah* (partition separating the genders) at the Shineveh Shtiebel, founded by her Uncle Israel and located in the back of a tenement building at 122 Ridge Street. It was not long after that she met and fell in love with twenty-five-year-old David Lander, an up-and-coming merchant in the *shmatteh* (clothing) business. Goldie saw in David a European-born Jew who had opted *not* to shed his heritage upon arriving at New York harbor. She admired his level of observance and his dedication to Judaic traditions and principles. Given the many *Amerikan-ishe* Jews she had met since her arrival, David Lander represented a breath of fresh air. Likewise, David was strongly attracted to this pretty young member of a venerated Jewish family.

The couple was married in August 1913 and established a household in David's tiny apartment. Within a few years the Landers had moved up to 13th Street and, soon thereafter, on June 17, 1915, Goldie gave birth to their first child. They named him Bernard after her father, Dov Berish Teitelbaum. The couple opened a fabric store on First Avenue, between 13th and 14th Streets, that was well received by the neighborhood's predominantly Italian residents. David Lander was an introspective man, regarded as decisive with an excellent head for business. Goldie was gregarious and friendly to everyone. Her people skills and her ability to speak some Italian served her well as she carried out her role as the store's sales manager.

The couple had two more children: Hadassah, born in 1917 and Nathan (Nissan), in 1920. By 1925 the family had moved to an elevator building across the street from Stuyvesant High School and a half a block from Stuyvesant Park. Beyond his emergence as a successful businessman, David Lander was active in the Jewish life of his community. He served for many years as the president of the Tifferes Yisrael Synagogue on 13th Street. He also supported the Shineveh Shtiebel as a member of its Chevre group. Sometimes these two worlds would come into conflict. On Shabbos and during Jewish holidays, David would walk with his children to the shtiebel. He made it a point, however, never to walk down First Avenue where the Lander's fabric store was located. A store like Lander's could easily do half a week's business on a Saturday. But because of his religious convictions, David Lander kept his store closed on Shabbos, and he did not wish for his children to witness this lost revenue.

"Shabbos should be filled with joy," was David's position, "and not filled with worry about lost business."

Although the Lander family prospered in America—by the late 1920s they had a sales staff, could afford to spend summers at a Catskill Mountain resort, and were able to pay for the children's yeshiva tuition—they never lost sight of their obligation to help other family members and to do their part in behalf of the community. When hard times hit, David Lander still found the funds to pay for the private yeshiva education of other children in the family. Coupled with their grace and generosity, the Landers were regarded as dispensers of wisdom and sound advice—both business-related and personal. Bernard recalled many an evening as friends and family would gather around the kitchen table and look to his father and mother for guidance in their personal affairs. Goldie, in particular, was the consummate hostess. Blessed with an infectious sense of humor, Goldie embraced her guests with a "fire in her eyes" and a genuine interest in their problems. Bernard recalled watching her offer a comforting word to her visitors as she escorted each one to the door.

By 1931 the Great Depression was wreaking economic havoc on the garment industry. David and Goldie were forced to close their store and move both their home and the store back to the old neighborhood. Although David tried his hand at becoming a wholesale supplier of exotic fabrics, most of the family's income during the 1930s arose from the retail store they operated on Orchard Street. The family lived modestly, but comfortably for many years on Second Avenue in the midst of the city's theatre district, moving eventually to a triangular building at 240½ E. Houston. The Depression years were stressful, but the family did not really suffer great deprivation.

As World War II erupted, David Lander opened a business on West 36th Street, Manhattan's Fashion Avenue, importing and wholesaling velveteen fabric, a cotton cloth that is often mixed with silk in order to simulate the feel of velvet. The business was generally successful, although it was continually at the mercy of the ever-shifting winds of the fashion world.

In 1941 the family relocated to a home on Bennett Avenue in Washington Heights. They were the first observant Jewish family in the building, located within walking distance of the well-known Breuer Shul.

David Lander would go to work by train each day where he would meet Bernard and his brother Nathan. Both young men worked with their father during much of their adult lives. Goldie, by this point, was less active in the business. She missed the one-on-one customer interaction of the retail trade and did not feel that she played as much of a role in the wholesale end of things.

Along with his business and synagogue activities, David had also been a member of Mizrachi since 1913. Mizrachi was the major religious Zionist movement that sought to recreate a Jewish presence in Eretz Yisroel as delineated in the Torah. The American Mizrachi movement had been founded by Goldie's cousin, Ben Koenigsberg. Not surprisingly, Ben had enlisted his cousin's husband, David, to the cause. David soon became an ardent advocate for a Jewish homeland in Palestine, a value he passed on to his son, Bernard and to his siblings.

David and Goldie finally were able to visit Israel in 1968. Later, David commented to Bernard about the great privilege he experienced by "walking in the footsteps of our patriarchs; the very roads that Avraham Avinu had traveled."

Both of Bernard Lander's parents were blessed with a lengthy lifespan. David died on April 6, 1980 at age ninety-two, after having continued working at his profession until his retirement at age eighty-eight. His funeral was attended by many of New York's Hasidic leadership, including Grand Rabbi Shlomo Halberstam, the Bobover Rebbe.

Goldie remained in Washington Heights after David's death and often made visits to Touro College, the institution her son Bernard had founded. Bernard Lander cherished those visits above all else, invariably interrupting his involvement with the business of the day in order to welcome her and provide her with an honored seat by his side. Well into her nineties, Goldie was known to offer lucid comments and dispense sound advice as she sat in on her son's business meetings.

She prayed for, and was granted, a clarity of mind for the length of her days. She prayed that the Divine Presence should not forsake her while she remained alive and her prayer was answered. Goldie Lander died, with both sound mind and unwavering spirit intact, on July 17, 1991, at age ninety-nine. She lived long enough to witness much of her son Bernard's story unfold, a story that begins during the 1920s in that most unique cultural cauldron known as New York's Lower East Side.

CHAPTER TWO

The Boy on the Platform

The world exists only by virtue of the breath of schoolchildren.

—Talmud, Shabbat 119b

The dreaded day had arrived at last. Dreaded by Bernard's mother, Goldie, that is. This day of trauma and trepidation had, in fact, long been anticipated by Bernard himself. For the Orthodox Jewish nine-year-old boy, standing on the elevated train platform a few steps from Stuyvesant Park and his family's 15th Street apartment—looking down on the peddler-packed streets of the Lower East Side—today was Independence Day. The summer of 1924 had lain for weeks like a stifling comforter across the city's immigrant neighborhoods, but today Bernard felt light-hearted and liberated. He was on his way. He was leaving one mother's embrace for that of another.

Goldie Lander was instinctively overprotective. This was, perhaps, for good reason. Bernard, her first-born, had not uttered a word in any of the three languages that permeated the Lander household (Yiddish, Hebrew, and English) until he was four years old. By then Goldie and David Lander had shuttled their quiet son to numerous doctors and therapists, the last of whom suggested that Bernard have his tonsils removed. His parents did so, and this helped a bit, but the boy remained silent. Then, as if by magic, Bernard suddenly began speaking fluently shortly after his fourth birthday; a trait that was shared many years later by his own son and grandson. This congenitally delayed speech development seemed to be no impediment to future success, however, and all three Lander men became accomplished orators upon reaching adulthood.

Although Bernard's childhood family was far from affluent, Goldie always harbored a slightly irrational fear that someone would kidnap her young boy and hold him for ransom. The fact that the family lived across the boulevard from New York's infamous Hell's Kitchen only added to her nervous apprehension. The area was notorious for its *A Manu Neura* or Black Hand operators who would extort protection money from illiterate immigrant families by sending them threatening notes consisting of only a palm print dipped in black ink.

Goldie had finally overcome some of these maternal misgivings and had agreed to allow Bernard to ride the elevated train uptown *by himself.* His destination was to be his second home.

David and Goldie Lander had decided that it was time to pull their precocious son out of the New York public school system and en-roll him at the RJJ religious school. RJJ stood for Rabbi Jacob Joseph, a distinguished religious leader who, during the 1880s, was lured away from his post as the Maggid of Vilna in Lithuania to serve as the chief rabbi of New York's Association of American Hebrew Congregations, a federation of Eastern European synagogues. Rabbi Joseph's nickname was "Rav Yaakov Charif (sharp)" because of his facile mind. It was this quality that prompted the school's founder, Rabbi Shmuel Yitzhak Andron, to bestow Rabbi Joseph's name on his new institution when its doors opened in 1900. In short order the RJJ school became a driv-ing force in promoting Torah learning and teaching religious obser-vance to transplanted Orthodox Jews and their offspring in America.

A strong factor in the Landers' decision to enroll their son at the RJJ was a man who would become a towering figure in the life of Bernard Lander. Benjamin Koenigsberg was Goldie Lander's cousin and since 1923 had served as the chairman of the RJJ's Board of Trustees. Ben Koenigs-berg was the American-born son of Goldie's uncle (more of a grandfather figure to Bernard), Israel Koenigsberg. Israel assiduously maintained the lifeline between the old world and the new by managing the *Kollel Chibas Yerushalayim*, a support group for Galician Torah scholars in Palestine. In 1924 Israel took the perilous step of embarking on a sea voyage to British mandated Palestine or, as traditional Jews referred to it, *Eretz Yisrael.* The sight of his great-uncle Israel's picking up, at age sixty-four, and his travel-ing to the holy city of Tsefat, left a deep and lasting impression on young Bernard.

But it was Uncle Yisroel's son Ben who was to become Bernard Land-er's major role model. Ben, as a young man in 1905, had caused an uproar among the Orthodox Jewish community when he sat for and was admitted to the New York Bar. At that time there were no Orthodox attorneys, and such a worldly occupation did not seem appropriate for the son of a respected Torah scholar like Israel Koenigsberg. But Ben would have none of this. He believed, as did many of his generation, that G-d had deposited him onto the soil of this new land for a distinct purpose. And that purpose could best be fulfilled by adapting somewhat to the ways of his new homeland. Benjamin Koenigsberg spent his life building a solid foundation for American Orthodox Judaism. Among his many initiatives, Ben organized the first Friday night English language Torah lecture series. This was done to counter the efforts of Rabbi Stephen Wise, who was planning to establish an English language Reform synagogue on the Lower East Side. The lectures were held at the massive Kavalirer Synagogue, more popularly known as the Pitt Street Shul. The inaugural address was delivered by Rabbi Judah Magnes from the Clinton Street Reform synagogue and the head of the New York City Kehillah. More than 5,000 Torah-hungry listeners packed the synagogue. The Pitt Street lecture series was an immediate success and served as the cornerstone for the Young Israel movement that continued for more than forty years under the passionate leadership of Ben Koenigsberg. Naturally, Bernard Lander would, in a few years, become an active member. But on this day, it was not thoughts about his cousin and future mentor that inhabited the boy's head. Instead, he was no doubt experiencing some apprehension and excitement at this watershed moment in his life. As he peered down the elevated track into the dusty morning daylight, Bernard must have imagined that it was his future that was barreling down the rails at breakneck speed.

At his new school, RJJ, Bernard would be but one of hundreds of students—an order of magnitude expansion from his cloistered public school universe. Standing on that platform, with Goldie keeping both her distance and a watchful eye, he was saying a private goodbye to his frivolous childhood. At PS 19, Bernard's academic prowess had shone brightly, but his independent temperament and his impatience with his teacher's slow pedagogic pace, resulted in frequent "deportment" issues. He invariably impressed his teachers with his boundless energy and self-confident aplomb. This self-confidence also served him well when dealing with his non-Jewish classmates. The student body was an ethnic reflection of the Lower East Side neighborhood it served. Bernard, at that point in his life, believed that one half of the world was composed of Italian Catholics, one quarter was Jewish like him, and the rest was a mixture of other ethnic groups.

Like most immigrant parents, David and Goldie Lander viewed the public school system as a means of acculturation and a portal to success in the wider, secular society. While many observant families trained their children to shun the glittering opportunities represented by American modernity and stay devoted to traditional Torah study, this was not the case with the Landers. They encouraged young Bernard to read secular books and were pleased that he spent much of his free time at the public library. His parents even went so far as to purchase, for Bernard's edification, a set of the premier children's encyclopedia of the day, *The Book of Knowledge*—the only known set ever sold in the entire neighborhood. Bernard consumed all twenty volumes with a passion, reading and rereading the dog-eared volumes time and time again. This lust for learning, not surprisingly, resulted in his emergence as a top academic student.

Although they initially sent him to public school, Bernard's parents had no intention of neglecting his Judaic education. As soon as he started at PS 19, David and Goldie had arranged for Bernard to study every day with a private tutor named Mr. Himmelfarb. Mr. Himmelfarb worked as the *shamash* (deacon) at Tifferes Yisroel, the synagogue across the street from the Lander home. Beginning with the basics of Chumash and Mishna, Bernard quickly advanced to studying the more advanced Gemora. Bernard's parents wished for him to focus on his Jewish studies in order to channel some of his inventive and at times, capricious, tendencies. They were only partially successful.

Bernard was every bit as accomplished at pulling off pranks as he was at his studies. After spending the summer collecting grasshoppers at "Stuy" Park, and then feeding them in captivity, he surreptitiously released fifty of the lively insects in class, causing a major panic. Adding luster to this accomplishment was the fact that he was never apprehended. He was careful to cover his (and the grasshoppers') tracks so as not to be sentenced to the demonic "rat hole"—in actuality, a dark broom closet where a student being punished was forced to stand and contemplate his sins. But Bernard was as clever as he was precocious and, despite his frequent infractions, he never saw the inside of the rat hole.

Before moving to 15th Street, the Lander family lived in a cold-water flat at 336 E. 13th Street, directly across the street from Tifferes Yisrael, the synagogue where Bernard's father, David, served as congregational president. The family's *shmatteh* business was located on the next block and one block farther was Stuyvesant Park, with its lush shade trees and many wooden benches. Down the street, on First Avenue, stood PS 19. Each ethnic group in the neighborhood held dominion over its own well-defined turf, with the park and the school serving as common ground areas. It was a true "East Side Story" environment.

Growing up on this borderline boulevard had molded Bernard into a street savvy kid who knew his way around the block. On the last day of third grade, Bernard had listened to the school kids singing their devilish refrain on his way home from school: "No more teachers, no more books. Hang the teachers up on hooks!" As he hurriedly made his way past the trattorias and cannoli shops, he turned quickly to hear the crack of a gunshot ring out. Ducking close to the ground, Bernard got a glimpse of a hand releasing a smoking pistol and watched as it fell to the ground next to the body of the victim. Wide-eyed, his heart pumping wildly, Bernard focused on the perpetrator as he watched him smoothly blend into the crowd that was quickly forming around the prone body. When the police arrived, the shooter behaved casually, like an innocent passer-by and was not detained. Bernard considered approaching the police, but then thought better of it. Who would believe an eight-year-old boy, especially a Jewish kid from the other side of 15th Street?

Despite his mother's overprotective nature, there was no shielding Bernard from the rough-cut culture of the street. Like other kids his age, he would spend hours playing punch ball and stickball. This culture also had a particular rite of passage whereby boys were called upon to prove their manhood by jumping from a fifth floor window of one building down onto the fourth floor roof of a neighboring one. Bernard did not engage in this particular bit of bravado, although he was willing to occasionally jump directly from one fourth floor window to another. He survived all these high jinks without a scratch, although similar encounters left him somewhat worse for wear. One day he arrived home with all the buttons of his shirt ripped off. He explained to Goldie that he had had a run-in with a Jew-hating Ukranian tough they called "The Giraffe." The Giraffe had used his switchblade knife to remove Bernard's buttons one by one and then dared him to do something about it. Bernard walked away, but he already understood the value of alliances and managed, a few days after his encounter with The Giraffe, to round up a group of friendly Italian boys who agreed to "take care of him." Bernard never lost another button after that.

But all this was behind him now. At RJJ there would be no more immigrant melting pot. He would become immersed in time honored study techniques developed in Lithuania and administered by Rabbi Shmuel Yitzhak Andron. Most of the other students at RJJ were from Hasidic families. Bernard knew some of them from the *Shineveh Shtiebel*. The *shtiebel*, or "little house," was an artifact from the old world that had been transplanted into the Hasidic communities of New York. These were not merely rooms set aside for communal Jewish prayer but also served as community gathering spots. In contrast to a formal synagogue, a shtiebel is far smaller and approached more casually. In the Hasidic communities of Eastern Europe prior to the Holocaust, it was in the *shtiebelekh* where disciples, or *Hasidim*, could get close to their revered and beloved *rebbe*. The Shineveh Shtiebel was where the Lander family would often visit to pray and reconnect with their heritage. This particular shtiebel was immortalized in the writings of the beloved Jewish composer Ernest Bloch, who visited there and then wrote about how the sacred singing had deeply affected him: "I assure you that my music seems to me a very poor little thing beside that which I had heard! And that all the kings on earth … appear to me as very vulgar people beside these old ones, proud in their poverty, rich in their certainties." Bernard grew to cherish the camaraderie and nurturing warmth of the shtiebel. But inexorably, the rapidly changing world outside this insulated environment would soon begin to impose itself onto the youngster's consciousness.

Bernard Lander had heard his father comment many times: "Shver tsu zayn a Yid." The world makes it hard to be a Jew. One could argue that this was, at the same time, both true and not true in the milieu of Jewish New York in the 1920s. It was truly a Dickensian period—encompassing both the best and the worst of times. The Eastern European Jews who had fled persecution and pogroms to arrive to "Der Goldeneh Medinah" had, for the most part, found what they had been seeking: life under a regime that did not interfere with their religious practices. The early decades of the twentieth century saw something of a renaissance in Jewish culture centered in New York and as evidenced by the growth of the Yiddish theatre, a host of Jewish newspapers, book publishers, and—among the most observant—bustling new communities in places like Williamsburg and Boro Park in Brooklyn. These Orthodox strongholds maintained strong links, both spiritual and financial, with their European counterparts, while at the same time support flowed from both sides of the Atlantic to religious Zionist movements, such as Mizrachi, in Palestine. This intercontinental Torah triangle defined the Jewish world up through the 1930s. But at the same time, as this flowering of Jewish culture was taking place in some quarters, the bile of anti-Semitism was spewing across Western nations, including here, in the Home of the Brave and the Land of the Free.

The economic boom that had helped to elevate the living standards of immigrant families like the Landers brought with it a dark side. The era was marked by a decided provincialism and a narrowing of the heart. Most Americans understood that "The War to End All Wars" had been, in fact, nothing more than a mere slogan. The National Origins Act, passed in 1924, put an end to the flow of immigration from Southern and Eastern Europe as America turned increasingly inward and isolationist. The Ku Klux Klan reached the pinnacle of its power during this period by combining pagan ritual with its message of hate-tinged white supremacy. And while Henry Ford had, through the advent of the assembly line, placed the automobile and many other consumer goods within the grasp of the average working man, he used the fortune he amassed to underwrite his virulent anti-Semitic agenda. Ford purchased the Dearborn Independent newspaper in 1919, and it was soon running a daily feature called "The International Jew," in which he published vicious anti-Jewish rants and reprinted excerpts from the infamous bogus tract promulgated in Czarist Russia known as "The Protocols of the Elders of Zion." All the Jew baiting paid off handsomely. The paper was soon selling 700,000 copies a week across the country. Meanwhile, as Harvard and other major universities began imposing Jewish student quotas, an obscure radio evangelist named Father Coughlin gained a national following by lambasting the "Jewish Conspiracy" with regularity to the nation's fast-emerging radio audience. Fueled and reinforced by the wave of political anti-Semitism spreading across Europe, American-style anti-Jewish sentiment was causing Jews to be barred from academic positions, banks, hospitals, and other white-collar occupations. Housing restrictions were also imposed with many neighborhoods posting signs identifying themselves as "Christian Communities."

As a nine-year-old boy, standing alone on a New York train platform, waiting to be whisked off toward his own destiny, Bernard Lander was no doubt oblivious to these macro sociological and political forces. But he was soon to encounter their effects. The antipathy and antagonism that was building against American Jews would soon be felt by Bernard as he went to and from his ten-hour study-filled days at RJJ. He was required to pass the grounds of an Irish Catholic parochial school, where the students were taught daily about how their Savior had been murdered through the treachery of Jews. Epithets would be hurled and fistfights would erupt as the age-old bugaboos of classical anti-Semitism were conjured up on the mean sidewalks of New York.

The streams of hatred that young Bernard Lander was required to traverse would, over the coming decade, merge into first a torrent and then a flooding river, rampant with Jewish blood and tears. From the RJJ school, Bernard Lander's next stop along his Judaic odyssey was the Talmudic Academy high school. He graduated from the TA in January of 1933, within weeks of the ascension to office of both Franklin D. Roosevelt and Adolph Hitler. The stage would then be set for the defining confrontation of the twentieth century. It is against this backdrop and from the flames of that historic conflagration that Bernard Lander first emerged as a driving force in the frontlines of education and civil liberties. His story is the American story, and it began the day he first rode the train by himself to the end of First Avenue and toward the beginning of his life's work as one of America's most influential and innovative educators.

But all this lay ahead. For now, the young boy on the platform could only contemplate the experiences that awaited him at his new school. What sort of friends would he make? What would his teachers expect of him? Was he good enough to study Torah and Talmud beside the sons of rabbis and Hasidic scholars? These doubts crossed his mind as Bernard opened his school bag to make sure he had plenty of pencils and notebooks. He had decided not to bring along the jar full of grasshoppers.

CHAPTER THREE

The Path of Learning

The Holy One, blessed be He, gives wisdom only to one
who already possesses wisdom.

—*Talmud, Berakhot 55a*

What Bernard Lander discovered, once he began classes at the
Rabbi Jacob Joseph School, was a world that clearly delineated the sacred from the profane. The demarcation line
arrived during each long school day precisely at 3 pm when *limudei
kodesh*, the school's Jewish studies curriculum, ended and *limudei chol*,
its general studies program began. During the *limudei chol* classes, that
ran until 7 pm, students progressed as they did in the New York public
schools, according to their age group. In *limudei kodesh*, however, pupils
were grouped according to their abilities. A child who was brilliant at
Torah and Talmud, for example, could find himself moved ahead regardless of his actual age. So it was for Bernard, who typically was placed
with other students two to three years his senior.

But while Bernard soon demonstrated his prodigious academic skills,
he just as soon proved that he had not left his wild ways back at PS 19.
His report cards were resplendent with *A*s for both religious and general
subjects, but also contained *D*s—as in deportment—when it came to conduct. The fact that Bernard was frequently found fighting with the other
students no doubt stemmed in part from the teasing he was forced to endure as a "Mama's Boy." Goldie would often appear at the school during a
break to bring her son a hot meal or a warm muffler. These visits did not
go unnoticed by his older classmates.

"What's the matter?" they would taunt, "did little Dov Berish forget
and leave his *tsitsis* at home?" Such mockery would easily provoke the
scrappy lad to retaliate with his fists until he was pulled off forcibly by

his teachers and dispatched to the Rosh Yeshiva's office to cool his heels and his temper.

Young Bernard was indelibly influenced during his years at RJJ by its president Julius Dukas, a true giant of the New York Jewish community. Dukas was one of the founders of the Orthodox Union and served as president of RJJ from 1913 until his death in 1940. Bernard recalls how Dukas's Sundays were spent raising funds to support the poorer students. His devotion to the most needy at RJJ was legendary.

Bernard Lander was blessed with a host of outstanding instructors at RJJ. Foremost among these was Rabbi Jacob Reimer, who taught advanced Gemora. Rabbi Reimer bestowed upon his more advanced students, such as Bernard, not only the details of the Talmud, but also the analytical skills required to master it. He provided Bernard with a *derech* in learning—the defined path towards a life of study. Rabbi Reimer was blessed with an extraordinary intellect and had actually memorized the entire *Tanach* (Torah, Prophets and Writings — the Jewish Bible). He would challenge students to stump him by asking them to recite a passage that he would be unable to identify. None ever did. Rabbi Reimer was a warm and loving teacher who left an immutable mark on the emerging scholar.

But not all of Bernard's influences during those years arose from school. He maintained a close friendship with a neighbor boy he had known since early childhood, Leonard Berkowitz. After a long school day, Bernard would look forward to palling around with Lenny at their nearby apartment on 15th Street. Unlike the Landers, the Berkowitzes were not an observant family. Like many secular young Jews of that period, Lenny's parents were avowed socialists, active in the Young People's Socialist League. Through his contact with Lenny and his family, young Bernard was exposed to the Jewish intellectual community. It was this sort of knowledge that would serve him well in future years.

Bernard Lander graduated eighth grade as part of the Rabbi Jacob Joseph School class of January 1929. The school had just inaugurated a new high school program that Bernie attended for only half a year. In the fall of 1929, he transferred to the Talmudical Academy, the affiliate high school of Yeshiva College, where his parents felt he would be exposed to much broader academic opportunities.

Entering the gates of the Talmudical Academy was Bernard's first contact with Yeshiva College, an institution that would profoundly shape the course of his life. By the time Bernard began his studies in 1929, "Yeshiva," as it was commonly referred to, was already the American Orthodox movement's flagship institution of higher learning. Achieving this position of prominence was primarily due to the accomplishments of one man, Rabbi Dr. Bernard (Dov) Revel, a Torah giant and brilliant scholar. Rabbi Revel brought Yeshiva into being in 1915 and served as its guiding light until his death in 1940. Though physically slight, Revel was considered a giant among his peers and his presence dominated Yeshiva during the years that Bernard Lander studied there. Rabbi Revel's influence on Bernard Lander was profound and his story is one that is unquestionably worth telling.

Emerging from Lithuania at the close of the nineteenth century, Bernard Revel was early on a free thinker. After achieving *semicha* (ordination) at the age of sixteen, he earned a Russian high school diploma through independent study and then became caught up in the revolutionary movements of that time. It was a period of earth-shaking political unrest. The pursuit of social justice and the improvement of the human condition motivated Revel to become active in the General Jewish Worker's Alliance (the "Bund"). His published articles, considered subversive by the regime, led to Revel's arrest by Czarist forces in 1905. Released the following year, Revel wasted no time immigrating to the United States.

Upon arrival he immediately enrolled at New York's RIETS (Rabbi Isaac Elchanan Theological Seminary), the only Orthodox rabbinic academy in the United States. RIETS had been established in 1897 as a yeshiva for advanced Torah study, meant to attract European scholars who had fled to America. Not neglecting his general studies, Revel was also awarded a Master's degree in Medieval Jewish Ethics from New York University in 1909. Two years later he earned his Ph.D. when he became the first graduate of Philadelphia's Dropsie College and its noted Jewish civilization program.

Ever the iconoclast, upon completing his education, Revel decided to heed Horace Greeley's advice and "Go West, young man." He opted to join wife Sarah's family business in the rich oilfields of Oklahoma. Even as he amassed a small fortune thanks to the black gold pumping from the family oil wells, Revel's heart and soul continued to flow with the words of Torah and Talmud. He realized, due to his exposure to the far horizons of Oklahoma, that Torah teachings and modernity could successfully co-exist in this vast new land.

Revel returned to the New York educational milieu as a relatively wealthy man just as the waves of Jewish immigration from Eastern Europe were reaching their crest. He witnessed how the children of these mostly Orthodox immigrants were soon being drawn away from their traditional heritage as they were lured toward America's new native strains of Conservative and Reform Judaism. He recognized, probably before anyone else, that American Orthodoxy needed to be modernized in order to retain the religious affiliations of its children. He set out to recast European Orthodoxy into a New World mold.

Choosing "Torah over oil," Revel's first act was to meld two struggling New York yeshivas. His alma mater, the Rabbi Isaac Elchanan Theological Seminary (RIETS) was merged with the Yeshivat Etz Chaim into one successful school where Orthodox students could study the Talmud *and* the worldly philosophers without undergoing a conflict in their loyalties. Revel became the new school's first Rosh Yeshiva (principal) in 1915, introducing such subjects as homiletics (sermon preparation), pedagogy, and some secular instruction.

Revel's first priority after taking over the helm at Yeshiva was to organize the Talmudical Academy, or TA. Opening in 1916, the TA was the first high school in America to combine Jewish and general studies. Similar to the structure of the RJJ School, it was Torah studies in the morning and a general curriculum, based on the courses being taught at New York public high schools, in the afternoon. Revel soon recognized that as students graduated from TA, those who wished to pursue a general education left for other schools, leaving only the rabbinic candidates behind to study at RIETS. Even among those who remained at RIETS, many, he discovered, were taking courses elsewhere at night and over the summer in order to shore up their general education. Revel realized that Yeshiva needed to provide concurrent parallel courses in both rabbinics and general studies. Under Revel's leadership, Yeshiva announced in 1923 its intent to establish a four-year comprehensive liberal arts college to operate parallel to RIETS with a dual curriculum according to the model of the Talmudical Academy high school.

The third leg of Yeshiva College actually came into being a few years earlier in 1921. That was the year Yeshiva agreed to incorporate a teacher's training school from the Mizrachi Organization of America that was unable to keep it afloat. When Mizrachi established the school in 1917, it sought to populate the growing number of afternoon Hebrew schools around the nation with professionally prepared teachers who were advocates of religious Zionism. After the Teachers Institute, or TI, as it was known, fully became part of Yeshiva, it continued its mission with a curriculum stressing modern Hebrew and Bible study. Incorporating such a modern-style institution as the TI into the traditional Yeshiva environment was viewed as something of an anomaly by the prevailing heads of RIETS. Yet it was precisely this type of bold innovation that earned Revel his reputation as the Rabbi who saved Orthodox Judaism in America.

The school grew in prestige and with time became Yeshiva College, the first Jewish liberal arts institution in the United States. Revel's successor added the Albert Einstein College of Medicine with a faculty that included not only Reform and Conservative Jews, but non-Jews as well.

As America enjoyed a period of post-war prosperity in the 1920s, Revel was a tireless and highly effective fundraiser, collecting more than $5 million in support for the new Yeshiva College that included the TI, the TA and RIETS. In 1924, he used the funds to purchase two square blocks in Washington Heights on a site three hundred feet above the Harlem River. His fundraising was effective because of its outreach to the non-Orthodox world, where he spread his message of academic openness. In a 1926 solicitation letter to a prominent New York attorney, Revel wrote:

> Other (non-Orthodox) students who desire the knowledge of the Torah and Hebrew culture as a part of their general development, who wish to acquire their education in a thoroughly Jewish atmosphere, will be welcome to its influence, and such non-Jews as may seek to add to their own, the knowledge of Judaism, may also come.

In recruiting faculty, Revel was again a pioneer and an innovator. Seeking to engage the best instructors available regardless of their religious orientation, he preferred Orthodox Jews who would serve as positive role models for his students, but not at the expense of quality instruction. On September 25, 1928, Yeshiva College opened its doors to thirty-one students, mostly graduates of the TA. A few weeks later, 15,000 people gathered at the dedication of Yeshiva's stunning new building, which was to house the Yeshiva Liberal Arts College, RIETS, the Talmudical Academy and the Teachers Institute. Together, these schools, soon to be known collectively as Yeshiva College, encompassed Rabbi Revel's vision of a solid foundation upon which to build the future of Orthodox Judaism in America.

To say that Revel's groundbreaking accomplishments served to inspire Bernard Lander would be a gross understatement. As we shall see, Lander's course, while played out on a global stage, was to be marked by the same fearless dedication and inspired innovation as was displayed by Rabbi Bernard Revel in the establishment of what would become Yeshiva University.

Bernard came under Rabbi Revel's wing not only as a student, but also as a family friend. It was Rabbi Revel who tested each student personally at the Talmudical Academy and it was he who decided when a student was prepared to move to a higher level Talmud class. Bernard became friendly with Rabbi Revel's two sons, Norman and Hirschel, and was a frequent visitor in the Revel home. Rabbi Revel took a real interest in his budding student and appreciated Bernard's intellectual brilliance and outstanding memory. During one visit, he asked Bernard what he was planning to study over the summer. He then placed a formidable challenge before his student: to study and memorize the Talmudic tractate of Nedarim with the commentary of Rabbenu Nissim. Bernard was flattered that Rabbi Revel would think him capable of such a challenging task. He applied himself vigorously over the summer and returned to class in the fall having perfectly memorized, word-for-word, the ninety two-sided folios of *Nedarim* plus commentaries. Dr. Lander could still recite passages from the tractate when he had reached his nineties.

Bernard soon fell in love with Yeshiva's new campus. In particular he adored the steep cliffs overlooking the Harlem River. On each day that the weather permitted, Bernard would visit the cliffs during his lunch break. There he would make the perilous climb down to the riverbank and then hike back up in time for his afternoon classes. He was a swift and energetic climber and loved to challenge his friends to see who could more quickly ascend to the heights. While Bernard never sustained any injuries, other students, attempting to emulate his climbing prowess, would often come away bruised and battered. Tragically, several years after Bernard had left the school, a Yeshiva student would lose his life along those very cliffs.

Those enthusiastic bolts up the mountainside were emblematic of Bernard's precocious personality in high school. He was a young man in a hurry: in a hurry to compete with his classmates and moreover, in a hurry to challenge himself to stretch and press against the boundaries of his world, both physical and intellectual.

This fire in the belly was certainly present when it came to religious studies, and it also drove his thirst for general knowledge, although perhaps with not quite as much fervor. Many evenings were spent reading in the public library, where he amassed a vast independent knowledge base about Western Literature. Bernard's favorite general studies class by far was World History, in which he became a star pupil. He was able to easily manage that temporal balance that allowed him to devour the latest copy of the New York Times aboard his school-bound train each morning and then delve into the most venerated Talmudic tractates once he arrived.

It was during this period that his political outlook was being shaped, not only by world events, but also by his friend Leonard Berkowitz's socialist parents. He looked forward to their political discussions and found himself attracted to their notions of "redistribution of wealth" and "fair working conditions."

Friday nights would often find Bernard attending Shabbos services at a Hasidic shtiebel on East Houston Street and then staying afterwards for the camaraderie and spirited discussions. Relishing the atmosphere of learning, Bernard regarded the shtiebel as a place to pray, to study and to replenish one's soul.

Another pillar of Bernard's early teenage years was *Bachurei Chemed,* a youth group to which he was introduced shortly after his Bar Mitzvah, by Ben Koenigsberg's brother, Chaim. Most of the other boys in *Bachurei Chemed* were from transplanted Galician Hasidic families. The group stressed learning and piety and conducted its business in Yiddish.

Emerging from Bachurei Chemed, Bernard soon gravitated to the burgeoning Young Israel movement. He found its distinctly "Americanishe" orientation appealing and would often attend services at its first storefront shul on East Broadway. The Young Israel movement grew rapidly, establishing a presence in the Orthodox communities of Williamsburg and Boro Park in Brooklyn. By the late 1920s, they were in twenty U.S. cities. Bernard liked the fact that the classes were conducted in English and that the services reflected a new and decidedly American sensibility. In distinct contrast to the immigrant "greenhorn" shuls he had attended all of his life, at Young Israel there was no sale of Torah honors (*aliyot*) or other such old-world trappings. At Young Israel, with its focus on attracting young observant Jewish men, Bernard would occasionally attend holiday social events. No social butterfly, Bernard far preferred the company of his friends who chose to devote their time and energies to intense Talmudic learning.

Bernard Lander completed his studies at the Talmudical Academy in January of 1933, along with forty-four of his classmates, and began taking courses immediately at Yeshiva College.

The decision to follow the path of Jewish learning beyond high school was an almost automatic one. With Bernard's evident aptitude and his already established breadth of knowledge of religious texts, any other course simply would not make sense. While he certainly entertained thoughts of following his father into the business arena, the world in which Bernard found himself had no place for such a scholar/entrepreneur. *Parnassah*, or one's livelihood, was one thing, and Talmud study was quite another. Both required a consuming commitment, passion and dedication. They were, for the most part, mutually exclusive. As they had done for centuries, religious scholars would still need to depend upon the generosity of others to sustain themselves. At this point in his life, this stark practical reality did not disturb Bernard Lander very much. But as the young man continued on his path towards Rabbinic ordination, he would begin to question this dichotomy. "Why not?" he pondered. "Why can't I combine a life of religious learning with a profession that provides me with a livelihood?" It was a question that would become the hallmark of his future career.

CHAPTER FOUR

The Road to the Rabbinate

Scholars are builders, builders of the world.
—Talmud: Shabbat 114a

Bernard Lander felt right at home after he advanced from the Talmudical Academy to Yeshiva College. The daily schedule was identical to the one he had grown used to in high school: learning at the seminary (RIETS) until 3:00 pm, followed by four hours of general study. During his first two years, Bernard's class of roughly forty students remained together as they delved into the core curriculum of social sciences, mathematics, the physical sciences, literature, and history. But during their junior and senior years, students were permitted to branch out and enroll in elective courses. And Bernard signed up for as many as he could.

Even within the relatively small student body, there existed a certain stratification and a distinct hierarchy among its students. Roughly half of Bernard's class was composed of young men like himself: graduates of Yeshiva's TA high school. A handful, who had emerged from New York City's public high schools, suffered during their first years at Yeshiva due to their limited knowledge of Hebrew. Then there were the out-of-towners, who typically came from observant families outside of New York. Many were sons of rabbis and were sent to Yeshiva to follow in their family's rabbinic tradition. While most members of Bernard's class were enrolled at RIETS (including all of the out-of-towners), a sizable group was instead enrolled at the Teacher's Institute. These students were often less observant and lax when it came to attending prayer services.

Bernard listened to all the common complaints about the TI guys, but his attitude was more tolerant and understanding. It wasn't the student's fault, he believed, that he happened to be born into a less observant family. At least he, or his parents, had chosen Yeshiva to provide a quality education in an intensive Jewish environment. Perhaps the pendulum would swing the other way, and TI students would emerge more, rather than less, committed to Torah values. Bernard suspected that the kiddush cup could be viewed as half full.

This growing phenomenon of weakened Torah observance—among even the most allegedly "advanced" Talmudic scholars in his class—gnawed at the young rabbinic candidate. Bernard suspected that perhaps the problem could be traced to the methodology employed by the school's teaching staff. Rabbi Revel, in his quest to broaden the horizons of Orthodox Judaism, had populated the college's teaching staff with some free-thinking faculty members, including those who, according to Bernard, perpetrated and enabled this lapsed level of observance.

It is clear that Revel, in hiring faculty in departments such as philosophy, was trying to achieve a certain balance: a harmony between religious and secular wisdom. These faculty members served as a substantial counterweight to what some might regard as the dogmatic approach favored by the RIETS instructors. Revel held strong to the notion that Yeshiva serve as a true liberal arts college and not institute a controlled academic environment of the type that existed at Catholic parochial colleges.

Bernard, however, came to believe that certain professors recklessly utilized critical methods of philosophic inquiry to undermine principles of religious belief and that their presence on the faculty was a mistake. This belief would guide Bernard Lander years later as he assembled the faculty for his newly established institution of Jewish learning, Touro College.

Like many young idealistic Jews, Bernard took the mandate of Tikkun Olam—the healing of the world—to heart. Such beliefs, when coupled with the utopian visions he encountered at the Berkowitz home, helped to formulate Bernard's worldview as it took shape in the crucible of the Great Depression. It was this growing sensibility that led him to the emerging discipline of sociology.

Yeshiva was one of the first schools in America to introduce a department of sociology. It was there, while studying under noted sociologist Theodore Abel, that Bernard discovered the field that would define his course over the coming years. Sociology held the promise of scientifically understanding human group behavior—something Judaism had been concerned with for centuries.

Dr. Theodore Abel was Yeshiva's first associate professor of sociology during the 1930s. He later served on the faculties of Columbia University and Hunter College. A non-Jew, Abel was intrigued by the social dynamics that led to Hitler's ascension to power in 1933. After gaining the cooperation of the new Nazi regime, Abel traveled to Germany and advertised small cash awards to members of the NDSAP who would agree to write an essay about why they decided to join the party and support Hitler. He received more than 700 responses. Translating, compiling, and analyzing the results over the next four years, Abel published them in the landmark 1938 book: *Why Hitler Came into Power* (346 pages, Harvard University Press). The book, still in print some seventy years later, is today a widely respected treatise on the social and political forces leading up to Hitler's rise.

Bernard Lander's college days were also colored by an association he had been developing throughout his entire life. Mizrachi was a religious Zionist movement into which Bernard's parents had enlisted back in 1913. The movement was founded by Rabbi Yitzchak Yaacov Reines in Vilna, Latvia in 1902. Its name is a Hebrew acronym for *Merkaz Ruhani* (religious center). It advocates that Torah should be at the core of all efforts to establish and maintain a Jewish homeland in Eretz Yisroel. Rabbi Meir Berlin exported the Mizrachi movement to the United States in the early years of the twentieth century. Among those he reached with his message were David and Goldie Lander and Rabbi Bernard Revel.

During his junior year at Yeshiva College, Bernard and a group of young Mizrachi rebels, including his friend Charles Bick, established the first American chapter of *Hapoel Hamizrachi*, a socialist religious workers' movement within a movement. *Hapoel Hamizrachi* campaigned for social justice and espoused *Torah va-Avodah* (Torah and work). Its ideology was an amalgam of socialist political dogma imbued with highly interpreted Torah and Talmudic wisdom. The group gained momentum thanks to the darkening spread of fascism across Europe, but, like many other such international *Bundist* organizations, it dissolved when the Molotov-Ribbentrop Pact between Russia and Germany was revealed. Nevertheless, Bernard's association with Hapoel Hamizrachi, which included his serving as its president, shaped and solidified his lifelong leadership commitment to social justice.

It was also during this *Hapoel Hamizrachi* period that Bernard began his lifelong association with Dr. Pinkhos Churgin, who acted as the group's faculty advisor. Churgin would go on to become president of the national Mizrachi Organization of America in 1949 where he conceived and planned the creation of Bar Ilan University in Israel. He moved there in 1955 to serve as the new school's first president. Bernard's friendship with Dr. Churgin would prove to be of major importance in the coming years.

It was also during his early years of involvement with Mizrachi that one of Bernard's more bizarre life episodes occured. He and a college classmate, Avi Greenberg, decided that they would attend the Mizrachi national convention being held in Washington D.C. One of their most favored speakers, Rabbi Shragai, was going to address the mostly conservative grand plenum, and both young men wanted to be there to relish what promised to be a fiery moment. Unfortunately, they did not have the funds to pay for their travel expenses from New York. Relying upon their thumbs, the duo managed to hitchhike as far south as Baltimore, but there they ran out of luck and willing drivers. Pooling what little money they managed to scrape together, Bernard approached the driver of a long black vehicle parked near the main highway. Desperate, he managed to negotiate the price of a ride with the driver of what turned out to be a hearse, although the two passengers had to remain prone in the rear bed of the vehicle all the way to Washington. "We were dying to get to that speech," quipped Dr. Lander years later, proud of the fact that he has attended almost every Mizrachi convention since then, although usually arriving in a more traditional manner.

During his senior year, Bernard Lander made an unsuccessful electoral bid for the presidency of his Yeshiva College class. Falling short of that, he was, however, elected to serve as president of the Students' Organization of Yeshiva or SOY, an older social organization that saw Bernard involved with organizing the RIETS Purim festival, among other responsibilities. He also fulfilled his social justice agenda at SOY by distributing cash stipends to students in financial need during the darkest days of the Depression. The experience left its mark on Bernard, who would never forget the struggles of pride and compassion he encountered when helping those facing serious financial challenges.

In June, as America prepared for the upcoming Olympic Games in Berlin, Bernard Lander was granted his undergraduate degree with honors from Yeshiva College. Roughly half of his graduating classmates went on to secure jobs in the field of Jewish community service (teachers, social workers, fundraisers, etc.) while the other half went into business or sought out advanced training in the professions. A handful, including Bernard, decided to continue their studies at RIETS for two more years of postgraduate work that would, if they were successful, earn them *semicha* or ordination as members of the Orthodox rabbinate.

It was at this point in his life that Bernard Lander entered the more rarefied atmosphere of advanced Judaic learning. Bernard's intellect had provided him with a serene conviction that a better world could be achieved through the modern application of social policy guided by venerated Jewish teachings. It was during these seminal years that Bernard's world truly began to expand and unfold.

While continuing at RIETS, Bernard developed an enduring relationship with one of the most revered and distinguished rabbinic families in the Orthodox Jewish world. The Soloveitchik dynasty traces its lineage back to Aaron and the Biblical Levite tribe. Hence, when, during the European Enlightenment it was necessary for Jewish families to adopt an official surname, they selected "Soloveitchik," or nightingale, a reference to the ancient role of the Levites as singers in the Holy Temple in Jerusalem.

Bernard began attending the *shiurim* (lectures) of Rabbi Moshe Soloveitchik, the Rosh Yeshiva or Head of RIETS, during the fall of 1936. "Reb Moshe," as he was known by his students, was a leading figure in European Jewry when he was recruited by Rabbi Revel in 1928 to head the seminary. Reb Moshe was the son of the legendary and charismatic Rabbi Chaim Soloveitchik of Brest-Litovsk (Reb Chaim of Brisk) who revolutionized the study of Talmud with a popular form of analysis that would become known as "The Brisker Method" or "Derech Brisk." Reb Chaim based his method on the teachings of the Rambam (Maimonides) as laid out in his Mishneh Torah. It is viewed as a "conceptual" or "reductionistic" technique, aimed at resolving apparently contradictory Talmudic passages. The Brisker Method represented a departure from the more holistic, or "face value," approaches in use at the time. Reb Chaim's innovative methods garnered a large and fervently loyal following.

Reb Chaim's son Reb Moshe was born in 1879 and spent his early years studying alongside his brother under the guidance of their illustrious father in Brisk, in what is today Belarus. After the Communist takeover in 1920, the family moved to Warsaw where Reb Moshe served as the head of the Talmud department of the Tachkemoni Seminary. His reputation as something of a genius and an educator par excellence soon spread throughout the Yeshiva world. It was in Warsaw in 1928 that Reb Moshe was recruited by Rabbi Revel, who convinced him to immigrate to New York and accept the Rosh Yeshiva position at RIETS.

At RIETS, Reb Moshe's reputation as a master of logic and legal constructions began to soar. His deep knowledge of the Talmudic tractates, plus his extraordinary powers of ratiocination, as he developed layered streams of precedence to represent both competing sides of a given religious issue, were considered to be nothing short of artistic in their flow and texture by those, like Bernard Lander, who were fortunate enough to attend Reb Moshe's *shiurim*.

This was an intense time for Bernard Lander. Long days, and often longer nights, were devoted entirely to his Torah and Talmudic studies. In addition to absorbing Reb Moshe's elaborate legal constructions, Bernard directed a good portion of his time towards Jewish law in preparation for his ordination exams. Dr. Lander recalled those days as both exhausting and exhilarating. But they were not without their rewards. Reb Moshe did not make it a secret that he considered Bernard Lander to be his most accomplished student. The opportunity of being so consummately focused on Torah study while in the close proximity of giants like Soloveitchik, Revel, Benjamin Aranowitz, and others was, for Bernard Lander, a near nirvana—the best of all possible worlds.

Bernard approached his *semicha* examinations with his usual high level of confidence, bordering on bravado. The actual final exam typically took about ninety minutes to complete. In Bernard's case it lasted for six hours. This was because the oral examiners delighted in repeatedly tossing on-the-spot questions at the young scholar, peppering them with often obscure references, and then observing as he again and again demonstrated his broad knowledge and his amazing ability to correctly think through each question to its proper solution. He acquitted himself with distinction and was granted the appellation of "Rabbi" Bernard Lander.

But saying good-bye to RIETS, even after receiving tacit ordination, was no trivial matter. Rabbi Lander continued at RIETS by way of ongoing post-graduate courses in Jewish studies. Reb Moshe's son, Rabbi Dr.

Joseph Soloveitchik, who would assume his father's position at RIETS in 1941, was, at this time maintaining his own yeshiva in Boston. He would visit New York regularly to see his parents and, while there, conduct a philosophy seminar at RIETS. It was via these postgraduate seminars that Bernard developed a magnetic rapport with Rabbi Joseph and was thereby introduced to the works of the neo-Kantian German philosopher, Hermann Cohen. In later life, Dr. Lander counted Cohen among his major philosophical influences.

During his forty-five year tenure at RIETS, Rabbi Joseph Soloveitchik, or "The Rav" as he was known, ordained more than 2,000 rabbis, many of whom became prominent leaders of American Orthodox Judaism. He was known as a brilliant, preeminent talmudist, master teacher, eloquent speaker, and profound thinker. He was a staunch advocate for more intensive textual Torah study for females and helped to inaugurate New York's Stern College for Women. The Rav was open to the idea of offering advanced degrees in nonreligious disciplines. Blessed with an enlightened outlook, the Rav succeeded in attracting and inspiring several generations of spiritual leaders and Jewish educators. Among the first of these was a freshly minted young rabbi named Bernard Lander.

Rabbi Isaac Elchanan, the namesake of Bernard Lander's Yeshiva seminary, was born on March 24, 1813. One hundred and twenty-five years later to the day, Bernard was officially bestowed with *semicha* during the annual RIETS ordination ceremony. The occasion was a festive one, but that fact did not fully conceal some of the cracks that had begun to appear in the Yeshiva edifice. Rabbi Joseph Soloveitchik, the putative heir to the school's Rosh Yeshiva position, was invited to speak as a special guest. In his keynote remarks, a subtle exposition of the proper way of conducting rabbinic training, Rabbi Joseph referenced the law stipulating that a kosher Torah scroll must be written using only black ink on a white parchment.

"A Torah whose parchment is inscribed with letters of silver and gold is undoubtedly a beautiful work of art. But it is still an invalid Torah."

Bernard understood the Rav's true meaning. It was a thinly-veiled criticism of the concept of a "yeshiva college" that seeks to blend secular and rabbinic studies on a single scroll. A lovely thing, perhaps. But a true yeshiva? No. Soloveitchik's remarks that day were also similarly interpreted by Rabbi Revel, who found them irritating and immediately stopped inviting the Rav to lecture at RIETS. Despite this temporary banishment, Bernard and six other of Soloveitchik's students continued their philosophy studies in the dormitory instead of in the classroom. This act of loyalty is reflective of a comment that Rabbi Soloveitchik made many years later: "When I first came to America, I had two close friends. Dr. Bernard Lander was one of them."

So, as Bernard Lander was officially ordained as an Orthodox Rabbi, he once again found himself standing at a threshold. This time there was no fast-moving train charging his way. This time he found himself approaching a crossroads with one signpost pointing towards Baltimore and the other towards Boston. Which one would the young Rabbi choose? He was torn since he recognized that this decision would critically determine the course of his future life and career.

CHAPTER FIVE

The New Rabbi

Who are the ministering angels? The rabbis ....
—Talmud, Nedarim 20b

While Bernard Lander's outstanding abilities at deciphering the most complex Talmudic tractates had led to his success at attaining *semicha*, he now faced an intricate puzzle that gave him profound pause: what to do with his life? At age twenty-three, Bernard did not envision himself serving as a spiritual leader of a synagogue. The pastoral life did not provide the excitement and opportunities for social change that he relished. Following in the footsteps of his cousin and mentor Ben Koenisgsberg, Bernard applied to and was accepted at Harvard Law School. "As an attorney I could become involved in community affairs and possibly politics," he thought to himself. It would also provide a better livelihood than that of a junior rabbi.

Bernard also considered attending graduate school and earning an advanced degree in sociology. He was animated by the lofty promise that sociology held out—nothing less than the restructuring of society in order to better serve mankind. Professor Theodore Abel encouraged Bernard to apply to the doctoral program at Columbia University, home of the nation's leading sociology program. He heeded the advice and became the first Yeshiva College alumnus to be accepted at a Columbia graduate school. As Bernard stared at the two letters of acceptance from Harvard and Columbia, many considerations weighed upon the young man›s mind.

Acceptance is one thing, but finding the funds to pay the tuition fees at an Ivy League school is quite another. Bernard could no longer in good conscience rely upon his parents' ongoing financial support. They had already sacrificed so much to provide both him and his brother Nathan with the finest educational opportunities possible. Bernard recognized that he was an adult now and therefore fully responsible for his own future. Despite his antipathy towards working as a congregational rabbi, he began to seek out just such a rabbinic position, one that would permit him to draw a salary while, at the same time, enabling him to pursue his studies at Columbia. Not surprisingly, Bernard turned to Rabbi Moshe Soloveitchik for advice. Rabbi Moshe suggested a position at the Blue Hill Avenue *shul* in Boston where his own son *davened* (prayed). The position would require delivering sermons in Yiddish.

Bernard found this requirement unappealing. While he was certainly capable of sermonizing in Yiddish, he preferred a younger, English-speaking congregation. But there was another reason that Bernard was reluctant to accept the position at Blue Hill. Many years later, he explained his thinking in the following way:

> At the time, I had been accepted at Harvard Law School and was seriously considering the move to Boston. However, I rejected the proposal because I questioned my fluency in delivering sermons in Yiddish to a crowd of several hundred worshippers, and the thought of delivering a sermon in the presence of the Gaon Rav Yosef Dov was daunting. In the end I became a rabbi in Baltimore, and switched my area of study from law to sociology.

Despite his reluctance, Bernard did not entirely close the door on this opportunity, since it would allow him to easily attend Harvard Law School.

At the same time, Bernard sought out the advice of one of Rabbi Revel's closest confidants at RIETS, Dean Samuel Sar. Rabbi Sar was involved with placing Yeshiva graduates at Orthodox synagogues around the country. He had recently placed one of Bernard's classmates at Congregation Beth Jacob in Baltimore. The synagogue, unable to come to terms with the new rabbi, informed Dean Sar that the position remained open. Sar immediately contacted Bernard, who indicated that he was interested. Bernard visited Beth Jacob and conducted services during a "trial Shabbos." The congregation loved him, and likewise, Bernard felt very much at home there. The salary was sufficient and the schedule commitment such that it would allow him to work on his thesis and travel back to New York to carry out his doctoral studies at Columbia. He reached an agreement in principle with the synagogue board and now sat facing a critical decision. Boston versus Baltimore. Columbia versus Harvard. Older Yiddish versus younger English-speaking congregations. These were all factors, but at its core, the choice lay between the disciplines of law versus sociology. In Bernard's mind the road to Boston represented an old-world sensibility. There he would be following a family tradition, exercising his well-honed Talmudic skills in the legal arena while ministering to the spiritual needs of an established, more senior congregation. By contrast, the road to Baltimore meant breaking ground in a new and exciting field, while serving in the pulpit of a *shul* with a younger, more Americanized demographic. He took the road to Baltimore.

Like many American synagogues, Congregation Beth Jacob, Rabbi Lander's new home, was born amidst discord and disagreement. A contingent of congregants at Shearith Israel, a venerated Baltimore Orthodox *shul* established in 1879, had vociferously expressed its unhappiness with the direction the *shul's* twenty-nine-year-old German-born rabbi, Shimon Schwab, was taking the congregation. Rabbi Schwab had fled Nazi Germany and accepted the Baltimore pulpit despite the fact that he spoke little English. The vocal group was unhappy with the *mechitsah* (barrier between the genders) and was distanced further when the rabbi ruled out synagogue membership for those who were not Sabbath observant (*Shomer Shabbos*). The dissatisfaction had been building for several years, and by 1938, the splinter group took action, breaking away and starting its own new synagogue, Beth Jacob. After renting a former school building at the corner of Park Heights and Manhattan Avenues, a block and a half from Shearith Israel, the new *shul* now needed a new rabbi. Their first attempt did not go well.

The new synagogue's president, Hungarian-born Abraham Schreter, was a charismatic and dynamic Shearith Israel congregant who had become a leader of the breakaway group when he learned that his son, who had chosen not to be *Shomer Shabbos*, was denied membership. As his first act as president of Beth Jacob, Schreter was charged with the task of hiring a rabbi for the new *shul*. He selected Dr. Louis Kaplan, an innovative teacher who had been serving as the executive director of the Baltimore Board of Jewish Education. He was initially well received by the new congregation, but when he used the term "Jonah and the fish story" in a sermon, he offended the traditional sentiments of many. Dr. Kaplan's short-lived tenure as spiritual leader of Congregation Beth Jacob was over. Enter Bernard Lander.

As he stepped off the train in Baltimore's Central Station to begin his new position in the pulpit of Congregation Beth Jacob, Rabbi Bernard Lander was, at the tender age of twenty-three, a *musmach* (ordained rabbi) of RIETS, a graduate of Yeshiva College, and a doctoral student in the sociology department at Columbia University. He also possessed the good sense and sensitivity not to commit the same type of faux pas that had scuttled his predecessor.

Rabbi Lander was fully aware of the circumstances that had given rise to the formation of his new home synagogue. Despite his tender years, Lander was aware that the same forces that had given birth to this *shul* were at work all across the country: Americanized second-generation young Jews coming into positions of power within their congregations versus the traditional leanings of their old world parents. Beth Jacob represented a microcosm of this nationwide struggle. Rabbi Lander observed how the younger members, mostly public school and college-educated, were typically less observant than their parents. There was less of an attachment to authentic tradition and, as a result, there was a widespread weakening of the "spirit and vital message of Judaism." This was the precise situation for which Yeshiva College had been established and, as one of its new exponents, Rabbi Lander felt he could effectively serve to bridge this generational gap—the gap between "intellectualism and faith," as Rabbi Revel often put it. He was correct, but it wasn't going to be easy.

Before agreeing to accept his new post, Rabbi Lander had insisted that his appointment first be approved by Shearith Israel's Rabbi Schwab. Rabbi Schwab granted his approval after meeting with Lander, advising him that Beth Jacob needed a rabbi, and it would be better that *he* accept the position rather than a rabbi with liberal tendencies.

Rabbi Lander quickly set to work hammering home the message that Judaism is indeed relevant to both young American Jews as well as their immigrant parents. As a member of their generation, he spoke the language of his younger constituents. Like them, he too was interested in social justice and building a better American society. Like them, he felt that Judaism should be manifested beyond the cloistered halls of learning. Like them, he believed that merely studying Torah without acting upon its principles was inadequate. While his younger congregants were impressed with his vast knowledge of Western culture and civilization, their parents were equally impressed with their new rabbi's encyclopedic range of Jewish texts and traditions. Rabbi Lander soon engendered a level of respect that often resulted in shock when a congregant learned he was only twenty-three years old.

Rabbi Lander remained in the pulpit of Congregation Beth Jacob for five years. During those years, the world was plunged into the abyss of war and the history of the Jewish people entered its darkest period under a portal marked "Arbeit Macht Frei." Despite these global forces, Rabbi Lander, during this period, blossomed as an inspiring speaker as he deftly applied Jewish teachings to the burning issues that were quickly engulfing the world. Week after week, during his regular Shabbos morning *d'rasha* (sermon), Rabbi Lander would stitch the week's events into the tapestry of Jewish history and tradition. He focused on the micro as well as the macro events, demonstrating to congregants how to apply Torah teachings in their personal, social, and business affairs.

"*Leshon hora* (malicious gossip) is a weapon more powerful than a Howitzer," he would declare. "With a gun, a soldier shoots once and it's either hit or miss and he's done. With gossip the damage spreads from the lips of one victim to the ears of the next."

When Shabbos arrived earlier in the day during Baltimore's winter months, Rabbi Lander would offer his sermons during Friday evening services. Word soon spread as young intellectuals from across the northwest quadrant of the city were drawn in to listen and learn. As his renown as a brilliant lecturer grew, he began receiving invitations to speak at community events and to author feature pieces in the *Baltimore Sun*, Maryland's largest circulation newspaper at the time.

During his tenure, Rabbi Lander sought to expand the role of his synagogue within the community and within the lives of his congregants. He began to put in place the infrastructure that would shape Beth Jacob into more than merely a "Beth Tefillah" or house of worship. His vision cast the *shul* also as a "Beth Midrash," a place of study and learning, as well as a "Beth Knesset," a community center providing social, cultural and leisure programs for all congregants. "Our synagogue will become the heart and nerve center of Jewish life," he proclaimed repeatedly from the *bimah*.

Acting on this directive, and working closely with board president, Abraham Schreter, Rabbi Lander opened the doors to Beth Jacob's first afternoon and Sunday Hebrew school in 1940. The school would, under the inspired leadership of its president, Leon Rivkin, grow to an enrollment of more than 700 students.

By 1940 the events underway in Europe, as the Third Reich put into motion its "Final Solution," were in no way being understood by the American Jewish community. With a few notable exceptions, there emerged a deafening silence from America's Jewish secular leadership. This was due in part to Nazi subterfuge and sophisticated propaganda, but also by widespread fear that vocal protests and agitation would stimulate and stir up the specter of anti-Semitism that had been on the rise in American life during the 1930s.

Running counter to this trend was the brave voice of Yeshiva's devoted founder, Rabbi Bernard Revel. During a widely attended lecture in the fall of 1940, Revel proclaimed: "The lights of Torah are being dimmed across the seas. We must therefore light our torches all the more brilliantly." It was to be his last lecture.

Learning that his beloved teacher had suffered a series of strokes, Rabbi Lander rushed to his side. This was the man whom Lander had come to respect and perhaps even love. Rabbi Lander, in his role at Beth Jacob, was trying to emulate Rabbi Revel, a man who had dedicated his entire life to Torah and to the Jewish people. Having, by this point, been rendered blind, Rabbi Revel spent his last moments with Lander discussing from memory, the Talmudic tractates dealing with the laws of civil government. Finally leaving his teacher's bedside, Lander was one of the last nonfamily members to see him alive. Rabbi Revel, age fifty-five, died on December 2, 1940, and, despite his absence from this world, his memory would continue to inspire and guide Bernard Lander throughout his life. This was particularly true during the last years of Lander's life when he, too, was stricken with macular degeneration. He would often confide in friends how he drew great strength from his memories of Rabbi Revel during his final days.

Rabbi Lander returned to Baltimore and organized a citywide memorial service that saw Lander's friend, Hirschel Revel, eloquently eulogize his father. Yeshiva was still reeling from the loss of its founder when, a short two months later, another body blow struck the school. Yeshiva's crown and glory, Rabbi Moshe Soloveitchik, the school's head, heart, and guiding hand, took ill and died. For Bernard Lander, it was an incredible shock. The two people who had counseled and guided him during his most formative years were suddenly, and tragically, gone.

Rabbi Lander dealt with these losses by embracing his work at Beth Jacob with a renewed passion and fervor. He had developed a routine that saw him take the Monday morning train to New York to attend his Columbia classes. He would spend Monday evening with his parents who had, at this point, moved to Washington Heights. On Tuesdays he would typically visit the Yeshiva campus, reconnecting with his colleagues and former classmates, and then catch the midnight train back to Baltimore. He poured himself into his own ongoing religious studies as well as into the many congregational activities going on at Beth Jacob. He taught a class in Talmud to congregants that often attracted others from outside the synagogue family. Afternoons would often find Rabbi Lander engrossed in his studies at the public library, focused on his sociology studies. The path towards his doctorate led him to accept a position as a consultant, first with the Maryland State Commission on Juvenile Delinquency, and later with the City of Baltimore Youth Commission. He used these opportunities to collect data for his developing doctoral dissertation. Overall, Bernard felt energized and empowered by this active lifestyle and found that he was thriving in his dual role as congregational spiritual leader and budding sociologist.

Since the newly formed congregation's budget was not adequate to underwrite the rabbi's housing costs or provide a parsonage, Lander was required to seek out his own lodgings in Baltimore. He resided in a second-floor walk-up apartment on Clover Road. Finding a roof over one's head was simple, but locating a place to eat one's meals was another story. The level of *kashruth* (dietary law) observance of many congregants was below a standard that Rabbi Lander found acceptable. Sensitive to his role as a reconciler of factions within the *shul*, Rabbi Lander made it a strict policy not to eat in the homes of any of his congregants. This way no one would become offended—although *he* would still become hungry. Not knowing a tablespoon from a potato peeler, cooking his own meals was also not an option for Rabbi Lander. Fortunately, he located noncongregational families (the Mirvises and the Neubergers) who agreed to provide his meals. While he declined to accept dinner invitations from congregants, Rabbi Lander was a frequent and regular guest at their homes. As an available and attractive bachelor, Rabbi Lander was naturally the target of the community's local *shadchonim* (matchmakers). He was also a regular Shabbos guest in the homes of a number of Baltimore's leading rabbis, forging lifelong friendships with several of them.

Among the members of the Baltimore rabbinate befriended by Rabbi Lander and with whom he interacted during those years was Rabbi Mordechai Gifter, who would go on to serve as the Rosh Yeshiva of Telshe in Cleveland. Rabbi Gifter, who occupied the pulpit at Baltimore's Nusach Ari-Lubawitz Synagogue until 1943, had been studying in Europe when war broke out and was fortunate to slip back to the United States with his bride in the nick of time. Rabbi Lander served as a witness at Rabbi Gifter's wedding, and his signature may be found on the couple's *Ketubah*. Later, after the establishment of Touro College, Rabbi Gifter would joke that he could not be overly critical of Touro since its president had the power to invalidate his *Ketubah*!

Another of Rabbi Lander's Baltimore close contemporaries was Rabbi Naftali Neuberger. Rabbi Lander was often a Shabbos guest at the home of the recently-wed rabbi and his bride, Judy. Rabbi Neuberger had left his native Germany in 1938 and settled in Baltimore, where he first attended and later administered the Ner Israel Rabbinical College. Neuberger had overseen the construction of a new school building on Garrison Street and was on his way towards a leadership position on the national scene. In later years, Neuberger would gain recognition for his role in rescuing the Persian Jewish community that was being subjected to extreme persecution during the 1970s. Neuberger's school, Ner Israel, today boasts an enrollment of more than 1,000 students on a magnificent suburban campus. A few months before his death at age eighty-seven in 2005, Rabbi Neuberger attended the ninetieth birthday party of his old friend, Bernard Lander, in New York.

Perhaps Rabbi Lander's most unique relationship among those he developed while serving at Beth Jacob was with Rabbi Zvi Elimelech

Hertzberg, the leading Hasidic rabbi in Baltimore. Reb Zvi was a scion of a venerated Belz Hasidic family that emerged from Eastern Galicia. Considerably older than Rabbi Lander, Reb Zvi had fought in Emperor Franz Joseph's army during the First World War. He and his family immigrated from Poland to America in 1926 and settled in Baltimore.

Rabbi Lander loved the ambience at the Hertzberg home. He delighted in Reb Zvi's Hasidic tales as they sat around the large table in what was a true transplanted Galician Jewish home, filled with warmth, wonderful traditional food, and a sense of kindred fellowship that reminded Lander of his own childhood. Bernard and Reb Zvi's son, Arthur, became lifelong friends, despite (or perhaps because of) the fact that, since Arthur was destined to become a leading figure in the American Conservative movement, he and Bernard disagreed on almost every aspect of Judaism.

The relationships Rabbi Lander forged in Baltimore were true links of the heart. Lander looked back upon this era as one of significant personal growth and intellectual development. It was here, in Baltimore, as a raging war shaped the destiny of the world, that Rabbi Bernard Lander's own personal destiny took form. His nascent skills as a public speaker and a community leader began to blossom in Baltimore. It was here also that Rabbi Lander began to stretch and branch out to both the larger Jewish and the general communities. And it was here that Rabbi Lander began to connect with other emerging figures in the Torah world. All of these guiding factors would serve him well in the years that lay ahead.

As Rabbi Lander's world expanded, so did his level of happiness. He found that, except for one thing, he was extremely happy in this community. That one thing, not surprisingly, was his marital status. As he observed his contemporaries marching under the *chupah* (marriage canopy) one by one and begin building their families, Bernard could not help but feel some sense of remorse that his intense schedule did not permit him the time needed for socialization and courtship. He felt that he had met those few women in the Baltimore Orthodox community who were appropriately observant and that no sparks had flown. Adding to this sense of "I'll never find someone here in Baltimore," was the fact that his studies were nearing completion. He had originally accepted the position at Beth Jacob in order to afford the costs of obtaining his doctorate at Columbia. Now that this obligation had been met, there was no financial imperative at work and he was free to move on. There was also something else.

He was pleased about his emergence as a leading figure in the Baltimore Jewish community, but after five years, aspects of congregational life were beginning to wear on the "not-so-young" rabbi. As Lander wrote to his friend, Chaplain Norman Siegel, explaining his departure from Baltimore:

"I found I was spending all my time running from sisterhood meeting to sisterhood meeting and from congregation dance to brotherhood bingo." The final straw came when he was required to officiate at the funeral of the only child of two Holocaust survivors. "What can you possibly say in a situation like that?" he bemoaned to his friend. In later years, when asked why he never accepted another pulpit, although many were offered, Rabbi Lander would think back to his Baltimore years at Beth Jacob and respond simply: "I don't have the heart for it."

Rabbi Bernard Lander left Baltimore and the pulpit of Congregation Beth Jacob in 1944 and returned to New York, where he accepted a key position on a new commission established by Mayor Fiorello LaGuardia. The commission was charged with investigating and overcoming ethnic and racial tensions in New York City. It was the start of a new and important chapter in Bernard Lander's life, one that would both lead him towards an expanded leadership position and also place him on the road to romance.

CHAPTER SIX

Spiritual Sociologist

Master of Torah, master of *Hokhmah* (scientific wisdom).
—*Talmud, Megillah 13b*

B ernard Lander left Baltimore for New York after adding five years
of experience as a congregational rabbi to his résumé—along
with a great deal more. By the conclusion of those transformative
years, the young and energetic rabbi had emerged as an accomplished
force in the field of practical sociology. Lander had completed all of his
course requirements towards his doctorate at Columbia by the end of his
third year in Baltimore. The weekly trips to New York were no longer a
requirement, and his degree program encouraged candidates to acquire
professional experience in the field. Lander was, at this point, more than
eager to put the knowledge he had gained in the classroom into practical
use. He soon got his chance.

In November 1941, Maryland Governor Herbert O'Conor convened a commission to study the causes of, and recommend new methods for dealing with, the rising tide of juvenile delinquency in the state,
and particularly in Baltimore. The common wisdom was that the influx of war workers from the South, flowing into Maryland's shipyards
and factories, was the primary cause of this rapidly accelerating teenage
crime wave. The Maryland Commission on Juvenile Delinquency was
charged with investigating the matter and developing administrative
and legislative solutions. To assist them in this mission, the commission identified and recruited a Baltimore rabbi with the appropriate
credentials in sociology and who, by this time, was enjoying a growing reputation as an advocate for social justice. In early 1942, Rabbi
Bernard Lander received word that he had been tapped by Governor
O'Conor to serve as a special consultant to the Maryland Commission
on Juvenile Delinquency.

Rabbi Lander quickly surveyed the landscape and discovered that the state's management of children's welfare was a dismal, uncoordinated, and chaotic tangle of administrative and judicial neglect. State training schools, supposedly designed to rehabilitate wayward young offenders, were filled with mentally challenged children and others awaiting placement into foster care and were simply not doing the job they had been created to perform. The State Board of Public Welfare was focused exclusively on the funding of private institutions such as orphanages, with little, if any, attention directed towards teenagers who had been convicted of petty crimes. Most offenders returned to their original street gangs after incarceration and were soon back in the courts. Lander recommended a major overhaul of the state's child welfare system to effectively stem the tide of juvenile crime.

Another area that the commission investigated was Maryland's archaic juvenile justice system. Rabbi Lander pointed out that Baltimore was the only large city in the United States whose Juvenile Court judges were untrained justices of the peace. "We must have experienced jurists dispensing justice in our juvenile courts," he advised. Evidently the commission, as well as the state legislature, was listening. A constitutional amendment creating "… a Juvenile Court … for Baltimore City" and authorizing the General Assembly to "establish a Juvenile Court for any other incorporated city or town or any county of the State," was soon adopted in response to the commission's recommendations. The amendment required that only seasoned members of the state bar be placed on the bench.

In his role as commission consultant, Rabbi Lander visited several other states to investigate how they handled both the curative, as well as the preventative, aspects of juvenile crime. His observations led him to the conclusion that programs designed to prevent delinquency had proven more effective than those implemented after the fact. Rabbi Lander outlined a general approach for reducing youth-perpetrated crime in Baltimore in his report to the commission titled "The Prevention of Delinquency." He advocated the need for community-based programming to fill the idle time of youngsters in the many crime-breeding areas of the city:

> Behind the delinquent act, there is the home, the neighborhood, and the community conditions that caused the incipient

deviations from the conventions of society. It is to these roots of the crime problem that we must address any attempt to reduce the volume of delinquent behavior.

Lander's report made a strong case for state investment in recreational facilities, athletic centers, and the funding of neighborhood groups that would develop wholesome activities to keep young offenders occupied and less likely to engage in petty crime.

The activities of the commission soon began attracting public interest as they were reported in the Baltimore press. An interview with Rabbi Lander was published in the May 24, 1943, issue of *The Baltimore Sun,* in which he exploded the myth that the city's increased level of juvenile delinquency was due to the recent influx of war workers. "Organized activities for young people, through the schools and the community, are necessary to combat the influence of gangs," he stated. Lander pointed out that, based on his studies, the breakdown of social values that leads to juvenile crime is present in many neighborhoods, not just those populated by recent arrivals from the South.

Rabbi Lander's findings, particularly those laid out in his "Prevention of Delinquency" report, positively influenced the commission as it drafted its report to the governor. In addition to overhauling the state's juvenile justice system, the commission's findings also led to a total restructuring of its juvenile welfare system. Among its primary recommendations was the creation of a separate Bureau of Child Welfare, as part of the Department of Public Welfare, which would develop and manage programming aimed at rooting out the causes of juvenile crime. The concept was to replace the breeding grounds for crime—the pool halls where teenage gangs would congregate—with community centers and wholesome, supervised activities, such as sports and camping.

The commission further recommended that the envisioned Bureau of Child Welfare be charged with administering all state-sponsored institutions that housed young offenders. This recommendation was also heeded. Once the Bureau was in fact established, it included a Department of Institutions that placed the state training schools for delinquent children, reformatories, and other juvenile facilities under the Bureau's direct supervision and established standards of care, admission, discharge, and, most importantly, aftercare. The commission's recommendations were quickly adopted by the state legislature, and the new structure proved successful in reducing the overall juvenile crime rate in Baltimore. In an expansion of the Bureau's role in 1955, forestry camps for boys were established in western Maryland. These camps served to remove, albeit temporarily, young offenders from their urban environments and expose them to a healthful outdoor lifestyle. This program, first envisioned in Rabbi Lander's report to the commission, is credited with further reducing the teenage crime rate in Baltimore.

As Rabbi Lander's reputation in the area of juvenile delinquency grew, he was soon invited to offer his counsel in other similar capacities. In 1942, he took on a second position as a consultant to the Baltimore Youth Commission, a municipal social service agency also focused on combating teenage crime. In December 1943, Baltimore Mayor Theodore McKeldin appointed Rabbi Lander to the commission itself. During his service as a consultant, Lander helped to revise mandated high school curricula that added special racial and religious tolerance courses designed to battle the prejudice children often encountered in the home. These courses were highly unique and fully decades ahead of their time. Once Rabbi Lander became a commissioner, he served on the executive committee and became involved in empirically evaluating various means of reducing delinquency in one particular economically depressed Baltimore neighborhood. The methods of statistical analysis he developed in this role dovetailed perfectly with the research he was conducting for his doctoral dissertation.

There is little question that Bernard Lander's religious background influenced his service to the governmental agencies that sought his counsel in combating juvenile crime. His worldview, shaped by Talmudic tractates and both the written and oral traditions of Judaism, is clearly evident in the manner in which he approached his analysis. Lander regarded juvenile delinquency, at its core, as the by-product of society's deviation from normative social constructs. He observed that as adult family members moved further from their traditional roles, due to wartime and economic imperatives, a direct consequence was the loss of ethical socialization among their children. As he surveyed the social forces at work that produce societal ills such as juvenile delinquency, Rabbi Lander's conclusions demonstrated strong parallels with his ingrained views on the value of Jewish observance. While he never listed specific analogies, the sway of Orthodox Judaism is clearly evident throughout his written works. Such works were to include Rabbi Lander's Columbia doctoral dissertation that would eventually be published as a book and become recognized as a landmark treatise on juvenile delinquency in America.

While his pastoral duties and work as consultant and commissioner occupied most mornings during the war years of 1942 and 1943, Bernard Lander's afternoons were almost always spent at the Baltimore City Department of Vital Statistics or deep in the records room of the city's Juvenile Court. Here he would delve into census tracts, court records, and other arcane documents as he slowly began to formulate a new slant on the root causes of juvenile delinquency; an approach that would fundamentally challenge the prevailing wisdom.

Studies undertaken during the 1930s by social researchers Park and Burgess at the University of Chicago compared juvenile crime rates against economic census tract data. The studies had claimed to find a strong statistical correlation between delinquency levels and the average income level of a given neighborhood. Lower average income meant a higher juvenile crime rate, according to Park and Burgess. But Lander's immersion into Baltimore's crime and census statistics soon led him to question this widely held correlation. In studying some of the poorest areas of Baltimore, he observed that they experienced virtually no juvenile crime! His findings flew in the face of the U. of C. studies. How was this possible? Was Baltimore so different from Chicago? Lander did not think so. He determined that the statistical analysis methods employed by the Chicago social researchers were flawed. He suspected that the application of more advanced methods of statistical analysis might lead to different conclusions in the quest to understand the underlying causes of juvenile delinquency. This profound insight proved to be accurate and became the basis for Lander's doctoral dissertation research that would serve to shape governmental social policy for years to come.

But if family income was not a major factor leading to delinquency, then what was? What identifiable thread ran through the lives of young offenders that could be countered and thereby prevent the aberrant behavior before it occurred? This question hounded Lander as he strove to interpret the mountains of demographic and census data he was poring over. For example, he learned that from the years 1939 through 1942 there were 8,464 hearings in Baltimore's Juvenile Court. Lander extracted and recorded the essential data about each case on a single 3 x 5 index card. Next, each card was assigned to a census tract based upon the defendant's street address. The monumental task of analyzing these data would lead Lander once again into a realm that was decades ahead of his time: statistical data analysis via electronic computer.

The saga of the embryonic science of computing and how it was applied to analyze social demographic data at Columbia is a dramatic and historic one. The Bureau of Radio Research, a pioneering social science research group headed by Paul Lazarsfeld and funded by a Rockefeller grant, was actually founded at Princeton in 1937 and moved to Columbia at the outbreak of the war. In 1944, its name was changed to the Bureau of Applied Social Research (BASR). BASR at Columbia became the focus of the nascent field of quantitative sociology. From the time it moved to Columbia, the Bureau enjoyed access to a series of ever more sophisticated proto-computers. These electronic "tabulating machines" were operated via IBM punch cards and were capable of quickly (by the standards of the day) digesting large volumes of numeric data and running rapid linear regression analyses, for example. Of course it would take one of Columbia's IBM machines a full year to analyze the amount of data that any of today's personal computers could digest in a few minutes. But, in their day, these punched card "tabulators" represented a quantum leap forward from the "adding machine" methods in use at the time.

Bernard Lander painstakingly transferred the raw data he had recorded on his thousands of index cards over to IBM punched cards that could then be fed into the calculating behemoths at Columbia and appropriate statistical tests applied. Was there a statistically significant correlation between the number of years of schooling completed by a teenager and the likelihood of his being arrested for a felony? Was race a factor? Parental divorce? Lander even examined the question of whether taller youngsters were more criminally inclined than shorter ones.

Working with his mentor at Columbia, Professor William S. Robinson, Lander developed a solid foundation in the field of statistical analysis. Robinson, along with Scottish sociologist Robert MacIver, served as Rabbi Lander's dissertation advisors. Lander also was fortunate to work under the Bureau's celebrated director, Paul Lazarsfeld.

By the time he left Baltimore in 1944, Lander's research and dissertation were functionally complete. Since his results challenged the findings of the earlier University of Chicago study, he framed his work as an "ecological study," just like theirs. An ecological study is one that applies a series of statistical tests normally applied to an individual, to an entire population. Lander was aware, however, of the hazards involved in this approach. Professor Robinson, his advisor, had discovered what was called the "ecological fallacy," which wrongly imputed the characteristics of the entire group to each individual within that group in a form of statistical stereotyping. Lander did not make this mistake in the conclusions that he drew from his analyses. Utilizing the IBM tabulating equipment, Lander's results carried more weight than the U. of C. study because they were drawn from a much larger population.

After years of carefully organizing the results of his study, Rabbi Lander was finally able to complete and defend his dissertation in 1948. *Toward an Understanding of Juvenile Delinquency; A Study of 8,484 Cases of Juvenile Delinquency in Baltimore* represented a breakthrough in the field of applied social science. Building on MacIver's earlier work, *Social Causation*, Lander's treatise is radically innovative in its use of multiple and partial co-relational and factor analysis. But what did this advanced scientific approach to society's problems have to teach us? The conclusion was clear. Juvenile delinquency was not, as previously believed, primarily the result of unfavorable economic conditions. The main predictive indicator of delinquency, according to Lander, was a breakdown of social structure brought on by the encroachment of industry on established neighborhoods.

In his conclusion, Lander cautions that the results of his study must be regarded as "predictive," rather than "causative." Statistical correlations do not always imply causation. Umbrellas come out whenever it's raining, but umbrellas do not cause the rain to fall. He concludes his dissertation by offering the following disclaimer:

> The statistical findings in themselves do not supply the answer to the causal basis of the differential delinquency rate, but do provide a map, which if analyzed with care and caution, may suggest some directions and answers. They enable us to test and

suggest hypotheses. Statistical techniques and their results are effective aids in the quest for understanding. At best, however, they provide only clues, and if used without caution, may in many instances even be misleading.

Both Professors MacIver and Robinson strongly encouraged Rabbi Lander to publish his dissertation in book format in order to reach a wider audience. Lander agreed. *Towards an Understanding of Juvenile Delinquency* was, in fact, published by Columbia University Press in 1954. As MacIver notes in the introduction, he wrote for the book, "Lander has exposed the weaknesses of much of the work done in the investigation of the causes of delinquency, bringing out the defects of the methods on which certain conclusions have been based."

Lander's work became a widely read and widely cited monograph, both within and outside of the field of social science. At least five major studies applied Lander's innovative techniques to juvenile crime statistics in other large cities. The book was reprinted in 1955 and in 1958 and stands today as a pioneering landmark in the application of statistical analysis in the quest to further our understanding of social issues.

Bernard Lander's years at Columbia, devoted to his doctoral studies in sociology, came at a time when the field was undergoing its greatest expansion. This growth was driven by widely held optimism, bordering on naïveté, that the scientific method applied to societal ills could deliver solutions resulting in a better world. This noble and benevolent attitude had not always prevailed, however. The term *sociology* was originally coined in 1838 by French philosopher Auguste Comte, who had investigated the question of why certain societies endure and others decay. The Industrial Revolution's wide-reaching disruption of centuries-old social patterns and values sparked fervent academic interest in the social sciences. This era was marked by the work of Herbert Spencer, who gained fame as the father of "social Darwinism," a theory positing that societies evolve from primitive forms to more complex ones through a process that mimics human evolution. From this notion emerged a school of thought that opposed any form of social reform since it would interfere with the "natural selection" process that insured the survival of the fittest. Sadly, such notions would eventually serve as the misguided underpinnings of Nazi racial theories. Theories, that when put into deadly practice, would result in the destruction of the Jewish world in Europe.

The American school of sociology, as personified by figures such as Lester F. Ward and others, viewed sociology much differently—as an instrument of human benefit designed to unlock answers about social forces that would ultimately promote happiness and universal freedom. It was this school of "enlightened" sociology that attracted the young Bernard Lander to the field, and it was this variety that he encountered and later embraced as a doctoral candidate at Columbia.

Under the dynamic leadership of Professor Robert MacIver in the 1930s, Columbia emerged, alongside the University of Chicago, as the focal point of American sociological study. While the "Chicago School" became identified with social reform, it was at Columbia, under MacIver and his predecessor Franklin Giddings, that quantitative and statistical analysis of social phenomena was being carried out. Bernard Lander revered MacIver with great affection and respect, as did all of the professor's students. The relationship between MacIver and Rabbi Lander was a close and enduring one. As stated, MacIver served as Lander's dissertation advisor and provided him with the ongoing fatherly encouragement he needed to complete his massive study on Juvenile Delinquency. The two men would later work side by side on a major investigation of Jewish organizations that was hailed as a breakthrough at the time it was published.

Columbia was home to the one sociological study that received more attention than any other during this early period. *Middletown*, a detailed examination of a typical American small town—Muncie, Indiana—written by Robert S. and Helen Lynd in 1929, became a bestseller and served to introduce the field of sociology to the general public. The book is still required reading in most first-year sociology classes today.

A dispute erupted between MacIver and Robert Lynd during the time that Bernard Lander was at Columbia. The intellectual civil war was sparked by a critical review by MacIver of one of Lynd's books. Eminent German-born social researchers, such as Erich Fromm and Max Horkheimer of Columbia's Institute for Social Research, were forced to take sides in the academic tug-of-war. Bernard Lander, not surprisingly, elected to side with his mentor, Professor MacIver. The resulting friction led to the eventual departure of Fromm and Horkheimer.

But perhaps Rabbi Lander's greatest intellectual influence at Columbia was Professor Paul Lazarsfeld, a giant in the field of American sociology. Lazarsfeld fled Vienna in the early 1940s and eventually joined the

Columbia faculty as the director of the Bureau of Applied Social Research (BASR). It was at BASR that Lander gained access to the IBM tabulating machines used to compile the vast data employed in his doctoral dissertation. But it was not merely by the use of its proto-computers that Lander benefited from his work at the Bureau. Professor Lazarsfeld had expanded the work of BASR beyond pure research into the realm of the practical. The Bureau regularly worked with both corporate and governmental clients on a fee basis to carry out specific commissioned studies. To this end, Lazarsfeld had assembled a large and expert staff, adept at answering any question thrown at them using the latest empirical methods. Thanks to his relationship with Professor Lazarsfeld, Lander was able to employ these methods as he sought to draw valid conclusions from his data analysis.

While at Columbia, Lander also studied under Canadian social psychologist Otto Klineberg, who was known for discrediting racial theories based on intelligence testing. Klineberg conducted IQ tests on immigrants, American Indians, and black students and discovered no correlation between race and intelligence. His seminal studies greatly influenced the United States Supreme Court in its 1954 landmark *Brown v. Board of Education* decision that struck down racial segregation in America's public schools. Lander would often cite Klineberg's studies in his future work.

But while Bernard Lander toiled within Columbia's halls of academe, seeking answers to the burning social issues of the day, the world around him was igniting in flames. As U.S. troops fought bravely to bring down regimes built on racism and persecution in Europe and the Pacific, those same enemies of humanity were rearing their ugly heads on the home front. Violent race riots raged in Detroit and New York's Harlem during the summer of 1943. New York was further plagued that year by vicious anti-Jewish activity among the Irish teenage gangs that populated Washington Heights and the South Bronx. With shouts of "Kill the Jews!" these marauding gangs targeted synagogues during religious services, vandalizing them severely and attacking any Jewish children they encountered, in an Americanized version of *Kristallnacht*.

Entire Jewish neighborhoods were terrorized by these anti-Semitic gangs, inspired by the Father Coughlin–led Christian Front, and made up entirely of Irish Catholic teenagers. These gangs harassed Jewish storekeepers and had desecrated nearly every synagogue in Manhattan's Washington

Heights, an area that was home to a great many European Jewish immigrants who had fled Hitler, seeking sanctuary in "the home of the free." In December 1943, the *New York Times* reported that vandals had desecrated Jewish cemeteries throughout Brooklyn, Queens, and other areas of Long Island, overturning gravestones and painting obscenities and swastikas on them. This outrage garnered national attention, prompting U.S. Attorney General Francis Biddle to compare the damage done to New York's Jewish cemeteries to that witnessed in Nazi-occupied countries in Europe.

These atrocities were heavily covered in the press along with stories of individual Jews terrorized by roving bands of Irish thugs. For example, it was reported that three teenagers in the Bronx surrounded a fourteen-year-old Jewish boy and demanded to know if he was Jewish. When he nodded, they shouted: "He's a Jew! Let him have it!" They beat him and slashed him across the face leaving a deep scar from his ear to his lip. "Only one of the many attacks against Jews during the past week," cried the caption below the photo on the front page of the *Daily News*.

The media succeeded in arousing enough public outrage in New York City to prompt a public call to action. "Why are we fighting Nazis in Europe and letting them run free in New York?" characterized a growing popular sentiment. Prodded by both this public pressure and in response to the Harlem riots, City Hall initiated steps aimed at studying and reducing the epidemic of ethnic tension rampant throughout the five boroughs. On February 27, 1944, Mayor Fiorello La Guardia decreed the formation of a "Committee on Unity," whose mission, as announced with great flourish, was "to promote understanding and mutual respect among all the racial groups in our city." The committee was to be chaired by none other than former U.S. Solicitor General, Charles Evans Hughes, Jr., son of the former New York governor, U.S. Secretary of State, Chief Justice of the Supreme Court, and Republican presidential candidate in 1916. LaGuardia also selected a cross section of prominent black, Jewish, Catholic and protestant leaders to sit on the committee. Among these was a recognized expert in the field of juvenile delinquency who had recently returned to New York after spending five years in the pulpit of a Baltimore synagogue.

Bernard Lander's service to the Committee on Unity, as he was completing his Columbia doctoral dissertation, would forcefully shape the next major chapter of his life. It was during this chapter that Bernard's path would cross with that of another brilliant student of sociology who was studying at New York University at the time; a beautiful and engaging young woman by the name of Sarah Shragowitz.

CHAPTER SEVEN

Unity

Every assembly that is for the sake of Heaven will have
an enduring impact.
—*Pirkei Avot (Ethics of the Fathers) 4:14*

A t the time Bernard Lander was appointed to the Mayor's Committee on Unity in July 1944, he was no stranger to anti-Jewish
discrimination. In those years before films such as *Gentleman's
Agreement* began to alter public attitudes about anti-Semitism, Jews were
routinely barred from many aspects of American life. In areas such as
housing, public accommodation, university admission, professional employment, and even hospital admission, Jews had become accustomed
to quotas at best and complete exclusion at worst. When Lander was de-
liberating on the direction of his future career as he prepared to graduate
from Yeshiva College, he received a grim warning from faculty member,
Dr. Theodore Abel, who had first introduced him to the field of sociology. Abel, a non-Jew, was also a distinguished professor at Columbia
University. As a young Jewish intellectual, Abel warned, Lander would
not find a position in academia.

But that advice had been dispensed at a time that, at this juncture,
seemed like centuries ago. This was a new postwar world that was to be
marked by one overarching rubric: unity. Unity, as in the United Nations.
Unity, as in the United Negro College Fund. Unity, as in the Mayor's
Committee on Unity. It was this general sense of one-world optimism,
during that sweet slice of history between the end of World War II and
the onset of the Cold War—between Hiroshima blowing up and the Iron
Curtain coming down—that animated and motivated Bernard Lander as
he began his work on the Mayor's Committee.

A key part of committee chairman Hughes's mandate was to assemble a diverse governing board that included knowledgeable leaders

from each of New York's major ethnic communities. So it was no surprise that when seeking to fill the "Jewish" slot, Hughes turned to Maurice Hexter, the executive director of one of the city's foremost secular Jewish organizations: The Federation of Jewish Charities of New York. Hexter agreed to make inquiries and to assist Hughes in identifying a candidate with the appropriate credentials. When Hexter turned to his counterpart in Baltimore, Rabbi Bernard Lander's name was immediately suggested.

Hexter, who held a Ph.D. from Harvard in social ethics, was impressed with Lander's academic qualifications and during their first meeting, he was equally impressed with the young rabbi's excellent communication skills. Although Lander had been in Baltimore for the past five years, Hexter could see that the rabbi knew and fully understood the social dynamics present in New York City. He learned that Lander had worked extensively in Baltimore with black, Irish, and Jewish community leaders—exactly the type of work he would be required to perform on the Mayor's Committee. After conducting his due diligence, Hexter enthusiastically endorsed Lander to Hughes, and Hughes passed on the recommendation to Mayor LaGuardia with his blessing. The relationship between Rabbi Lander and Maurice Hexter that was initiated through this process endured for many years and would culminate with Hexter and Lander working together to establish a graduate school of social work at Yeshiva University.

As envisioned by Hughes and LaGuardia, the Committee's leadership was to include four positions with each seat representing one of the city's major ethnic constituencies: Protestant, Catholic, black and Jewish. The selected Catholic representative was Shuyler Warren, an African-American who had founded the Catholic Interracial Council and served on the National Urban League. The black representative was Edith Alexander, who was the community relations director at the city's Department of Public Welfare and had also served on the Urban League. The Protestant member was Dr. Dan W. Dodson, who was appointed to serve as the Committee's executive director by Chairman Hughes. Dodson, an assistant professor of educational sociology at NYU, was the son of a Texas sharecropper and understood racial prejudice from the viewpoint of someone who had successfully overcome it.

Despite their widely disparate early lives, Dodson and Lander shared much in common. They were both doctoral sociologists (although Lander was, at this point, still completing his dissertation), and they had both focused their work on the causes and prevention of juvenile crime. Both were deeply religious and found, within their respective spiritual lives, the impetus to deal with the task at hand: fighting racial and religious discrimination and improving relations among the city's ethnic communities. The two spiritual sociologists formed a strong team. Dodson, because he was not a Jew, was able to open certain doors that Lander was barred from entering. Lander, on the other hand, was adept at navigating the murky waters of New York City politics with its complex ethnic dynamics. Without Lander's hand on the tiller, Dodson would have found himself frequently adrift as the Committee's work got seriously underway. The two men conducted strategy sessions that met almost daily over the next four years. Although the remaining Committee members, Warren and Alexander, enjoyed different, less scholarly backgrounds, the four nevertheless worked effectively as a team to investigate and offer recommendations to defuse future crises in New York City's troubled neighborhoods.

The LaGuardia initiative proved to be a model for other cities to follow as a series of "human rights commissions"—many with an agenda borrowed from the Committee on Unity—soon became part of the emerging post-war urban landscape. The first item on that agenda was legislative reform, particularly in the area of employment. Bernard Lander had earlier been asked to work with a bipartisan state commission in drafting new legislation that would outlaw discrimination in the workplace. Now, as a member of the Committee on Unity's executive board, he helped to choreograph a delegation of concerned citizens who were dispatched to lobby in behalf of the proposed legislation in Albany. The delegation was headed by the Committee's chairman, Charles E. Hughes, Jr., who had succeeded in persuading Governor Thomas E. Dewey to publicly support the anti-discrimination bill.

Lander's efforts, via his role on the Committee on Unity, succeeded with the passage of the Ives-Quinn Bill in March 1945. The new law was essentially a codification of FDR's executive order No. 8802 that legally protected a citizen's civil rights in the workplace. The new law also established a watchdog agency, the five-member State Commission Against Discrimination in Employment, to enforce these rights. The impact of this landmark bill, the first of its kind in the nation, was far-reaching, and served as model legislation that was borrowed repeatedly by other state legislatures intent on eradicating employment discrimination in their own states. By the time of the passage of the Federal Civil Rights Act in 1964, twenty-nine states had placed similar fair employment laws on their books.

When the Mayor's Committee on Unity sought to address widespread racial discrimination in the professional sports arena, it was every bit as quick to step up to the plate. In the spring of 1945 the New York black community was becoming increasingly vocal in its call to "End Jim Crow in Baseball!" An ad hoc committee was formed, and its series of neighborhood street meetings was garnering increasing amounts of publicity as the weather turned warmer. Sensing that a fuse to future violence may have been lit, Committee Director Dan Dodson rapidly organized a meeting with the owners of both the Brooklyn Dodgers and the New York Yankees. The Dodgers' owner and fellow Texan, Branch Rickey, was sympathetic to the Committee's interest in integration and agreed to take immediate action.

Rickey recalled an incident that had taken place a few weeks earlier at Boston's Fenway Park. In an attempt to pacify the desegregationist sensibilities of a powerful city councilman, the Red Sox management pretended to open a tryout session to players from the Negro Baseball League. The tryout was a sham intended to demonstrate the negative consequences of putting black players on the field alongside white ones. The fans in the stands did not disappoint. One black player, Jackie Robinson, from the Kansas City Monarchs, was forced to endure a barrage of humiliating racial epithets and catcalls when he stepped up to the plate. What impressed Rickey, in addition to Robinson's obvious skills as a batter and fielder, was the way Robinson coolly handled the animosity of the racially charged crowd. If Rickey *was* to introduce a black player into the Dodger organization, it would have to be someone who could take it without flinching. Rickey met with Robinson to discuss signing him to the Dodgers' farm team, the Montreal Royals. In an oft-cited conversation between the two men, Rickey asked Robinson if he could face the racial hostility without taking the bait and reacting with anger. Robinson was taken aback. "Are you looking for a Negro who is afraid to fight back?" he asked.

"No," replied Rickey. "I need a Negro player with enough guts *not* to fight back." Robinson agreed to "turn the other cheek," and Rickey signed him to a $600-per-month contract.

Two years later, on April 15, 1947, Robinson was called up to the "big show" and played his first game as a member of the Brooklyn Dodgers. He had effectively broken the Major League color barrier exactly six months before Chuck Yeager would first break the sound barrier. At this point, Dodson, Lander, and the Mayor's Committee advised Rickey and offered him guidance as he pioneered the Major League integration process. Despite the anticipated racist reaction by many in the stands, other teams followed suit and began integrating their teams. Soon the racial barriers began to come down in all of American professional sports. The integration of the Brooklyn Dodgers is regarded by many cultural historians as a watershed event and recognized as the inception point of the American Civil Rights Movement.

While not as dramatic as instigating the desegregation of Major League Baseball, much of Rabbi Lander's behind-the-scenes work on the Committee was no less significant. Along with the Committee's Catholic director, Shuyler Warren, Lander met with church leaders and members of the Catholic press to stem the flow of anti-Semitic sermons and articles. As a result of these "moral suasion" efforts, newspapers such as *The Brooklyn Tablet*, which had been printing Father Coughlin's vile racist diatribes for years, were persuaded to stop doing so. The Committee was alerted that in a certain Brooklyn neighborhood, Italian police officers were failing to apprehend, and at times even found to be protecting members of, Italian street gangs involved in racial attacks. Lander visited the police station and informed the chief that his precinct was being watched by the Committee, a simple warning that convinced the involved officers to begin properly carrying out their duties.

Rabbi Lander recognized that the one area of the Committee's mandate of greatest importance to the Jewish community was the field of education. He naturally took a leading role as the Committee devised ways to eradicate the religious quota system that had become ingrained in America's educational infrastructure. Historically, the politically empowered establishment, alarmed by the rising numbers of immigrants reaching its shores, as well as the large numbers of blacks moving northward, instigated quotas during the 1920s that served to effectively restrict higher educational opportunities for Jews, Catholics, and blacks. Catholics, and to a lesser degree blacks, had built their own colleges. But aside from religious seminaries, such as Yeshiva, Jews looked entirely to private colleges and state universities as providers of the degrees required to secure the best professional careers. Thus Jews felt the sting of discriminatory admission quotas more sharply than did other minorities who enjoyed alternative options.

Rooting out and exposing these policies would not be an easy task, Lander soon learned. Many schools conducted their admissions programs in a clandestine fashion, well concealed from public scrutiny. This cloak of secrecy was primarily the outgrowth of a scandal that rocked Harvard in 1922 when it was revealed that its president, A. Lawrence Lowell, had laid down specific quota figures for the number of Jews to be admitted to the school's incoming freshman class. Lowell was alarmed by the ever-increasing percentage of Jewish students he had observed at Harvard and other Ivy League schools over the prior decade. As large numbers of European Jewish immigrants, absorbed by the United States since the beginning of the century, became assimilated and successful, their highest priority was to secure a top quality education for their children. By 1922 the percentage of Jewish students at Columbia had peaked at 40 percent. Jewish enrollment levels at the other Ivy League schools, including Harvard, also stood at record levels.

Lowell viewed this situation as "Harvard's Jewish problem" and decided to openly take action against it by implementing the admissions quotas. The reaction was swift and strong. Working in alliance, groups such as the American Jewish Congress and the American Federation of Labor grabbed the headlines and succeeded in pressuring the governor of Massachusetts to investigate Harvard's violation of state equal opportunity laws. Lowell and Harvard caved in, and the quotas were lifted, but the victory was a pyrrhic one.

While officially professing open enrollment policies, Harvard, and the other schools who followed suit, simply went underground. Via various subterfuges, such as geographic quotas and preferential treatment for students exhibiting so-called "leadership potential" (typically the children of wealthy and politically connected families), America's elite colleges and universities continued to successfully limit the admission of ethnic, religious, and racial minorities. In just one example, acceptance at the top tier medical schools for City College graduates, 80 percent of whom were Jewish, fell dramatically from 58 percent in 1925 to 15 percent in 1943.

The educational landscape that Rabbi Lander surveyed in the late 1940s had been effectively shaped, primarily via deception, to staunch the free flow of qualified Jewish students into the halls of ivy. Lander's job, as he saw it, was to remove the blockage of bigotry in order to once again permit merit, rather than religious orientation, to determine who would receive a college education and who would not.

Rabbi Lander began his investigation by examining the admissions policies and practices of New York City institutions. He likewise looked at educational opportunities for local Jewish students who attempted to enroll at schools outside the city. When he met with admissions officers and deans at several of New York City's private colleges, he would hear them admit "strictly off the record" that they were regularly implementing quota systems to restrict the number of Jews at their schools. Some of the responses used to defend this practice were startling. "We are building a national school here," he was advised by one law school dean. "We limit the number of New Yorkers to make room for the kids from Indiana and Texas." When Lander asked one medical school's admissions officer why the school did not even consider applicants who had graduated from New York's heavily Jewish City College, he was told that they lacked an "appropriate bedside manner!"

In an incisive report detailing the insidious methods used to limit minority admissions, Lander pointed out that the harm caused by such prejudicial practices was not limited to merely the prospective student being denied admission. "Our entire community is being ill-served when students capable of becoming our top surgeons, jurists, and government leaders are being denied access to a college education because of their religion."

Lander's report went on to urge the state's educational sanctioning agency, the Board of Regents, to investigate these collegiate discriminatory practices and take strong action against them. He sadly noted that New York was spending less per capita on higher education than any other state in the union. This shocking situation needed immediate attention and, going beyond simple criticism in his report, Lander advocated the establishment of a new state university system that would provide appropriate educational facilities to all New York residents regardless of financial status in order to "assure all qualified applicants, regardless of race, creed, color, or national origin, their full educational opportunities."

Upon completing his report, and convinced of the urgency of its message, Lander was concerned that it might languish in the Mayor's Committee for Unity for some time before any action was to be taken. To jumpstart the process, he employed some subterfuge of his own.

Lander enlisted the aid of another member of the Committee, social activist and best-selling author of *Imitation of Life*, *Backstreet*, and other novels: Fannie Hurst. Neither a radical nor an intellectual, Hurst was a close friend of Eleanor Roosevelt and had vigorously supported the New Deal. As a director of New York's Urban League, she enjoyed easy access to the city's newspaper editors. At Lander's behest, Hurst leaked the report to Benjamin Fine, the Pulitzer Prize–winning education editor at the *New York Times*, who saw to it that the blistering report received front-page coverage in the following day's edition. Lander's ploy worked; the story was a bombshell. Due to the intense public interest generated by the report's findings (among other factors), it was quickly published and widely distributed both within and outside of the New York academic community. Once again Governor Dewey responded by appointing a commission that would eventually do exactly what Lander's report had advocated: establish the State University of New York (SUNY). The report also spurred the New York state legislature to pass the Quinn-Olliffe Bill, the first fair educational practices law enacted in the United States. The Dewey commission went further by instructing the Board of Regents to deny public funding to any college or university found guilty of minority discrimination, regardless of how such practices were depicted by the school itself.

The legacy of Lander's work in this area can best be appreciated by reviewing the establishment and current profile of SUNY, an educational system that was created in direct response to his tenacious and inspired advocacy.

The State University of New York lists its founding date as February 1948 when New York became the last of forty-eight states to finally create a state university system. The new university consolidated twenty-nine unaffiliated institutions, including eleven teachers colleges. Today SUNY has grown to include sixty-four colleges on geographically dispersed campuses that are all within commuting distance of New York. SUNY provides access to virtually every field of academic or professional study through 7,669 degree and certification programs. As of January 2008, 20 percent of SUNY's 418,000 enrolled students were members of minority groups. Although most are from New York, SUNY students come from every state and from 160 nations. A full 40 percent of New York's high school graduates enroll at SUNY each year resulting in over two and a half million SUNY alumni living in New York and around the world. These alumni are indeed indebted to Rabbi Bernard Lander and his pioneering work to eradicate ethnic and racial quotas and to enlarge the scope of educational opportunities in the state of New York.

Lander came to understand that the work of the Mayor's Committee was not destined to be an overnight struggle. His breakthrough success in the area of combating the higher education quota system must be regarded as a crack in the firmament that would, after some time, result in the elimination of all such quotas. The following year, the Association of American Colleges, in a dramatic mea culpa, acknowledged "with a troubled conscience" a history of discrimination against Jews among America's academic establishment. Under the guidance of this professional association, questions about a candidate's race and religion—questions that had been there for a quarter century—began to slowly disappear from college entrance application forms. Over the ensuing twenty-year period, the level of discrimination in American higher education steadily declined, a fact that is also a proud component of the Lander Legacy.

Of course the Mayor's Committee was first and foremost dedicated to investigating and understanding the social forces at work in those areas that had prompted its formation in the first place. In this capacity, Bernard Lander's background in researching the juvenile delinquency statistics of Baltimore proved invaluable. Under the auspices of the Mayor's Committee, Lander initiated and oversaw an in-depth survey aimed at gaining an understanding of a long series of anti-Semitic outbreaks centered on Coney Island. For this task he enlisted the services of the newly formed Congress on Community Interrelations. or the CCI.

The CCI had been established as a social research group by one of America's three leading Jewish advocacy organizations, the American Jewish Congress (the American Jewish Committee and the Anti-Defamation League being the other two). Lander had learned about the group's plans to set up the CCI from his friend and AJCongress leader, Rabbi Irving Miller who, like Lander, had also earned ordination from RIETS. As Miller explained, the CCI was being formed in response to calls for more proactive efforts in fighting anti-Semitism that arose during a recent AJCongress conference held in New York City. The CCI's mission was to study the causes of anti-Semitism in America in order to combat and eliminate them. Lander suggested that Miller consider noted German émigré social scientist, Kurt Lewin, to head the new group. Often recognized as the "founder of social psychology" and a pioneer in the study of organizational development, Lewin was, at this point, heading the Research Center for Group Dynamics at M.I.T. Rabbi Miller passed on Lander's recommendation to AJCongress president Stephen S. Wise, who contacted Lewin. Kurt Lewin was in fact hired as a consultant by the CCI based partly on Lander's suggestion. Lewin's work on behalf of the CCI led to significant advances and led to the CCI's coming key role in many aspects of the civil rights movement.

Working under the auspices of both the Mayor's Committee and the CCI, Lander designed a survey used to conduct in-depth interviews with residents of the Coney Island neighborhoods under investigation. He employed interview techniques that had been developed by Lazarsfeld and Merton at Columbia in order to unearth the structure of the prejudice that permeated the community. The surveys revealed that the anti-Jewish disturbances were merely one of a constellation of anti-social behaviors carried out by Italian gangs. The study concluded that in order to combat the racial and anti-Jewish manifestations, alternative socially acceptable channels for youthful behavior had to become available. The Mayor's Committee, acting on these recommendations, assigned a field worker the task of developing such programs similar to those that Lander had used in Baltimore. While no miracles resulted, the number of racially motivated teenage crimes in the area continued to decline over the coming years due, in part, to the youth programs put into place by the Mayor's Committee at Rabbi Lander's behest.

The significance of these types of sociological studies was extolled by many in the field at the time. Noted gestalt theorist Goodwin Watson, referring to the CCI study, commented, "The social power of self-directed, cooperative fact-finding in its potential contribution to strengthening democracy, ranks higher than the discovery of atomic energy!"

The Mayor's Committee also turned its attention to Washington Heights. Working with the City College department of sociology, Lander discovered that a full 30 percent of parents interviewed reported that their children had been involved in clashes with other ethnic groups. Again, the Committee issued a report to the city that urged investment in neighborhood recreational centers as well as a program of in-school tolerance education. Both recommendations were acted upon and, in a follow-up study, the number of such clashes had substantially diminished.

Having been formed amidst the shadow and smoke of the Harlem riots, it is no surprise that most of the work of the Mayor's Committee focused on improving conditions in the black community. The Committee's efforts in securing equal employment legislation impacted blacks enormously since they were often the "last hired and the first fired" when times were tough. But something also needed to be done about not only how black people earned their money, but also how they spent it. Allegations of price gouging by Harlem shopkeepers and merchants was one of the factors that had sparked the riots. The Committee looked into pricing practices during both 1945 and 1946, tracking prices up and down 125th Street. They worked closely with neighborhood consumer groups and responded to claims of not only price gouging but also reports of discrimination in employment and cases of public accommodations and transportation services being denied to blacks.

The experience of serving on the Mayor's Committee on Unity had a deep and lasting effect on Bernard Lander. While always firm in the principle that each individual has infinite intrinsic value and that all people are equal in the eyes of G-d, he now had personal first-hand experience to support this belief. By working closely and effectively with blacks, protestants, and Irish and Italian Catholics, Lander had gained a personal appreciation for their concerns and had come to value their friendships. While never neglecting the needs of his own people, Lander gained the respect of his non-Jewish colleagues because of his empathy and devotion to their needs.

In 1947, as he continued to fine tune his Columbia doctoral dissertation, Rabbi Lander accepted a part-time evening teaching position at CUNY's Hunter College in midtown Manhattan. His work on the Mayor's Committee continued unabated. The following year, Charles Evans Hughes, Jr. submitted his resignation as chairman of the Mayor's Committee on Unity. Hughes's successor was Edward Lazansky, who felt that

Catholics and Jews were capable of taking care of themselves and that the Committee on Unity should concentrate solely on improving opportunities for the city's black population.

The Committee's director, and Rabbi Lander's close colleague over the previous four years, Dan Dodson, soon thereafter returned to his post at NYU. Having identified many of the root causes leading to urban violence and after having submitted a series of administrative and legislative recommendations adopted by City Hall and the State of New York, the Committee now saw its role evolve into that of an enforcement arm that would act to secure these new civil rights protections on a more permanent basis. Eventually the Committee on Unity was replaced by just such a standing city agency, the Commission on Human Rights, which was granted the authority to enforce the newly enacted civil rights legislation.

As he saw the activities of the Committee winding down, Bernard Lander decided that the time had come for him to move on. With more time finally available, he was able to complete, submit, and defend his doctoral dissertation at Columbia, which awarded Lander his Ph.D. degree in late 1948. Although Dr. Lander became a full-time member of the Hunter College faculty the following year, he soon found that he was not cut out for merely a pedagogic career. The yearning for social service still burned strongly in his heart and so, shortly before the decade ended, Bernard Lander sought and accepted a new position with the New York City Youth Board.

Since returning to New York from Baltimore, Bernard Lander had devoted himself to the ideal of building unity among the diverse ethnic factions of New York. But it was another sort of unity that captured his attention during the winter of early 1948.

Bernard, at the time, was not only investigating religious tensions in Washington Heights; he was also living in the neighborhood. An advantage of having returned to New York as a single man was that he was able to reside with his parents, whose home sat only a few short blocks from the Yeshiva campus. During the long winter nights, Bernard was in the habit of retiring to the warmth of Yeshiva's *beis medrash* (house of learning) following Shabbos. There he would indulge in intense learning and lively discussion until the early hours. He found these weekly sessions both spiritually and intellectually invigorating, providing him with renewed energy to face the coming week's challenges.

So it was no doubt the case that Bernard was deep in study at Yeshiva on the Saturday night that Sarah Shragowitz attended a party at a friend's apartment. Fortunately for Bernard, his brother Nathan, who was also living at their parents' home at the time, did attend the gathering that night. There he met Sarah, blessed with the same wholesome natural beauty of her Biblical namesake, who impressed Nathan with her character and intelligence. When Sarah explained that she had one semester remaining at New York University where she was majoring in sociology, Nathan instantly mentioned his brother who was, by this point, a few months shy of earning his doctorate in sociology from Columbia.

Nathan understood, perhaps better than Bernard himself, what his older brother was seeking in a wife, and after spending some time exposed to Sarah's poise and charm, he concluded that here was an excellent candidate. Nathan began to inquire about Sarah's family background and learned that she was the daughter of the only rabbi in Port Chester, New York, a village in the town of Rye off Long Island Sound.

When Nathan later reported his encounter to Bernard, he urged his brother to not let this opportunity pass him by.

Bernard greatly respected his younger brother's opinion on all matters, including matters of the heart, so he swung into action. His first step was to call on his friend Dr. Abraham Katsh, chairman of the Department of Hebrew Studies at NYU to learn, if by chance, he knew a student named Sarah Shragowitz. Dr. Katsh informed Bernard that Sarah was a student in his class—a very bright student—and fully supported Nathan's opinion of her. He invited Bernard to sit in on the class so that he could introduce them. Bernard agreed.

But, alas the fates that had caused them to miss each other at the party were still at work, and when Bernard arrived to Dr. Katsh's class, he was informed that Sarah was absent that day because she was studying for a major test in another subject. After speaking with Dr. Katsh about Sarah for a second time, and receiving yet another strong endorsement, Bernard felt that he had completed his due diligence and decided to phone Sarah directly. The over-the-phone introductions went well, and the two agreed to meet the following day.

Sarah was naturally apprehensive, but once they met, she found that she had a great deal in common and much to talk about with this energetic, highly intelligent young man. Although they did not breach the subject at that first meeting, they both quickly saw in each other the potential for marriage.

As the courtship moved forward, it soon became time for Bernard to visit Sarah's family in Port Chester, where he met Sarah's father, Rabbi Moshe Shragowitz, a stately man who exuded an air of old-world dignity. Rabbi Shragowitz had emigrated from Kletsk in 1923 with his wife, Hinde, and their young son, Jacob. Before coming to Port Chester, Rabbi Shragowitz had served for ten years as a congregational rabbi in Somerville, New Jersey. It was there that the couple's third daughter, Sarah, was born in 1926. The family moved to their current home in this quaint shipbuilding town in 1936 where, over the course of the ensuing forty years, Rabbi Shragowitz would serve the small Jewish community as its rabbi, *chazzan*, *shochet* and *mohel* (spiritual leader, cantor, ritual slaughterer, and ritual circumciser).

From his very first encounter with the Shragowitzes, Bernard Lander had nothing but the utmost respect and affection for Sarah's parents. Moshe Shragowitz was a true rabbinic scholar, steeped in Torah tradition, and an outstanding community leader. Hinde, he regarded as a pillar of *chesed* (kindness), ceaselessly engaged in charitable acts throughout their community.

In Sarah, Bernard had found the life partner who had eluded him for so long both in Baltimore and in New York. Sarah was likewise drawn to this highly intelligent and devoted man who was clearly intent on repairing the world around him. She was also impressed with Bernard's level of religious observance. After being surrounded by the highly assimilated young Jewish men she encountered at NYU, meeting a serious, knowledgeable and committed Jew like Bernard was like a breath of fresh air. Bernard proposed marriage and Sarah agreed to meet him under the *chupah* of marital unity.

The wedding date was set for Monday, November 1, 1948. The following day, the politician who had been the most instrumental in implementing the panoply of social programs that Bernard had been advocating over the past four years, Governor Thomas E. Dewey, was defeated in his bid for the presidency in an upset victory carried out by President Harry S Truman. A new era had surely begun.

CHAPTER EIGHT

New Horizons

Your eyes shall behold a land stretching afar.
—Isaiah 33:17

It was the first day of November 1948, and the well-trained catering staff of the Riverside Plaza Hotel was busy readying the main hall for a traditional Jewish wedding celebration. The venerable establishment, located on Manhattan's West 71st Street, had hosted many such *simchas* (celebrations) in its day, but there was something unusual going on at the Lander / Shragowitz nuptials. In the wedding invitations that Bernard and Sarah had sent out, the ceremony time was listed as 5:30 pm. At exactly half past five a distinguished Columbia University professor, Dr. Robert McIver, had entered the hall, peering about expectantly. He was soon followed by a contingent of other academic and political types, all looking a bit mystified. Bernard's non-Jewish Columbia colleagues and Mayor's Committee members were evidently unfamiliar with J.S.T., Jewish Standard Time, which typically added at least fifteen minutes to any scheduled appointment time. Over the next half hour guests began filing in steadily and by 6 pm the hall was filled with a diverse and potent blend of personalities from all quarters of Bernard and Sarah's lives. The interfaith and inter-racial guest list included Lander, Shragowitz and Koenigsberg family members, Mayor's Committee members and city officials, learned Yeshiva scholars, Urban League leaders, congregants from Beth Jacob in Baltimore, RIETS professors, researchers from Columbia and BASR, NYU classmates and faculty members, childhood friends, and many more.

The non-Jewish guests, many of them attending an Orthodox wedding for the first time, were easily swept into the atmosphere of the evening at the *Kabbalas Panim* (bride's reception) and the groom's *tisch* (literally: table) as they observed the signing of the *K'tubah* (wedding contract) and the ceremonial breaking of the wedding plate. All guests came away with a new or renewed appreciation for the warm Jewish spirit, or *Yiddishkeit*, that permeated the event.

Rabbi Aharon Kotler, the same respected rabbi who had married Sarah's parents some twenty-five years earlier in Kletsk, and a relative of Sarah's family, officiated under the *chupah*. As a custom and a courtesy, any other rabbis in attendance were invited to stand alongside the couple during the wedding ceremony. In all, nine rabbis crowded under the *chupah* as the bride circled the groom seven times and the *Sheva Brachos* (seven blessings) were recited. Such honors were bestowed upon one of the *Roshei Yeshiva* (heads) of RIETS, Rabbi Dovid Lifshitz, as well as Rabbi Samuel Sar and Rabbi Joseph Lookstein from the Yeshiva faculty. Sarah's grandfather, Rabbi Joseph Shragowitz, from Fitchberg, Massachusetts and her sister Bessie's husband, Rabbi Aaron Kra, the rabbi in Ansonia, Connecticut, were also so honored, as were Bernard's brother, Rabbi Nathan Lander; his cousin, Rabbi Herschel Koenigsberg; and his brother-in-law, Rabbi Max Posnansky.

As custom dictated, a wineglass wrapped in a cloth napkin was placed under Bernard's foot at the conclusion of the ceremony. The popping sound that arose as his foot came down—a perpetual reminder of the destruction of the ancient Temple in Jerusalem—was met with cheers and shouts of "Mazel Tov" and "Siman Tov" as the gathered guests pelted the newlyweds with a shower of candy. Some of the honored dignitaries in attendance who were introduced during the *Simchas Chasan v'Kallah* (the wedding feast) included leaders of the American Mizrachi Organization such as its president, Pinkhos Churgin; Dr. David Petergorsky, executive director of the American Jewish Congress; Isaiah Minkoff, executive director of the National Community Relations Advisory Council; and Rabbi Ahron Soloveichik.

As Bernard Lander scanned the long tables filled with family and friends from his seat of honor at the head table beside his beautiful young bride, he felt supremely blessed and fortunate. At the same time, he could not suppress a feeling of urgency. He felt an insurmountable impetus to move ahead and pursue both his personal and professional destinies. While he understood that a new chapter of his life had been opened, he was unsure where life's road would lead him. His only certainty was that from this point on, he would no longer be traversing that road alone.

As Rabbi Lander pondered his life's path, he sensed that his destiny would take him beyond New York's five boroughs and out into the larger world. He recalled how, in recent years, he had already stretched his horizons and had begun to act on a global stage. In January 1946, at the behest of the American Jewish Committee, he had travelled to Mexico City. The group had established a local agency there to combat anti-Semitism, and Lander was asked to examine and report objectively on its effectiveness. He remained in Mexico well into February as he conducted an in-depth investigation of the fascist forces at work in the capital and throughout the nation. As he conducted interviews with community leaders, local politicians and U.S. embassy staff members, Lander soon learned of a strong and sinister force known as the Sinarquista.

The Sinarquista was an outlawed fascist political organization that promoted *synarchy,* a structured hierarchical social order intended to transcend conflict between economic classes through an ideology known as *synarchism.* Synarchism was born as a reaction to the pro-anarchy political movements popular during the late nineteenth century, but the term had now come to serve as a euphemistic code word for fascist and anti-communist ideologies. The Sinarquista, active in Mexico since the mid-1930s as an extension of the Roman Catholic extreme right, was violently opposed to the populist and secularist policies of the ruling Mexican regime. The group, somewhat dormant since the 1938 assassination of its leader, José Urquiza, had recently regrouped and was being revived under the banner of the extremist Popular Force Party (PFP).

The more Lander learned about the politics of Mexico, the more evidence he saw of PFP influence in Mexican life. He brought his concerns to the U.S. ambassador to Mexico at the time, George S. Messersmith, to whom Lander explained that the PFP's rising level of influence was posing a real threat to Mexico's Jewish community. He presented evidence that numerous former Nazis, who had secretly fled to Mexico after the war, were exerting their sinister influence within the Sinarquista movement and implored the ambassador to raise the issue with the Roman Catholic archdiocese. "I'm asking that you urge the church to halt its support of the PFP." Messersmith turned a deaf ear and showed Lander the door.

Lander concluded that Messersmith, along with a cabal of government officials, was sympathetic towards the Mexican fascists. Upon his return to New York, Lander decided to report his findings directly to

Washington. He recalled that during an outbreak of anti-Semitic incidents in 1930, when an economic slump prompted Mexican storekeepers to target Jewish bankers—whom they blamed for the crisis—that the U.S. State Department had intervened and had pressured the Mexican government to quash the protests. Lander presumed that the State Department would again respond in kind. He quickly drafted a report and dispatched it, along with supporting documents, to Spruille Braden, the Assistant Secretary of State for Latin American Affairs. Disappointingly, his efforts were met with polite indifference. In 1946 the United States State Department was preoccupied with the emerging spread of communism. Fighting fascists was old history. Hadn't the United States just won the war in order to rid the world of fascism?

Lander's report succeeded in one regard, however; it resulted in his being labeled as a "communist sympathizer" or "comsymp" by the U.S. State Department, a sobriquet that would dog him for years and result in his ostensibly being denied needed government funding during the following decade's McCarthy era.

As Bernard Lander recalled the disappointments of this first foray onto the international stage, he was buoyed by the fact that his second attempt was one he could look back upon with some pride. The Partition of Palestine vote that had taken place at the United Nations exactly one year before, in November 1947 was a monumental event marking the end of the nearly 1,900-year exile of the Jewish people. Fifty-six countries were then represented in the U.N. and the vote to partition passed with thirty-tree in favor, thirteen against, and ten abstentions. This vote was closer than it may have appeared since, in order to secure passage, the measure required a two-thirds majority of those nations voting. As anticipated, the European nations voted as a bloc in favor of partition and the Arab nations also voted en masse against it. This placed the decision squarely into the hands of the nonaligned nations with no obvious interest in the outcome. In what seemed to some observers as an inexplicable act of solidarity, thirteen nations of the Caribbean, Central, and South America also voted as a bloc in favor of partition. These votes made the difference and succeeded in bringing the State of Israel into existence.

Much has been written about figures such as David Ben-Gurion and Chaim Weizmann and their roles in forging the new Jewish state. But there remains a short list of unsung heroes whose activities outside the spotlight were every bit as vital. One such individual was Samuel Zemurray, the Russian immigrant to the United States, who rose from dire poverty to become the owner of the United Fruit Company, the world's largest purveyors of bananas. A devout Zionist, Zemurray not only donated a banana boat to the *Sochnut* (the Jewish Agency, the recognized "government in exile" of the Jewish people) that would later be famously renamed the Exodus and used to transport Holocaust survivors to Eretz Yisroel, he also used his economic clout to convince the Latin American governments he had been dealing with for decades to cast their votes at the U.N. in favor of the partition motion.

Another name that should unquestionably be placed on the unsung heroes list is that of Bernard Lander. Spurred into action by the Sochnut, which had early on recognized the pivotal role to be played by the Latin American nations, Lander, at the behest of the Sochnut called upon the contacts he had been cultivating for the prior three years. In those early years of the struggle for civil rights, Jews and blacks regarded each other as soulmates, both victims of institutionalized racism and discrimination. This bond was manifested as a political coalition that would endure through the mid-1960s. Lander became a member of a Pro-Palestine committee and began knocking on the doors of the black leaders he knew through his work on the Mayor's Committee on Unity and elsewhere.

Lander first pled his case to Walter White, the Secretary of the NAACP who agreed to go into action. White, who had a particular interest in Haiti, spent months lobbying the Haitian U.N. delegation in an ultimately successful effort to gain its vote in behalf of the Zionist cause.

Lander also contacted a black member of the Mayor's Committee with whom he had worked closely. Channing H. Tobias, who held a doctorate of divinity, had spent his life devoted to the YMCA, a role that often led him to Latin America as he strove to resolve racial issues with local political leaders. Tobias had been appointed to the Committee on Civil Rights by President Truman in 1946 and sat on the national board of the NAACP. Once again, Lander made his case to a respected black leader, asking for his intercession on behalf of Partition among his many contacts in Latin America. Tobias was sympathetic and assured Lander that he would give it his best effort.

The narrowly won U.N. vote was regarded as a victory for Jewish diplomacy. Pro-partition advocates had managed to summon the support of black national and international leaders who enjoyed close ties to Jewish activists, such as Bernard Lander, through their years of working together in behalf of civil rights. In the final tally, the thirteen of the thirty-three aye votes at the U.N. General Assembly tendered by non-aligned Latin American members were the result of outside influence. Lobbied by banana peddlers and black civil rights leaders, the votes cast by these Roman Catholic countries, far removed from the affairs of Jews and the Middle East, made all the difference in the world.

One characteristic that benefited Rabbi Lander's effectiveness as a civil rights activist and Zionist was his modesty and willingness to remain out of the limelight. When a harsh article criticizing Jewish settlements in Palestine appeared in the *Reader's Digest*, Lander did not respond directly. He called upon his colleague Dan Dodson. Dodson, at Lander's request, wrote to a friend who was a senior editor at the magazine, asking him to publish the other side of this issue. The editor agreed, and the rebuttal piece soon appeared. Lander, throughout his career, firmly believed that a bridge is often a better defense than a wall. He urged his rabbinic colleagues to reach out to other local clergy when taking on social issues or community relations. "A public statement on an issue by an Episcopalian or Methodist Bishop from Kentucky has more sway over the State Department than the largest mass convention in New York City sponsored by the most well-known Jewish organization," he once commented. Lander's distaste for self-aggrandizement was also a decided asset in his new role as a husband.

Bernard and Sarah transitioned into married life as many young couples do. They rented a small apartment in Long Beach as Sarah embarked on her studies towards a master's degree in sociology at the New School for Social Research. The NSSR, founded in 1919, was located in downtown Manhattan and served as the home of the "University in Exile" in 1933 for Jewish scholars driven from Nazi-controlled Europe. Bernard was still involved with the Mayor's Committee on Unity during the day and continued teaching at Hunter College in the evenings. One evening, Bernard again complained to his friend, Morris Lifschitz, about the long commute that both he and Sarah had to endure each day. Lifschitz, who lived in

Queens, urged the Landers to consider Forest Hills, with its many vacant tracts of land, easy commute to Manhattan, and young Jewish community. The rabbi of the community, Morris Max, was a scholar of stature. He was originally from Baltimore, and Bernard had been friends with his brother there. After spending one year in Long Beach, Bernard and Sarah relocated to Forest Hills in Queens. It was to remain their home for the remainder of their marriage.

When Bernard Lander arrived to Forest Hills in late 1949, he was met by a dismal picture of a struggling Torah community in disarray. It was becoming obvious that Lifschitz had encouraged Lander to move to Forest Hills not only because he wanted his friend as a neighbor, but also out of respect for his outstanding leadership and organizing abilities. Lifschitz, a gifted and community-spirited lawyer, had served with Lander for several years on the Executive Committee of Mizrachi and recognized that his skills would make him a first-class collaborator in Lifschitz's push to "remove the shame, the helplessness, and the hopelessness" that characterized the Torah-true Jewish community of Forest Hills.

The community's only visible organization was the *shul*, known as the Queens Jewish Center and Talmud Torah (QJC), which was housed in a pitifully overcrowded storefront on 66th Avenue. This was supposed to serve as the synagogue's temporary quarters at the time it was first established in 1943, but the congregation had been unable to make any real progress. It had, at one point, purchased land, Lander was told, but was forced to halt construction of a new building due to a lack of adequate funding.

Dr. Lander immediately joined the congregation and soon found himself on the board. Within one year of his arrival, he was elected president and quickly appointed Morris Lifschitz to head a new building fund campaign. The October 1950 edition of the QJC's newsletter heralded the news under the banner headline: "DR. LANDER ELECTED PRESIDENT." The article's depiction of the Landers is noteworthy:

> A quiet and unassuming young fellow, (Dr. Lander) immediately impresses all those with whom he comes in contact with his level-headed logic and his ability to address an audience in a man-to-man, friendly tone that is most engaging. Although he and the charming Mrs. Lander moved into our neighborhood

only about a year ago, they are generally regarded as old and familiar friends.

Some exercise leadership by shouting: "Follow me!" while others shout "Wait for me!" Still others are forced to drag their followers, often kicking and screaming, to the place they wish to lead them. It was this third situation that characterized the early days of Dr. Lander's tenure as QJC president. Lander soon discovered that every discussion about building a new facility was soon dominated by a single issue: the cost. Where will the money come from? How will we be able to afford the upkeep? We already tried this, and it almost put us into bankruptcy!

With his ally Morris Lifschitz at his side, Lander fought valiantly to convince a battered congregation that the cost of doing nothing was even more expensive than building a new home. The two succeeded in slowly generating community support for a new building that would include a school for the children, a sanctuary for prayer and study and a social hall. Lander laid out a two-part plan designed to spread the costs over a longer period. Phase A, for which the funds could be raised from within the community itself, would provide only the school building. The sanctuary and social hall would be added later with funding raised from outside sources. It was Lander's vision that the school building would provide adequate space for a day school, an institution that he felt was absolutely essential for Jewish survival in America.

As the plans were drawn up and attractive elevation renderings were displayed to the congregation, enthusiasm for the project accelerated dramatically. It was clear that Morris Lifschitz had performed a great mitzvah by enticing Bernard Lander into joining the Forest Hills community. The rabbi—and now, doctor of sociology—not only understood the priorities of survival required by a Torah community like Forest Hills, but he also possessed the skills to vigorously articulate those priorities in the greater context of Jewish history. This talent is clearly demonstrated in his dramatic plea for support that included the following heart-stirring passage:

> In the last two decades we have witnessed, first, the saddest and, then, the happiest moments of almost two thousand years of Jewish history. In the wake of Buchenwald and Dachau, the song of our pioneers and builders again arises from the plains of Sharon and hills of Judea.

Whilst we exalt in the victories and rejoicing of our brethren in Israel, we must not forsake our Jewish Communities in the Diaspora. We cannot surrender five million American Jews and American Jewish life to religious assimilation and desiccation. As we work for an expanding economy and community in Israel, we must simultaneously strive for the building of a creative and self-respecting Jewish life in America.

In the building of our Synagogue and Center, we are making a significant contribution to a vital Jewish life in Forest Hills.

A variety of topics were capturing the attention of the American public on August 13, 1951. In Jerusalem, the World Zionist Congress was convening to re-examine its future role in relation to the State of Israel, while in East Berlin more than one million German youth took to the streets in a frightening government-directed "peace festival" marked by anti-American slogans and banners professing their devotion to communism. Closer to home, golfer Ben Hogan blazed to a stellar finish in the biggest single purse of his career as his six under par performance earned him an astounding $12,500, while Babe Didrikson-Zaharias took home the LPGA World Golf Championship trophy. The New York Giants were on their way to winning the pennant and black center fielder Willie Mays was completing his first season in the majors that would result in his winning the League's 1951 Rookie of the Year award.

But there were also two landmark events that coincided on that date in the lives of Bernard and Sarah Lander that overshadowed all of the other news of the day. It was on this bright summer afternoon that ground was broken on 108th Street in Queens for the QJC's new school building, and it was also on this day that the Lander's first child, Esther, arrived into the world.

The school building was completed in June of the following year, and since it could comfortably accommodate more than 300 worshippers, regular services were soon scheduled. The use of the school building was a temporary measure, intended to last only until funds could be obtained to complete Phase Two of the project that would see a sanctuary and social hall added to the floor plan. But a Jewish institution is not merely built with bricks and mortar. Under Lander's vision for the future of the Forest Hills community, this new facility was to be the home of a day school that would provide Jewish learning and transmit Torah values to each succeeding generation of young people. So, months before the building was dedicated, Lander had turned his focus to the vital goal of establishing just such a school.

Assembling a group of activist congregants and enlisting the enthusiastic support of Rabbi Morris Max, Lander created a founder's group that would evolve into the day school's first board of directors. Lander felt that the school should be autonomous, with its own distinguishing name and identity. He suggested naming the new school after his Yeshiva mentor, Rabbi Dr. Bernard (Dov) Revel. The others agreed.

Yeshiva Dov Revel opened its doors for the fall semester of 1952 in the QJC's newly constructed school building, offering a first and second grade curriculum. The school added classes each year and eventually served children from kindergarten through eighth grade. With the exception of Talmud and Torah classes in the middle school that were segregated by gender, classes were mixed. Under the leadership of its first principal, Rabbi Dr. Morris Charner, the school soon developed a reputation for academic excellence. Attracting students through the high quality of both its Judaic and general curricula, Yeshiva Dov Revel grew rapidly, eventually reaching an enrollment of more than one thousand students in its expanded building on 112th Street.

Bernard Lander continued to serve as president of the congregation for another five years, but it would be nearly ten years before the synagogue component of the QJC building would be completed. Much to the sorrow of his congregants, the *shul's* beloved Rabbi Max made *aliyah* to Israel a few years later. He was succeeded by Rabbi Joseph Grunblatt, who would serve as QJC's spiritual leader for the next forty years.

Bernard Lander's work in restoring vitality to the Forest Hills Jewish community reached beyond the day school and the synagogue, institutions with which he was directly involved. Taken together these facilities constituted a solid cornerstone for the entire Queens Jewish community. Over the coming years, their presence attracted a class of highly committed Jews to Forest Hills. The neighborhood was marked by an ambience of reverence and serious dedication to Jewish values, as evidenced by the thirty QJC families headed by ordained Orthodox rabbis. The community became home to the leaders of major Jewish organizations such as the Orthodox Union, the Rabbinical Council of America, and Mizra-chi. It was in Forest Hills that these observant families could confidently send their children to school and enjoy the Torah lifestyle they preferred. The growth of the Forest Hills Jewish community soon led to a second Orthodox synagogue opening its doors and, as housing prices began to escalate, the community expanded into adjoining neighborhoods such as Kew Gardens.

The transformation of the Queens Jewish community from one eking out an existence in a ramshackle storefront to a vital center for the nation's most Torah-devoted families is a dramatic one that Bernard Lander could deservedly look back upon with pride. But while Lander was perhaps one of the most tenacious and goal-oriented leaders to stride across the stage of American Judaism, he was fundamentally a modest man who did not thirst for glory. The driving impetus that characterized the Queens trans-formation was driven not by Lander's search for acclaim, but rather by his intrinsic devotion to Judaic expression. It was these motivations and instincts that would guide Bernard Lander over the coming decade as he attained leadership positions at the national level among several major Jewish organizations. They would guide Lander's course in the days ahead as his influence was starting to be felt in circles far beyond his Queens neighborhood. Lander felt he was ready for the formidable challenges that lay ahead and so, armed with his confidence and convictions, he set out to fulfill his destiny in the broader panorama of national leadership.

CHAPTER NINE

Learner to Leader

Let all your actions be for the sake of Heaven.
— *Pirkei Avot (Ethics of the Fathers) 2:12*

Watching the evening news in 2012, one would assume that the question of Jewish settlements in the Middle East is an entirely "au courant" issue. But, in fact, the struggle to reclaim the ancient Jewish homeland dates back to the days before Theodore Herzl first conceived and articulated the Zionist dream in the late nineteenth century. There have traditionally been two streams flowing from the Diaspora that have fed the Zionist current over the decades. The two constructs of this dichotomy are labeled Political Zionism and Religious Zionism. It was the latter stream, with its precepts of redemption based on Biblical scripture, into which Bernard Lander was immersed, and it was from this movement that he emerged as a leader of the Mizrachi movement.

Mizrachi originated at the dawn of the twentieth century at a world conference of religious Zionists held in Vilnius, Lithuania. The gathering, called by Rabbi Yitzchak Yaacov Reines, was initiated in direct response to Theodor Herzl's recent rekindling of the ancient Jewish dream of territorial redemption. Reines had attended the 1899 Third Zionist Conference in Switzerland and was responding to Herzl's call for European rabbis to support his fledgling movement. Not an observant Jew himself, Herzl nevertheless clearly understood that for it to gain acceptance, the Zionist endeavor must contain a religious, not merely a political, dimension. Rabbi Reines passionately concurred and expounded on the Torah underpinnings of the Zionist vision during the Vilnius conference. Inspired by his words, the delegates were moved to action and voted to create an entity that would place Torah squarely into the heart of the Zionist movement. In determining a name for this newly forged religious

Zionist group, Reines recalled a term coined by his colleague Rabbi Samuel Mohilever years earlier: *Mercaz Ruhani* or religious center. Shortened to Mizrachi, the movement has been a potent force in the development of the Jewish homeland.

While Mizrachi is perhaps best known for being the first religious political party in the new state of Israel, where it vigorously campaigned for laws enforcing Kashrut and Shabbat observance, it was in the American vineyards of Mizrachi that Bernard Lander toiled, primarily due to the efforts of Rabbi Meir Bar Ilan. As the American Jewish community sought to rebuild its leadership in the wake of World War II, Bar Ilan began actively recruiting young blood to serve in the Mizrachi movement. In 1946, he succeeded in attracting both Rabbi Lander and his friend Morris Lifschitz to serve on the organization's executive board. Lander soon became a popular and articulate advocate for Jewish settlement in Eretz Yisroel. As he spoke before newly founded Mizrachi groups in cities across the country, Lander became an impassioned exponent of the Zionist dream, presenting the case for religious Zionism to an increasingly receptive audience. "The clock of Jewish history is moving rapidly before our eyes," he would exhort. "It is our duty as serious and stalwart Jews to insure that Torah is not abandoned in the rush to meet our destiny." Within two years, Herzl's Zionist dream would become a reality, only six months shy of his 1898 prediction that a Jewish state would emerge within fifty years. With the establishment of the sovereign State of Israel, the Mizrachi movement's primary mission shifted to one of *shomer* (watchman), guardians making sure that traditional Judaic law and observance would be woven tightly into the new nation's legal structure and social fabric.

In 1949, Rabbi Lander's friend and former faculty advisor Dr. Pinkhos Churgin was elected president of the national Mizrachi Organization of America. His first order of business was to begin work towards establishing a new university in Israel that would combine both religious and general studies—similar to the Yeshiva University model in New York. Churgin needed an outspoken and energetic spokesman to carry the banner for his vision and, not surprisingly, he turned to Bernard Lander. Churgin invited Lander to join a founder's group that convened in Atlantic City in 1950. There, the concept of creating an Orthodox-affiliated institute of higher learning in Israel was overwhelmingly endorsed, and the name Bar-Ilan

University, honoring the founder of the American Mizrachi movement, was selected.

Churgin and Lander's enthusiasm for the new project was soon met with widespread scorn among the non-religious Jewish press in both the United States and Israel. While this was to be expected, the reaction among Israel's Orthodox community was not. Churgin encountered strong pressure from the country's rabbinic leadership, including Tel Aviv chief rabbi Isser Yehuda Unterman to abandon his notion of exporting American-style Yeshiva learning to Israel. The idea of combining religious and secular studies under the same roof was anathema to the European-trained rabbis who now constituted the new state's religious hierarchy. Churgin was persuaded to abandon his original concept and, instead, modified his plans to establish a secular, coeducational Israeli university. The school would be sponsored by American Orthodox Jewry, and while it would not include a seminary, it would offer a full-fledged Jewish studies department. It was this concept, as modified, that succeeded in gaining acceptance in both Israel and the United States.

By 1952 the Israeli government agreed to allocate land for Bar-Ilan University in Ramat Gan. At the same time, Dr. Lander was named to the new school's board, where he urged his fellow directors to purchase the orchards and other properties adjacent to the site. This investment advice proved to be indeed prescient since the school has today become the nation's second largest university with a growing enrollment of some 27,000 students. Construction began the following year, and the doors were opened in 1955. Because of the recruitment and fundraising efforts conducted by Lander and others, most of the school's financing and the majority of the original students came from North America. When Lander was asked by the board—whose members greatly respected his foresight and erudition—to conduct screening interviews with prospective American applicants, he agreed and discovered that he greatly relished this role, taking pride in his own ability to accurately discern the most promising of candidates.

Bar-Ilan University articulated its mission in this way: "to blend tradition with modern technologies and scholarship and teach the compelling ethics of Jewish heritage to all. To synthesize the ancient and the modern, the sacred and the material, the spiritual and the scientific." It is this transcendent quest for *ichud* and *havdalah*—determining the points of unification and lines of demarcation of the sacred and the secular—that would come to characterize the rest of Bernard Lander's professional life and eventually form the cornerstone of his lasting legacy to the Jewish people.

Pinkhos Churgin died in 1957, shortly after Bar-Ilan University started its third year of operation. Prior to his death, however, Rabbi Churgin had attempted to point his protégée, Bernard Lander, towards deploying his talents to benefit his alma mater, Yeshiva University. Churgin had repeatedly urged Yeshiva president, Dr. Samuel Belkin, to hire Dr. Lander to reinvigorate the school's flagging graduate programs. Eventually Belkin saw fit to act upon Churgin's advice.

The call came in November 1954 when Belkin, who had assumed the helm at Yeshiva in 1943 after the death of founder Bernard Revel, told Lander that he wanted to discuss bringing him onboard to help administer Yeshiva's two postgraduate schools. The first was a Jewish studies program initiated by Revel himself in 1935 and renamed the Bernard Revel Graduate School subsequent to the founder's death. The second program was established in 1948 as the School of Education and Community Administration or SECA. SECA's founding dean was a member of Yeshiva's first graduating class, Dr. Jacob Hartstein, who had fielded a small but outstanding faculty and fashioned a curriculum offering advanced courses in psychology, education, and social work. Hartstein left Yeshiva in the early 1950s before either of the graduate programs had been accredited for the issuance of postgraduate degrees. Lander greeted Belkin's invitation with enthusiasm and, after resolving a potential conflict with his employer at the time, Hunter College, he accepted his first post as part of Yeshiva University's administration, that of Visiting Director of Graduate Studies (see next chapter).

But promoting his qualifications to Dr. Belkin was not the only time that Rabbi Churgin attempted to provide Bernard Lander with a career impetus. As Lander later learned from Professor Gershon Churgin, the professor's brother, Pinkhos, had privately named two possible successors to fill his shoes as president of Bar-Ilan University. One was Rabbi Dr. Emanuel Rackman, and the other was Rabbi Dr. Bernard Lander. The Bar-Ilan board floated the idea and asked if Lander was interested in being considered as its next president. After due consultation, Lander reported that while he was flattered by the late Rabbi Churgin's confidence and endorsement, he and Sarah were now the parents of three young daughters and could not easily leave their own parents behind were the family to pick up and make aliyah at that time. The board ultimately selected Rabbi Dr. Joseph Lookstein to succeed Churgin as president, who in turn, was succeeded in the post twenty years later by Churgin's other choice, Rabbi Rackman.

It would be Lander's leadership role with another major Jewish organization that would propel him even further across the national stage. While he was serving as rabbi of Congregation Beth Jacob in Baltimore, Lander's cousin, Benjamin Koenigsberg, had urged him to become involved with the Union of Orthodox Jewish Congregations of America. Also known as the Orthodox Union, or simply the OU, the group continues to serve as the major sanctioning body for Kashruth observance among America's food processors. But this was not its sole, nor even its primary, role.

Founded in 1898, the OU, one of America's oldest Jewish institutions, was established by the same rabbis who created the Jewish Theological Seminary or JTS, America's first acknowledged Judaic school of divinity. The OU was established as a bulwark against the rising hegemony of Reform Judaism in America. It served to establish and strengthen Orthodox synagogues, youth programs, and day schools and became known as the nation's leading exponent of Orthodoxy and Religious Zionism in America.

By 1902, rifts between the OU and JTS became pronounced. In order to buoy its flagging fortunes, a group of JTS supporters that year succeeded in attracting a well-known European scholar, Solomon Schechter, to the United States to head the school. Schechter immediately set about to "liberalize" the seminary, hoping to attract enrollment from among American-born rabbinic candidates. Exactly 100 days after Schechter's arrival, the OU broke with JTS, charging that it was leading Jews in the very direction that the OU had been established to avoid. It was announced that the OU and its affiliates would no longer recognize as legitimate the *semicha* (ordination) bestowed by JTS upon its rabbinic graduates. This move prompted Schechter and others to found the Conservative movement as a sort of "middle path" between the traditional course of Orthodoxy and the modernist road of Reform.

In 1923, the OU Kashruth Division was initiated when it contracted with the H.J. Heinz company to oversee the preparation of the company's condiments and other food products. The familiar OU *hekhsher* (seal of approval), Ⓤ was first displayed that year on bottles of Heinz Ketchup. The OU grew rather slowly until the 1950s when it actively sought to enlarge its scope of affiliated Orthodox synagogues. As rabbis trained by Rabbi Joseph Soloveitchik and ordained at Yeshiva's RIETS seminary were dispatched to OU-affiliated synagogues across the country, Orthodox Jewry saw its influence spread beyond the confines of New York and the eastern seaboard. Today the OU remains the largest Orthodox Jewish organization in America. It has survived and flourished due to an ability to adapt effectively to American-style pluralism without forgoing Halachic principles.

Bernard Lander began attending the OU's biannual conventions in the 1940s. Over the ensuing years he witnessed and keenly understood how demographic forces were causing Jews to rush to the suburbs and abandon their Orthodox synagogues in the old neighborhoods. Lander lent his support as the OU fought valiant battles on behalf of Orthodoxy—through such programs as the Torah Umesorah network of Jewish day schools—seeking to preserve and further expand Orthodoxy amid the new post-war American Jewish landscape.

At the OU convention held over Thanksgiving weekend of 1954, Dr. Lander joined a group of young activists as a new generation of leadership was swept into office. Lander, along with Samuel Brennglass of Massena, New York, was elected national vice-president while Lander's good friend, Forest Hills attorney Harold Boxer, became national secretary. Boxer, in his professional travels throughout the country, had made a point of visiting not only Orthodox, but also Conservative synagogues. He shared with Lander his observations that while the Conservative movement had been operating a successful national youth group (United Synagogue Youth) for more than three years, nothing of the sort yet existed under the Orthodox umbrella. Lander, Brennglass, and Boxer placed the creation of just such a national synagogue youth movement at the top of the OU's agenda. Brennglass drafted the resolution that called for the immediate establishment of the National Conference of Synagogue Youth (NCSY), and while some debate ensued, support for the resolution was overwhelming. Boxer was named as the NCSY's first chairman, and Bernard Lander stepped up to serve on the new group's governing body, the NCSY Youth Commission.

The enthusiasm that brought the NCSY into existence soon gave way to the realities of trying to manage a nationwide entity without benefit of adequate funding. Despite increasing dissension and frequent calls for disbanding the organization that arose from within the OU's upper leadership, Boxer and Lander became unwavering advocates for maintaining support. "What would be the purpose of the OU itself if we were to abandon our Jewish youth?" Lander asked rhetorically.

NCSY struggled to remain viable throughout the 1950s, and in 1959, under the direction of a new national director, Rabbi Pinchas Stolper, it finally turned the corner. Stolper assembled a cadre of yeshiva student volunteers and dispatched them to communities around the country to set up teenage *Shabbatonim* (Sabbath retreats). The tactic worked, as students recruited from the major New York Orthodox religious schools set to work and began introducing an exciting brand of Judaism to America's disaffiliated young people. The wheels that were put into motion through Lander, Boxer, and Stolper's pioneering work have continued to turn. Over the ensuing decades, NCSY Shabbatonim have ignited dormant feelings of *Yiddishkeit* (Jewishness) appreciation and religious observance among countless Jewish adolescents across the nation. The program is today considered one of the most successful outreach initiatives ever developed by the American Orthodox community.

In his impassioned work to establish and maintain the fledgling NCSY, Bernard Lander emerged as a national leader committed to investing in Jewish youth. His advocacy over the ensuing years served to place and keep NCSY at the top of the OU agenda. As vice president, Lander also fought repeatedly to increase funding allocations to college campus programs, convincing the more reluctant that investing in such youth programs would yield higher returns than any other.

Because of his work in the civil rights arena and his stature as a sociologist, Dr. Lander was tapped to serve as the OU representative to the Synagogue Council of America. The SCA was established as an expression of Jewish shared community known as *Klal Yisroel* (the entire Jewish people). Its primary agenda was in the area of community relations, where it worked with other Jewish agencies to promote civil rights, foster urban development, and improve conditions for the less fortunate. While the SCA's mission was in keeping with Lander's commitment to social justice, he soon began experiencing second thoughts as the group moved further and further from basic Jewish principles, a drift that was attributable to the increasing influence of the SCA's Reform leadership. This religious dynamic expressed itself in political terms since Rabbi Joseph Soloveitchik had repeatedly resisted calls from the organization's leaders to withdraw OU's membership in the SCA. Such a bolt, Rabbi Soloveitchik feared, would be perceived as a failure of Jewish unity by the general community and act to harm overall Jewish interests.

In 1967, Dr. Lander was offered the presidency of the SCA and again found himself at a crossroads. He could either accept the position and strive to change the course of the organization from within, or he could resign rather than head a group that was leading Jews away from Torah values. In a quandary of conscience, Lander turned to the man known simply as Reb Moshe. Rabbi Moshe Feinstein was a world-renowned Torah scholar and *posek* (an adjudicator of Jewish law). His expertise in Halakha was unparalleled, and he was regarded by most as the de facto rabbinic authority for Orthodox Jewry in North America. Reb Moshe counseled Lander that he could not, as an observant Torah-true Jew, agree to become the head of an organization dominated by the Reform and Conservative movements. Lander understood the wisdom of Reb Moshe's advice and immediately resigned his position on the Synagogue Council. The group continued, with limited effectiveness, through the 1990s when it disbanded after the Reform movement acted to sanction mixed marriages between Jews and non-Jews and publicly condoned unions between gay partners.

By the early 1950s, Bernard Lander felt that the arc of his career was starting to turn downward. He faced increasing frustration that his work in areas of social advocacy was not leading him anywhere. He began to pay attention to the repeated overtures he was receiving from congregations urging him to accept a pulpit position. The irregular schedules and uncertainties of his situation were beginning to take their toll. Sarah informed him that she wanted to see him at breakfast and dinner each day but not at lunchtime. Unfortunately, none of the congregational posts he investigated would allow him sufficient time and opportunity to continue his social activism and academic work. And he was not prepared to give those up merely in exchange for a regular work schedule.

Throughout those years, Bernard Lander continued to enjoy the many public speaking opportunities that his position with the OU and Mizrachi had afforded him. He loved traveling and observing Jewish life outside of New York. In turn, he began to develop a strong following as word of his oratorical skills spread throughout the Jewish world. Yet, while the speaking tours were exciting, they failed to satisfy his deeper yearning to conduct a truly meaningful life. He continued to listen for opportunities that would allow him to fulfill his passion to promote Orthodoxy in America. The fateful call from President Belkin, asking Lander to consider returning to Yeshiva in order to head the school's graduate program, was exactly what Bernard Lander had been hoping to hear.

CHAPTER TEN

The Yeshiva Years

Not study is the main thing, but action.
    —*Pirkei Avot (Ethics of the Fathers) 1:17*

B ernard Lander had never fully left Yeshiva University, either spiritually or physically. He had maintained close ties to many of his former professors and classmates, several of whom were now members of the Yeshiva faculty. Even during his years in Baltimore, it was a rare week that did not find him traversing the short distance between his parents' home and the Yeshiva campus. Now he was being summoned to come aboard in a new role that he felt would overcome the angst and anxiety he had been experiencing in recent years. His hopes were high as he prepared for his return to the halls of Yeshiva.

Dr. Lander knew Dr. Samuel Belkin and had met with him several times over the prior decade since Lander's return to New York City. Lander viewed himself as a member of the Yeshiva family, and thus he had never been reluctant to share his opinions about the school's mission with Belkin. While Lander applauded Belkin's plans to establish a new medical school as "a great leap forward," for example, he also let Belkin know, by means of personal correspondence, that a day-college program, serving students not qualified for or not interested in the 9:00 AM–3:00 PM program of intensive Talmud study at RIETS, would be even more effective in strengthening Orthodox Judaism than a medical school. Lander concluded his missive with "One can accomplish more with regard to the inculcation of a religious spirit, in a college atmosphere than in a medical school situation." Ironically, it was the successful quest for a Touro College medical school that marked the final years of Dr. Lander's life.

Dr. Lander responded to Samuel Belkin's invitation to serve as dean of Yeshiva's Graduate Division with humble enthusiasm. As a Yeshiva alumnus, he wrote back that he considered it "a great honor and privilege" to be able to build Jewish life through service to his alma mater. He recognized that this opportunity had arrived at the perfect moment in his life, and he told Belkin that he was ready to assume his responsibilities immediately. But there was one obstacle.

At this point, Dr. Lander held a full-time faculty position at Hunter College that he intended to maintain. An awkward situation would arise if a member of Hunter's faculty also held the title of dean at another school. The matter was easily resolved, however, when Belkin agreed to change his title from dean to "Visiting Director of the Graduate Division."

As a key figure in the Yeshiva hierarchy, Samuel Belkin had followed closely in the footsteps of the school's founder, Bernard Revel. Like Revel, Belkin had served as *rosh yeshiva* (principal or head) at RIETS, gave brilliant *shiurim* (lectures) in Talmud and Codes (codified books of law), and sat on the school's rabbinical ordination committee. As president, Belkin strove to see Yeshiva University take its place among the great American institutions of higher learning. At the time Bernard Lander became a member of its senior administration in November 1954, the school was in full expansion mode. The Albert Einstein School of Medicine was being organized and set to open its doors in the fall of the following year.

The atmosphere of energetic activity was infectious as Dr. Lander took up his new responsibilities, hitting the ground running with a dazzling burst of new initiatives. Lander immediately implemented a new departmental structure at one of the graduate division's two units, the School of Education and Community Administration or SECA. SECA now would consist of four faculties: psychology, religious education, secular education, and social work. He promptly assigned four key tasks to each of the department heads:

1) Conduct research and determine which American schools are known to operate the best programs in your field. Then study their curricula for ideas on how to elevate the quality of your own program.
2) Determine the requirements for accreditation in order to allow for the granting of Masters and Ph.D. degrees in your field. Establish specific admissions requirements for your department.
3) Develop a defined program of study for your department that will facilitate accreditation.

Lander next set the same requirements for the faculty at the Bernard Revel Graduate School of Jewish Studies, the other division of Yeshiva's graduate school. By June 1955 both deans had developed programs with clearly defined admission requirements, designed course curricula, and identified needed faculty. The effect of these measures was immediate and highly positive, particularly in the area of faculty morale. Professors at both graduate schools understood that accreditation would enhance the academic standing of their programs and, as a by-product, elevate their own academic stature as well.

Once SECA's departmental structure had been defined and the curriculum developed, it served as a template for two separate graduate programs Lander had envisioned: a School of Education and a School of Social Work. Dr. Belkin supported these initiatives and agreed to consult with an expert in the field of education to prepare and submit a grant proposal to the Ford Foundation. Despite the consultant's promises, this tactic met with failure. Lander believed it was because the third party expert did not possess, and therefore could not adequately express, the passion for the project that only intimate familiarity could engender. Assuming the task himself, he prepared a detailed proposal that captured not only the cold statistics, but also the burning need for this project on the part of the school and the community. He successfully built a comprehensive case on behalf of a "pioneering school" of education and was eventually issued a $500,000 grant from the same Ford Foundation that had earlier turned the school down.

The news of this achievement spread quickly, and no one was more delighted than Samuel Belkin. "I will not forget what you have done for our school," Belkin told Lander sincerely. Ultimately it was one of these pioneering programs, the School of Education, which succeeded in putting Yeshiva on the map academically. Among the first to open its doors to liberal arts majors, the school broke new ground in developing alternative, practice-centered methods of teacher certification. Unfortunately, the School of Education that was to emerge as a result of the Ford Foundation grant, would become a major source of contention between the two men.

The problem lay in a divergence of vision for the new school. Belkin wished to see it fashioned in the mold of the medical school. "Our School of Education will produce the finest teachers who will serve the total American community," Belkin proclaimed. He saw this approach as furthering his dream of promoting Yeshiva to the status of "a great American university," ready to stand shoulder to shoulder with the best of the Ivy League. Dr. Lander believed that the Yeshiva Graduate School of Education should promote a primarily Jewish agenda, producing the finest teachers to staff the faculties of the nation's leading Jewish schools. It is conceivable that the school could have fulfilled both men's visions, but such hopes were shattered when an individual not committed to promoting a Jewish agenda was appointed as dean. Dr. Lander was by no means opposed to the general concept of serving the entire community, but he held strong reservations about placing people who did not adhere to Torah principles into leadership positions.

Overcoming his disappointment over the School of Education, Dr. Lander turned his attention to Yeshiva's social work program. Lander held out an ambitious agenda for this school as well. In surveying the national Jewish landscape, Lander had accurately observed that most of the executive leadership spots in Jewish community federations and their affiliated agencies were filled with conventionally trained social workers. These professionals typically held little sympathy for Jewish tradition or the Orthodox point of view. It was Lander's dream to produce a stream of Yeshiva-trained social workers who would provide the managerial manpower for Jewish federations, day schools, youth centers, nursing homes, and community centers all across America. Eventually, professionals steeped in Jewish values would work their way up the ladder until they assumed leadership positions in their organizations and in the community. Dr. Lander hoped to build a top quality program that would attract religious students who shared his passion for social justice. Graduates would be fully qualified to serve the general community, should they so choose, but they would also be well versed in the specific needs of the Jewish community.

As Dr. Lander continued to pursue his career as a guest speaker, he always kept a sharp eye out for talented individuals whom he might attract to the Yeshiva faculty. One particular Shabbos, Dr. Lander had been invited to serve as the scholar-in-residence at the Taylor Road Synagogue in Cleveland, Ohio. Over the weekend he observed an energetic young man running a Shabbos youth program organized by the local Jewish

Community Center. When he inquired, Lander was told that the young man's name was Solomon Green and that he was a trained social worker who had worked wonders since joining the staff of the JCC. Lander, acting mostly on instinct, approached Green and asked him a fateful question.

"How would you like to be the dean of a new school of social work at Yeshiva?" Green was stunned.

"Of course, I'm flattered by your invitation, Dr. Lander," Green replied, "but you should know that I have no training or experience as a teacher." Lander, recognizing the fact that his enthusiasm at finding a trained social worker with a strong Orthodox identity might have gotten the better of his judgment, invited Green to think things over and get back to him. Evidently Green heeded Lander's words, since one year later Solomon Green moved to New York to join the founding faculty at Yeshiva University's new School of Social Work. By 1966, Dr. Green was instrumental in designing the curriculum for Bar-Ilan University's Social Work School. He would go on to serve as the Yeshiva School of Social Work's third dean. Dr. Green often identified the first step of his career path as his fortuitous meeting with Dr. Lander during a Cleveland Shabbaton.

Dr. Lander did eventually identify and recruit a highly regarded Jewish scholar and social worker, Dr. Morton I. Teicher, from the University of Toronto, to serve as the school's founding dean. Teicher arrived at Yeshiva in 1956 and began assembling faculty, recruiting students, and developing curricula for the 1956–57 school year. Teicher headed the School of Social Work for the next fifteen years, during which time it was renamed the Wurzweiler School of Social Work. Teicher went on to join the faculty of the University of North Carolina's School of Social Work, where he also served as its dean. He today enjoys an active career writing books and articles on ethnology and other subjects and is a highly respected book reviewer for the Jewish press, both in print and online.

Jewish social work during the first half of the twentieth century was focused almost entirely on helping European immigrants adjust to their new lives in the American "melting pot." The Yeshiva school, as envisioned by Lander and implemented by Teicher, was established to look "beyond the melting pot," by directly addressing ethnicity as the primary source of value produced by American cultural pluralism. Social workers of this new school were no longer on a mission to erase every trace of the

"Old World" via cultural assimilation. Instead, Wurzweiler students were taught to cherish ethnicity as a manifestation of self-pride and empowerment among the communities they were destined to serve. This approach allowed for Jews and others to retain their religious and cultural heritage as they strove to improve the condition of their lives in America.

In the fifty-plus years since its founding, the Wurzweiler School of Social Work has awarded more than 6,000 master's degrees and more than 150 doctorates. Its graduates work today as therapists, managers, administrators, researchers, professors, college deans, and legislators serving in every venue from neighborhood community centers to the U.S. Capitol. The school's original curriculum, as developed by Dean Teicher under Dr. Lander's leadership, included courses designed to provide training appropriate for the specific needs of the American Jewish community. True to its original mission, Wurzweiler today has built on this historic foundation and places a strong emphasis on values and ethics, a respect for ethnicity, and the importance of religious beliefs and spirituality. The school stands today as a proud component of Bernard Lander's enduring legacy in behalf of the field of social work and the American Jewish community.

In addition to his groundbreaking work in establishing Yeshiva's School of Education and School of Social Work, Bernard Lander also labored intensively to bolster the standing of SECA's psychology department. Under his guidance, the department developed degree programs, recruited staff, attracted top-level faculty, and expanded its clinical services, working in tandem with the psychiatry faculty at Einstein Medical Center. The department's doctoral program was launched in 1957 and eventually was incorporated into the Ferkauf Graduate School of Psychology. Finally, Dr. Lander succeeded in establishing one of the nation's few accredited and comprehensive master's and doctoral degree programs in Jewish education, as part of the Graduate School of Education. The program quickly attracted high caliber degree candidates from across the country, many of whom already held top professional positions at Jewish day schools, high schools, and colleges.

In surveying the dynamic and rapid restructuring of the Yeshiva Graduate Division in the few short years since he had taken the helm, Bernard Lander could, were he not so busy, look back on his role with justifiable pride. His efforts had produced concrete results.

In January 1958, Dr. Bernard Lander wrote the following to Yeshiva president, Dr. Samuel Belkin:

> Approximately three years ago, you invited me to serve as Visiting Director of the Graduate Division, to help reorganize and develop the graduate program of studies at Yeshiva University. … I believe that this original task has now been completed.

With these words, Lander tendered his resignation as head of the Graduate Division. At the same time he requested that he be permitted to continue his affiliation with Yeshiva as head of the Bernard Revel Graduate School. Granted the position as head of the Revel Graduate School, he continued to serve there for the next eleven years.

When Bernard Lander took over the reins of the Bernard Revel Graduate School, it was already the leading Jewish Studies department outside of Israel. The school was home to a coterie of distinguished Jewish scholars and theologians in a wide array of disciplines. The faculty included Irving Agus in medieval Jewish history, Gershon Churgin in Jewish philosophy, Joshua Finkel in semitic languages, Nathan Goldberg in Jewish sociology, Sidney B. Hoenig in the history of the Second Commonwealth and the Dead Sea Scrolls, Issac Lewin in Eastern European Jewish history, Samuel K. Mirsky in geonic literature, Abraham Weiss in Talmud, and Hyman Grinstein in American Jewish history. Other distinguished scholars, including Rabbi Dr. Joseph B. Soloveitchik, taught in the school as adjunct professors. This high degree of specialization tended to not sit well with Dr. Lander as he established himself in the dean's office. He believed that the school's students would benefit from a more well-rounded education and so adopted a new class plan that included a core curriculum of four courses that all students were required to take in addition to those classes in their chosen area of specialization. These measures served to raise overall standards and tighten academic discipline. Dr. Lander was soon able to report excitedly on the outstanding results as seven candidates successfully sat for their oral exams in pursuit of their Doctor of Hebrew Literature degrees.

The door to Dr. Lander's office at the Revel Graduate School was always open to students wishing to confer about their studies or discuss particular problems they were facing. With the aid of his personable and efficient administrative assistant, Pearl Kardon, Lander gained the universal respect of the school's faculty and student body. Lander felt fulfilled in his role as dean and believed he was making a difference in the lives of his students and doing service towards improving the quality of American Jewish life in the process. The guidance he would offer students often resulted in a dramatic impact on their future lives. Rabbi Dr. Aaron Rakeffet recalls one example from his days as a doctoral candidate at Revel Graduate School.

Rabbi Rakeffet (then known as Arnold Rothkoff) had stopped by the dean's office in the early 1960s when Ms. Kardon pointed out that he had completed most of his coursework towards his doctoral degree.

"You had better start thinking about a topic for your dissertation, Arnold," she warned him. "Why don't I set up a meeting with Dean Lander and you two can discuss it?" Rakeffet agreed and he soon found himself seated in Dr. Lander's office holding a research plan for writing a biography of the Netziv, the distinguished Rosh Yeshiva of the Volozhin school in Lithuania. Lander paged through the plan and instructed Rakeffet to get back to him the next week. When he returned, Lander sat him down, looked him sternly in the eye and came right to the point.

"Arnold, I've discussed your ideas with the faculty, and we certainly have no objection to your topic," Lander explained. "But, we have a better idea. Something that really needs to be done." Rakeffet was mystified as Lander went on.

"We want you to write a definitive biography of Rabbi Bernard Revel." Lander became increasingly emotional and Rakeffet could see the tears welling up. "He was my *rebbe* and this will be his monument." Rakeffet agreed instantly, and Dr. Lander promised him his complete support. Lander next picked up the phone, called Revel's widow Sarah, and made arrangements for this young doctoral student to have access to Bernard Revel's personal papers. The dissertation was brilliant and was later published by the Jewish Publication Society under the title: *Bernard Revel: Builder of American Jewish Orthodoxy.* The book established Rabbi Dr. Rakeffet's reputation as an historian and did much to enhance Bernard Revel's name with the recognition it deserved.

In addition to counseling Revel Graduate School's doctoral candidates, Dr. Lander occasionally found himself mediating disputes among its distinguished scholars—and their distinguished egos. He proved to be an expert in the delicate art of dancing across the minefield of internecine politics in order to deliver a resolution that would invariably bring such conflicts to a harmonious conclusion.

The years flipped by swiftly as Dr. Lander patiently and steadily built the Bernard Revel Graduate School into an edifice of educational excellence that towered amidst the landscape of Jewish higher education in America. His work often extended beyond the campus walls, and he frequently found himself on the national stage, serving on governance boards and presidential commissions. Never content to restrict his focus to the mundane, day-to-day activities of collegiate life, Lander's attention often turned to Yeshiva University's long range strategic vision. This forward-thinking tendency grew more pronounced over the years as Lander shaped the Revel School into one of Orthodox Jewry's most cherished and respected institutions. He realized that as Yeshiva goes, so goes the future of American Orthodox Judaism. Both the school and the movement were integral components of Rabbi Bernard Revel's lasting legacy, and their fates were inexorably linked.

However, over the years he had witnessed a growing contingent of discontented faculty and alumni who were articulating their concern over what they perceived to be Yeshiva's growing secularization. They were unsettled by the growing trend of appointments of academically qualified, but nonobservant Jews to senior policy making positions. These appointments, while experts in their respective fields, held no regard for the traditional spirit that permeated the school's origins and its rich history. Turning over the leadership of Yeshiva University to those unfamiliar with and uncaring about its heritage was a dangerous mistake in the eyes of Lander and a number of others.

Dr. Lander also felt that Yeshiva had missed several key opportunities. For example, during the mid-1960s, Yeshiva was offered the opportunity of relocating its campus from Washington Heights to Manhattan's West Side under a proposed municipal redevelopment plan. Dr. Lander honestly observed how the Washington Heights neighborhood was deteriorating and argued in favor of the move. President Belkin, however, summarily vetoed the plan. It was a decision Belkin would come to regret many times, over the remaining decade of his tenure.

Another key opportunity presented itself a few years later. Lander had always championed the idea of extending Yeshiva's reach beyond New York City. By requiring serious yeshiva students to leave their hometowns behind, often never to return, if they wished to integrate their Torah studies with a quality college education, Yeshiva University was in fact draining these communities of their most Torah-dedicated young people. Why not, Lander asked repeatedly, establish Yeshiva branches in major Jewish communities such as Chicago, Baltimore, Miami, and St. Louis? When a very real prospect of establishing just such an extension campus in Los Angeles emerged, Lander became its strongest advocate. But Belkin demurred. "Does Harvard have campuses all over the country?" he asked, and the opportunity went up in smoke.

Samuel Belkin continued to serve as president of Yeshiva University for another decade, finally retiring in September 1975, bringing to a close his thirty-four year tenure at Yeshiva. He died the following year.

Dr. Lander had experienced disillusionment with the religious and academic directions of Yeshiva during this period. Not prone to dwell in the shadows of negativity, however, Lander forged his frustrations into a new vision of what a true Torah university would look like—were he ever granted the opportunity of leading one.

Starting in the early 1960s, Dr. Lander began describing, in private conversations to close friends, his dream of an authentic national Jewish college with campuses in major communities across the country. The response he encountered was predictable and hardly positive. "How can you think of starting another Orthodox Jewish school when the existing Orthodox school is tens of millions of dollars in debt!?" He did not have an acceptable answer, but he kept thinking as he continued to dream of a better way.

Dr. Lander eventually arrived at the unprecedented notion that a new Orthodox school could be financed strictly through tuition payments and some governmental support. He wished to create a college that would not be dependent upon the largesse of philanthropic Jews and foundation grants. As this vision took shape, he would cautiously unveil his thinking to trusted friends and colleagues. Even so, his ideas were usually met with scorn and ridicule once he was out of earshot, as illustrated in the following episode.

Bernard Lander had been invited to participate in the dedication of a new synagogue in Toronto by his friend, Rabbi Bernard Rosensweig. As they sat around the Shabbos table, Lander laid out his vision of a new national Jewish college, built and maintained without any fundraising activity. Rabbi Rosensweig recalls commenting to his wife afterwards: "For someone as seemingly rational as Bernie Lander, this is total *mishigos* (madness). It would be like me going to the moon." Of course within two years of that conversation, men did in fact land on the moon, and Bernard Lander's dream of a self-sufficient, national Orthodox Jewish institute of higher learning, moved one small step closer to reality.

Rabbi Rosensweig was hardly alone in his assessment of what he dubbed as "Lander's Lunacy." Fellow rabbis, community leaders and friends with whom Lander had exposed his thinking, believed, almost to a man, that his ideas were nothing more than a pipe dream—pure fantasy. It was during those days that Lander was frequently referred to as "the crazy genius."

By early 1969, Lander finally had put the pieces together so that the financial feasibility of his grand vision could conceivably be within his grasp. He asked for a meeting with Belkin during which he tendered his resignation as Director of the Bernard Revel Graduate School, effective September 1, 1969. Belkin listened politely as Dr. Lander explained that he was intending to start a new Jewish college in New York City.

Concerned that Belkin might become alarmed at the prospect of a competing institution, Lander was quick to explain that his new school would target only those students who were unlikely candidates to attend Yeshiva University. He was aware that his contract did not contain any sort of post-departure noncompete clauses. Such restrictions were rare within academic circles in those days. But it is unlikely that Dr. Belkin would be worrying about any undue competition originating from Bernard Lander's new college as he listened to his departing dean lay out his future plans. So he accepted Dr. Lander's resignation without protest, shook his hand, offered him a derisive smile, and wished him well.

A major chapter in Bernard Lander's life had now come to a close. Perhaps the esteem in which the Orthodox Jewish world held Dr. Lander could best be expressed through the words of the Doctor of Humane Letters degree bestowed upon him by President Samuel Belkin during the

Yeshiva commencement exercises in June 1969. The *honoris causa* degree was presented to Dr. Lander in recognition of the years of admirable service he had devoted to his alma mater and for his exemplary professional achievements. President Belkin read the words of tribute aloud:

> As a master of the domain of Sociology, and through your basic research in the field of juvenile delinquency, you have gained the esteem of our state and nation.
>
> As a distinguished alumnus and skilled administrator, you have rendered invaluable service to the advancement of your *alma mater*.
>
> As a brilliant teacher you have intellectually enriched and spiritually elevated all who have had the privilege of knowing you.
>
> We cherish you as an alumnus and respect you as a colleague.

As Bernard Lander, attired in mortarboard and gown, returned to his place on the platform and reread the words of the doctoral citation he had just been awarded, he could not help but think back to that nine-year-old boy standing on the rail platform on the Lower East Side of his youth. Like his younger self, Bernard Lander was once again peering anxiously into his onrushing destiny. He closed his eyes and leaned back slightly as the same feeling of rising anticipation swept over him like a fragrant west wind. He couldn't wait.

CHAPTER ELEVEN

Family Matters

> Privilege me to raise children and grandchildren who
> are wise and understanding, who love Hashem and fear
> G-d, people of truth … who illuminate the world with
> Torah and good deeds.
> —*From the traditional prayer recited after kindling the*
> *Shabbat lights*

As Bernard Lander's tenuous dream set sail—a dream of charting a new direction for Jewish higher education—his family's course was adeptly being guided by a capable and rock-steady hand at the helm. Sarah Lander was the consummate "balabusta," taking charge of every aspect of the family's domestic domain, from changing light bulbs to building the annual *sukka*. Her willingness to oversee all aspects of the household management enabled her extremely active husband to devote himself fully to his teaching, his ongoing research, and his community action commitments, all of which involved frequent travel. In addition, Sarah assiduously looked after the day-to-day needs of the growing family's four children: Esther, Hannah, Debbie, and Doniel.

The Lander children were an energetic and close-knit lot. Tearing through the Forest Hills neighborhood on foot or on bicycle, the children would often be seen rushing to meet their comrades in one of the community's many parks and playgrounds. Each of the siblings enjoyed a wide circle of friends, many of them drawn from the Yeshiva Dov Revel School, which all four attended. Sarah Lander also served as the family's sole driver and spent much of her time shuttling her children, as well as her husband, to and from various destinations both near and far. There existed a somewhat unconventional role reversal when it came to the delegation of domestic duties in the Lander household. If a faucet needed fixing or a gutter started leaking, it was Sarah who served as Madame Fix-It.

And if one of the girls needed a new dress for an upcoming special occasion, it was Bernard, who worked in Manhattan, who would typically stop at upscale Best & Co. to pick one out. While hardly a spendthrift, when it came to his children's clothing, Bernard had impeccable taste. He insisted that they be well-dressed and typically selected quality garments for them with little regard for price.

While Sarah's life certainly revolved around the needs of her husband and children, the orbit of her activities extended well beyond the family circle. Like her own mother, as well as her Biblical namesake, *Sarah Emeinu*, Sarah Lander was fully committed to the principle of *chesed* or kindness to others. Her days were filled with calling upon infirm members of the community, comforting those in mourning, driving her neighbors to doctor's appointments, and preparing delicious cakes that she would invariably deliver to each home she visited. And the traffic flowed in the other direction as well. The Lander home was known for its open door, where neighbors could stop in unannounced for a visit and, more often than not, solicit some needed advice. Sarah's many friends would naturally gravitate to her kitchen table, drawn by her gregarious nature and her reliably sunny disposition, as well as her highly charged energy level. Sarah was considered by her peers to be a real "classy lady." Her counsel was prized and sought out, not only by her friends, but also by the greater Jewish world.

Very active in all aspects of synagogue life, Sarah's dedication to community service often benefited the many other social agencies that operated in their Queens Jewish neighborhood. For several years, Sarah taught Torah studies in an afternoon Hebrew school populated by children from nonobservant families. She considered this type of outreach an act of kindness, introducing the true beauty of the Torah to those who had not been exposed to it at home. Her selflessness was directed also to a group of young Iranian students, placing them under her wing as they adjusted to American life.

Although she held clear dominion over it, Sarah was not the Queen of the Lander household. That designation was reserved for the one day each week that represented the spiritual zenith of every Orthodox Jewish household: Shabbos. The rules were well understood and strictly observed by even the youngest members of the Lander family. No discussion of politics or of Bernard's work week was permitted. Shabbos meal conversations usually revolved around the children's activities, both in and outside of school, and the many community programs in which the family members participated. The week's *parsha*, or weekly Torah portion, was often the topic of choice. Dr. Lander, seated at the head of the long and imposing dining room table, would issue pointed questions about the *parsha*, as well as inquiries into the children's current school assignments. Dr. Lander would sometimes provide an informal *shiur* (lesson) to his young dinner guests that served to highlight an interesting or less well-known aspect of the subject being discussed. Continuing with Jewish learning after the *benching* (grace after the meal) was completed, Dr. Lander might choose to invite Doniel and his friends to fill the rest of the long winter evening by joining him in study of the Talmudic tractates on *Brachos* (benedictions) or *Shabbos*.

The Lander's emphasis on dinner table Torah study had occasional far-reaching effects that, in one instance, brought the family some international acclaim. While in high school, daughter Debbie entered a North American Bible contest and succeeded in placing first in the national competition that tested students' knowledge of the *Tanach* (the Hebrew Bible). This accomplishment earned her the right to represent the United States as a high school freshman in the International Bible Contest (*Chidon HaTanach*), founded by David Ben-Gurion and which is still held annually in Jerusalem on *Yom Ha'atzmaut* (Israeli Independence Day). Sarah accompanied Debbie to Israel where she joined forty other contestants, representing twenty-four nations, who were required to answer questions drawn from the *Tanach's* more than 400 chapters. The first-prize winner is traditionally awarded a stipend towards a university studies grant. Dr. Lander served as his daughter's coach, continually prepping her with questions as she worked and studied to prepare for the world-class competition. Their diligence paid off as Debbie again succeeded and proudly brought home the Bronze Medal.

The steamy summer months, in the days before central air conditioning, often found families such as the Landers heading for Long Beach or extended stays in the Catskills Mountains. These areas were dotted with resorts, such as Grossingers, that specifically catered to observant Jewish families, offering a strict kosher cuisine, a Jewish day camp, and a fully functional synagogue on the premises. While the family vacationed, Dr. Lander would sometimes visit on weekends, but typically he would remain in the city, dividing his time between his research, his administrative duties, and helping out in his father's fabric business. Once in a while Dr. Lander was able to draw himself away for a somewhat longer period of rest and relaxation, but never for more than a two-week stretch. The summer of 1971, positioned between major chapters in Lander's career, was one such special occasion.

The family had arranged to rent an apartment on Ben Maimon Street in the Rehavia section of Jerusalem. The Holy City had been reunified after the 1967 Six Day War, and now Judaism's most sacred spot, the site of the ancient Second Temple, was under Jewish sovereignty for the first time in nearly 1,900 years. It was a heady and exhilarating time in Jewish history. It appeared evident, before the surprise Yom Kippur attack that was to take place two years' hence, that Israel's military might was invincible and its destiny inevitable. The Landers found themselves caught up in the zeitgeist of that optimistic era.

On Shabbos, Dr. Lander was able to walk with his children from their summer residence to the *Kotel* (the Western Wall), a retaining wall that serves as the only structural remnant of Herod's Temple, destroyed by the Romans in 70 CE. Donning *tefillin* (phylacteries), Dr. Lander and his son, Doniel, joyously and tearfully recited ancient prayers that articulated the centuries-old dream of redemption that would permit Jews to once again sing the praises of G-d in Jerusalem. The family also took bus tours and explored Jerusalem, the City of Gold, by foot and by taxi in an unforgettable journey of Jewish discovery.

Dr. Lander also enjoyed taking along family members as he traveled within the United States as a keynote speaker or a guest rabbi. Usually these engagements took him and his family entourage to points along the Eastern seaboard and Canada. Boston was a particularly popular family destination, where the Lander children would reconnect with their Aunt Bessie and their two cousins.

Perhaps the Lander children's favorite vacation spot was the home of their grandparents, the Shragowitzes, in Port Chester. Visits always included large family feasts with all the food being prepared from scratch. The Shragowitzes would regularly host community-wide Passover Seders that saw as many as forty seated around folding tables. Sarah's brother, Jacob, a physician; his wife, Joyce; and their four children, lived close by and would normally join the Landers whenever they visited Port Chester. These nurturing family get-togethers represent a shining highlight in the childhood memories of each of the four Lander children.

While Dr. Lander was perhaps less involved with household chores than most fathers, all of his adult children report that, despite his over-stuffed schedule, their father was invariably at their side whenever needed. Whether it was taking them to the doctor or attending PTA meetings, Bernard is remembered by his children with great fondness as a devoted and diligent parent.

During the formative years of Touro College in the early 1970s, the family home served as something more than a domicile. No longer possessing an office after his departure from Yeshiva, Dr. Lander held frequent meetings at the family dining room table. Working sessions, during which the future school's organizational structure was hammered into shape, took place amid the enticing aroma of Sarah's baked goods emanating from the kitchen. The Lander children looked on as a nonstop stream of leading academics, scientists, Jewish community leaders, and major philanthropists paraded through the family's living quarters. A typical meeting on any given evening might include one or two well-known luminaries convened to plot the future of Dr. Lander's educational vision (see following chapter). Among them were author Elie Wiesel, Rabbi Joseph B. Soloveitchik, real estate legend Larry Tisch, and former Miss America, Bess Myerson, who was serving as New York City's commissioner of consumer affairs at the time. Sarah, never one to be overly impressed by celebrities, offered the well-known visitors the same delightful "noshables" she typically put out for her next-door neighbors.

But Sarah's role during Touro's embryonic period was far more than that of a gracious hostess. During the intense strategy sessions where Touro's future hung in the balance, she would take her perch in the doorway leading from the dining room to the kitchen and listen intently to the spirited discussion. Whenever she disapproved of something she heard, she caught her husband's eye and admonished him with a simple: "Bernie, Bernie" and a subtle shake of the head. Lander would usually then announce to the group: "You hear what she says, folks. Forget about it!"

On other occasions, he would give her an apologetic look and mumble: "I've got no choice. I've got to do it." Either way, Sarah supported Bernie Lander unconditionally in every step he took towards the founding of Touro College.

During their teenage years, the Landers' three daughters attended Yeshiva University High School for Girls in Manhattan and then went on to study at Queens College of the City University of New York. Esther earned her Bachelor of Arts degree there and remained at Queens, taking courses towards a master's degree in education. Today, Esther serves as Director of Publications at Touro College.

Hannah was elected to Phi Beta Kappa, the national honor society for academic excellence, during her junior year. After earning her B.A. degree. she later studied business at Baruch College (part of CUNY) and received her M.B.A. degree. Today Hannah is an administrator in the Touro College Office of the Registrar and in that capacity would often accompany her father during his travels to Israel, Europe, and across the United States.

Debbie holds a master's degree from Queens College in educational psychology and worked in the New York City public school system as a school psychologist and mental health consultant. She currently serves as school psychologist for a number of yeshivas in Queens and on Long Island.

Like his father, Doniel Lander attended Yeshiva's Talmudical Academy, which became known as the M.T.A. or Manhattan Talmudical Academy. He joined the student body of Touro College during its third year of existence after studying during the summer under Rabbi Joseph B. Soloveitchik in Boston. Doniel was devoted to Rabbi Soloveitchik and opted to continue his studies with him at RIETS after he began his work at Touro. He devised a schedule that allowed him to participate in Rabbi Soloveitchik's Talmud *shiur* at RIETS in the mornings and then attend classes at Touro during the late afternoon.

Not surprisingly, this unusual arrangement that saw Doniel Lander, the son of the founder of a competing, breakaway school, attending classes at Yeshiva University, created some ripples. When this situation appeared on the radar screen of Yeshiva president, Samuel Belkin, he immediately approached his most illustrious faculty member. Belkin questioned how Dr. Lander's son could be enrolled as a student at Yeshiva University.

Rabbi Soloveitchik simply replied that Doniel was his personal student and that he wanted him to be in the *shiur*. Although Doniel's name did not appear on the class roster, the Rav continued to call his name and went out of his way to make Doniel feel welcome in his classroom. Eventually, when Doniel began his preparations for *semicha* (ordination), he was, in fact, officially enrolled as a rabbinical student at Yeshiva.

Upon completion of his studies, Rabbi Doniel Lander received *semicha* from his mentor, Rabbi Joseph B. Soloveitchik in 1976, after which he joined a postgraduate *kollel* (collection of advanced Torah scholars) affiliated with Touro College. He also enrolled at New York University in 1978, where he earned an M.B.A. and took courses towards a doctorate in finance. With his father's encouragement, Rabbi Doniel Lander, in 1983, founded Yeshivas Ohr Hachaim, an affiliate school of Touro College. Today he serves as *Rosh ha-Yeshiva* (head) of Yeshivas Ohr Hachaim, Chancellor of Touro College, and *Rosh ha-Yeshiva* of Touro's yeshiva high schools, Mesivta Yesodei Yeshurun and Mesivta Yesodei Yisroel.

The precious relationship that Bernard Lander, as an adult, enjoyed with his parents can best be described as dutiful and deeply devoted. On most days during this period, he assisted his father with the purchasing, accounting, and correspondence chores of the family wholesale textile business. Dr. Lander spoke with both his parents by telephone religiously. After David Lander's death in 1980, at age ninety-two, Bernard found strength in the strong and cherished ties he had established with his mother. Well into her nineties, Goldie Lander became a familiar figure in the hallways of Touro College. Whereas some other man might bristle at the sight of his elderly mother arriving unannounced at his office door, Dr. Lander's face would light up at the sight of her. With whomever he was meeting—or whatever major undertaking was being discussed—when Goldie entered the room, everything stopped as her son rose to greet her with a warm embrace and then escort her to a seat at his side before continuing with the business at hand.

On those days that Goldie chose not to stop by the Touro offices, Bernard would often visit her home, if only to look in on her briefly. This level of public parental devotion was acknowledged by all who knew Dr. Lander during this period, and it certainly enhanced the esteem in which he was held by his colleagues and associates. But many of Dr. Lander's actions on behalf of his parents remained private and sometimes left others a bit puzzled. For example, there was the matter of his regular trips to Notre Dame in South Bend, Indiana (see following chapter).

Lander was approached by noted Notre Dame president, Father Theodore Hesburg, who was puzzled by his esteemed research sociologist's habit of traveling by train from New York to attend his regular meetings at the South Bend campus (a sixteen-hour journey each way).

"I was wondering, Dr. Lander," he inquired privately, "why you take the train instead of hopping a jet in the morning. You could fly back home the same day after your meetings here. Do you have a fear of flying?" Dr. Lander smiled and gave the following response.

"It's my parents, Father. They would worry about me if I flew here for our meetings. So, I'd rather not upset them, and I take the train instead." The respect that Dr. Lander was earning in Father Hesburgh's eyes grew as he witnessed the man's faithful observance of the fifth commandment.

Dr. Lander's epic devotion to his parents was a trait shared by his two siblings, Nathan and Hadassah. Hadassah, a woman of demonstrable intellectual prowess, felt comfortable in the rarefied atmosphere of academics and theologians in which her brother, Bernard, circulated, causing one of her professors to comment after meeting her, "Hadassah is one of the most intelligent women I have ever met."

After attending Julia Richman High School, Hadassah studied education and economics at Hunter College and married Rabbi Max Posnansky in 1942. In her role as *rebbetzin*, Hadassah, along with the couple's three daughters, established Jewish homes in each of the communities where her husband was called upon to serve as spiritual leader or day school principal. She was an avid reader and a beloved and sensitive teacher. Denied "long days upon the land" despite her exemplary dedication to her parents, Hadassah's life ended in 1978 at the age of sixty.

Dr. Lander's brother, Nathan, served as Bernard's most stalwart supporter, always ready to offer a shoulder to the wheel or a shoulder to cry on, as the situation warranted. Both men shared more than merely a family background. Nathan, a respected sociologist, often worked jointly with Bernard, collaborating on investigative research projects such as the *El Bario* study. Deeply involved in Jewish affairs throughout his life, Nathan served, during the 1960s, as the director of research for the Synagogue

Council of America (S.C.A.). His role there often involved building bridges of understanding between Jewish and non-Jewish segments of American society. Nathan acted as S.C.A. liaison to such diverse groups as the National Council of Churches and the National Catholic Welfare Conference. In his role at the Synagogue Council, Nathan was among those charged with organizing the landmark August 1963 March on Washington. It was an address at this monumental outpouring that marked a seminal moment in the American civil rights movement when Dr. Martin Luther King stirred a nation with his historic "I Have a Dream" speech.

The March succeeded in attracting a broad spectrum of American religious leaders to the event, where they publicly proclaimed their opposition to the immorality of racial prejudice. This condemnation, based on religious grounds, and on display on television sets across the nation for the first time, played a decisive role in delegitimatizing segregation and building broad popular support for the civil rights legislation that Lyndon Johnson would introduce over the coming years.

When Touro College was founded in the early 1970s, Nathan Lander joined its nascent faculty as the head of the school's sociology department. Over the years, Bernard Lander had often come to look to his brother for prudent, pragmatic advice. That counsel, as well as Nathan's constructive criticism, did, on numerous occasions, prove pivotal in determining key policy issues and guiding the ongoing direction of Touro College.

Of the four Lander children, Debbie was the first to wed. While studying at *Machon Gold*, a Torah-based teacher's college in Jerusalem, she met Richard (Rafi) Waxman, a student at *Yeshivat Sha'alvim*, a nearby American-Israeli Torah study institution. The couple was married in 1976 shortly after Richard had completed his undergraduate studies at Touro as a member of the new school's charter graduating class. He went on to earn his doctorate in the field of psychology at Yeshiva University, with a specialty in neuropsychology. Today Dr. Waxman is a professor at Touro College and serves as a psychological consultant to several New York City hospitals. The couple has three children: Joshua, Shira, and Leora.

Doniel Lander and his bride, the former Phyllis Shuchatowitz, were married in 1981. Phyllis, a gregarious woman known for her outgoing manner and winsome smile, is the daughter of a well-respected Stamford, Connecticut Jewish day school principal. Rabbi Doniel Lander and

Phyllis are the parents of eight children: Rachel, Shoshana, Naomi, Dovid, Aharon, Moshe, Sarah Rivkah, and Yosef. In addition to her family responsibilities, Phyllis Lander coordinates student services at the Lander College for Men in Queens, a division of Touro College.

Esther met her future husband, Martin Greenfield, when both were assistant vice presidents at Philipp Brothers. Esther and Martin were married in 1984 and are the parents of three children: Shoshana, Yitzi, and Adina.

Bernard Lander reached a major milestone on June 25, 2004, when Debbie and Richard's daughter, Shira, gave birth to his first great-grandchild. Dr. Lander took a strong interest in the lives and many accomplishments of his progeny. He would *shep nachas* (derive pride) from the fact that many of his grandchildren have been educated at Touro-affiliated schools.

As the Lander family tree—a tree that took root in American soil one and a quarter centuries ago—continues to branch out into new areas of Jewish learning and achievement, it stands proudly as the sturdy core of Bernard Lander's lasting legacy.

CHAPTER TWELVE

The Founder

In a place where there are no leaders, strive to be a leader.
—*Pirkei Avot (Ethics of the Fathers) 2:6*

Wen, during the waning days of his administration, Ronald Reagan was asked to characterize his marriage to Nancy, he pondered for a moment and then commented: "I can't imagine life without her. There's nothing more wonderful for a man, but to know as he approaches his own doorstep, that someone at the other side of that door is listening for the sound of his footsteps." At age fifty-three, Bernard Lander could have easily spoken those exact words about Sarah, for it was then that she again listened for his familiar footsteps approaching their doorstep after his departure from Yeshiva University for the last time.

The summer of 1969 was a time of great triumph and even greater turmoil as the American flag was being planted on the moon's surface by U.S. astronauts and, at the same time, being burned by protesting college students at many of the nation's campuses. It was during this time of conflicting and converging forces in American life that Bernard sat down with Sarah to chart his future course.

The mission was clear: Bernard recognized an urgent need to create an institution—on a national level—that would provide college-age Jewish youth with a combination of liberal arts, career training, and religious studies that would deepen, rather than erode, their commitment to Judaism and the Jewish community. Dr. Lander was now fifty-three years old, but he was ready to actualize his dream, and he knew that Sarah was at his side. "Bernie," she said, "I have faith in you, and I am with you. Do it!" Buoyed by that support, Bernard Lander set out to build a new Jewish college.

Many who knew of Bernard Lander's far-flung notions about a new type of Jewish academic institution regarded him as a quixotic crusader.

Yet there were a few others, like Sarah, who understood his vision and of-fered him precious encouragement. Among these early supporters stood Father Theodore Hesburgh of Notre Dame University.

Through his association with George Shuster, the former president of Hunter College, Bernard Lander had, in the early 1960s, developed a relationship with Notre Dame's illustrious president. Shuster, after leaving Hunter, served as Hesburgh's assistant and headed the school's Institute for the Study of Man in Contemporary Society. Shuster invited Lander to conduct sociological research at Notre Dame and gave him a free rein to investigate any topic that caught his interest. Lander accepted. He set to work analyzing the causative relationship between a subculture's material-istic values and its juvenile crime rate. He posited that it was moral, rather than economic, deprivation that was behind the rising tide of delinquency and then conducted a four-year series of cross-cultural studies to examine his hypothesis. His findings, including the revelation that drug addiction was actually more widespread among teenagers with relatively higher fam-ily income levels, were groundbreaking and earned him the respect and friendship of Father Hesburgh.

As the decade drew to its close, student demonstrations protesting the war in Vietnam rocked the nation's campuses. Noting that many of the student organizers were Jewish, Father Hesburgh turned to Dr. Lander and asked him to study the phenomenon and examine the underlying causes. Bringing statistical analysis to bear on the problem, Dr. Lander reported that there was a direct correlation between the size of a university and the intensity of any demonstration that occurred there. Smaller, faith-based colleges, he observed, had suffered very few instances of student rebellion. He concluded from these findings that it was the impersonal nature of large universities that led to widespread student alienation and this undercurrent often erupted into violent campus outbreaks.

As he was reporting the results of his study to Father Hesburgh, Dr. Lander also laid out his vision of a nationwide network of colleges that would extend Jewish higher education beyond the boundaries of New York City.

"A chain of Jewish colleges and graduate schools where students will benefit through frequent personal contact with their professors," Lander explained. "It is that type of school that will not descend into chaos during difficult times." Hesburgh clearly agreed since it was this same type of environment that he was promoting at Notre Dame and that had, in his opinion, resulted in the absence of any type of disruptive student protests there. While other educators dismissed Lander's notion of building a new national Jewish university as nothing more than castles in the air, Hesburgh recognized the wisdom of Lander's vision and offered him his genuine and active encouragement. But that was not all. When Dr. Lander found his time and energies consumed by the full-throttle push to obtain a charter for Touro College—the key component needed to launch the new school—Hesburgh helped out significantly by reducing Lander's research responsibilities at Notre Dame while, at the same time, increasing his salary.

The concerns about circumstances on American college campuses that Bernard Lander had expressed to Father Hesburgh and to Sarah, consistently appeared as themes that he threaded throughout his frequent public pronouncements during this period. "Today's college campuses are a crisis area for Jewish survival," he would warn his audiences. "They are the crematoria of our people," invoking an extreme metaphor that equated Amherst with Auschwitz. His passionate remarks in Chicago, before the Union of Orthodox Jewish Congregations in November 1969 were characteristic of the dire message he trumpeted, often to less than sympathetic ears:

> Today's college student has been thrust into an environment for which he has been inadequately prepared intellectually—an atmosphere, alien and hostile to the traditions and moral values he received in childhood. We ask him to prevail against a campus culture and, in many instances, faculty members who take special delight in ridiculing the moral and traditional values of his parental or religious upbringing.

But Lander was not merely sermonizing to his audiences. His observations and conclusions were supported by hard data, scientifically collected, often by Lander himself. He would, for example, cite a study that showed that a shocking 26 percent of students at a particular Ivy League school who were raised as Jews, and who entered college as Jews, no longer so identified themselves by the time they graduated. He railed against the complacency of those who falsely believed that a Jewish day school and high school education would inoculate college students from abandoning their heritage. His own study of Yale undergraduates—all of whom had received an intensive Jewish education prior to entering college—found that nearly two thirds of them (65%) had broken entirely with the traditions of their upbringing by the time they received their Yale sheepskins.

"Do not delude yourselves." he would caution his audiences. "The early years are critical in the formation of a child's basic psychological structure and in the development of a healthy ego. But it is the college years that play the decisive role in determining an adult's sense of identity." Lander understood that the Jewish community's reliance solely upon elementary and secondary education providers as the socialization engines of its traditions, its culture, its peoplehood, represented a dangerous direction that was inevitably headed for disaster. He often discussed how it was during one's college years that his or her adult values and long-term lifestyle were molded. The undergraduate college years are the most critical when it comes to determining a person's ultimate course in life, he would argue. It is at this time that a personality becomes both introspective and malleable. Ponderous questions such as "Who am I?" and "What does it all mean?" are typically resolved during this seminal period in a young person's life. At the same time, Lander pointed out, it is during these years that one is more open to change than in any later period of life. For the majority of students, attitudes, values, and religious affiliation are permanently fixed upon graduation. That window of intellectual and spiritual opportunity, Lander firmly claimed, had to be exploited before it closed forever.

In his journal articles, Dr. Lander would at times refer to studies conducted by Theodore M. Newcomb of Bennington College dealing with peer pressure and the impulse to conform one's behavior to the perceived norm. Time and again, he used such studies to bolster his case in behalf of extending Jewish education beyond high school into the highly formative undergraduate years. Lander pointed out that not only were secular colleges stripping observant young Jews of their identity, but that the opposite effect would be encountered if the roles were reversed.

"We have seen how immersing a young Jewish man or woman into a 'youth culture' environment, with its emphasis on alienation, self-rejection, and New Left nihilism, makes it highly likely that the student will, before long, surrender the religious, cultural, and moral values absorbed through his or her family background," Lander wrote. "But it works the other way, as well," he was quick to remark.

"Place a young person with an assimilated Jewish background into a *positively* oriented environment that is committed to strong Jewish values, afford interaction with faculty members who personify those values, and the likelihood is great that he or she will be socialized into a proud, committed Jew and a productive American citizen." But where, outside of Yeshiva College, was such an environment to be found? Certainly not on the majority of American campuses of the day.

The so-called "counter-culture" that had emerged as the Baby Boom generation reached college age, was characterized by a wholesale rejection of core American values, alienation from religious traditions and an epidemic of mind altering recreational narcotic use. Was this an appropriate environment into which Jewish parents ought to dispatch their emotionally vulnerable children?

Lander's service to non-Jewish colleges, such as Notre Dame, provided him with a unique perspective within the Jewish academic world. He was able to assess fairly how the Christian educational infrastructure stacked up against the Jewish academic landscape. Once again, Lander applied his analytical skills and empirical training in order to conduct his comparisons. Looking at the sheer numbers, he discovered that up to that date, 58 Christian churches had sponsored more than 700 colleges and universities across America. Catholics alone had established 351 institutions of higher learning, among which were 65 accredited colleges and universities. The American Jewish community, in stark contrast, had created only two: Brandeis University and Yeshiva College. And of the two, only Yeshiva still embodied its Jewish character. Brandeis had, over the 20 years of its existence, shed much of the original Jewish character of the school. Not surprisingly, the self-rejection numbers among Brandeis students, Lander learned, were among the highest in the nation.

Yeshiva College, where Dr. Lander had spent the previous fifteen years as a member of the school's administration, was the polar opposite. Yeshiva students were required to matriculate in a double curriculum that included twenty hours of Hebrew and Talmudic studies each week. This, on top of a full-blown comprehensive college program! It was a rigorous and demanding schedule requiring an intensity that was well beyond the capabilities of an average Jewish college student. Hence, many young people who wished to pursue a mainstream college career while still continuing with their Jewish studies never even considered Yeshiva as an option. It was precisely this type of student—one who he felt represented the vast majority of Jewish college-bound teenagers—whom Dr. Lander wished to serve at the school he would someday establish.

But was there a market for such a school? After all, a college is a business, much like any other. One must accurately gauge the demand for the product or service involved before deciding whether or not to launch any new venture. Lander was convinced that the pent-up demand was enormous. Even with its extremely rigorous curriculum, Yeshiva College typically received more applications each year than the number of available openings in its entering class. There was no question in Lander's mind that a new college, established to meet the needs of all Jewish families, would enjoy a warm and welcome reception. It was this belief, based on the hard statistical data upon which he had come to rely throughout his career even more than the ideological rhetoric against the threats posed to Jewish survival, that ultimately propelled him into action. "If Yeshiva College cannot accommodate the number of students knocking on its doors today, what of the future?" he asked himself and those within his inner circle. And what about all those thousands of students who never even knock? What if we could prevent them from discarding their Jewish heritage while, at the same time, delivering the type of education they needed to become successful in mainstream America? How many more would flock to our doors then? All the questions pointed to the same answer. A new school—actually a new network of schools—was an idea whose time had not only arrived, but was, in fact, well overdue.

The challenges involved in such a bold venture are daunting, to say the least. How does one effectively weave Yiddishkeit into the day-to-day study patterns of a modern college curriculum? What about entrance requirements? Does one accept only students who began studying Hebrew and Torah in kindergarten and completed a full twelve years of Judaic study? This question was answered by Dr. Lander on philosophical grounds. He firmly believed that the new school must accept the obligation to educate offspring of the entire Jewish community, regardless of their level of observance or prior study. Special remedial courses would be established to bring the Judaically deficient freshmen up to speed, enabling them to study alongside their day school educated classmates by the time they began their sophomore year. Once a level playing field had been established, each student would be required to pursue a degree program that included the study of Torah, Talmud, ethics, and philosophy. The goal was to produce a graduate who was fully prepared to enter a professional career or enroll in graduate school for further study, as well as emerge with a solid foundation in the heritage and religious practices of the Jewish people.

While he was convinced of the enormous untapped demand for his envisioned new college, Dr. Lander was enough of a realist to admit that it would take several years for the school to become established, during which time enrollment levels would remain relatively low. How would they survive that critical start-up period as they waited for the revenue stream to grow into a sustaining river? Based on his prior research, Dr. Lander was certain that smaller colleges, where students could freely and frequently interact with their professors, were far more successful in preserving religious identity than those Big Ten behemoths. Being small was actually an asset that would prove compelling to prospective parents. "Your son will be mentored and guided by a faculty who will give him all the personalized attention his talents demand."

As Dr. Lander and his inner circle made concrete plans for the opening of the new school, he emphasized clearly that this was to be only the first of many such schools. Once it was up and running and all the bugs had been shaken out, the new college would serve as a template for the other such institutions across the nation that would be built in its image. This network, in Lander's grand design, would represent nothing less than the lifeblood of Jewish continuity and survival in America. It was, without question, a daring and daunting dream that would require every molecule of dedication from the group of founders he attracted to his side. Bernard Lander recognized the enormous obstacles he was facing, and he felt himself empowered by his faith in the Almighty as he faced the challenges that now lay ahead.

The first of these as the work got underway was the question of a charter. In America, individual states typically grant schools the authority to operate a college or university, to enroll students, and, most importantly, to award degrees. In New York state, this responsibility is assigned to the Board of Regents who, through the State Education Department Division of Higher Education (S.E.D.D.H.E.) evaluates each new school and, if it is found acceptable, issues the necessary charter. In conducting such evaluations the office is charged with determining whether the new school's operations will serve "the public good." In addition to examining the school's proposed curriculum, mission statement, faculty structure, physical facilities, and the like, the office also places great importance on its prospects for long-term financial solvency and stability. A bankroll in the millions—or the clear ability to raise such sums—was an a priori requirement needed to obtain a higher education charter from the state of New York. Bernard Lander had neither. He was not personally wealthy, and he had a strong distaste for the indignities of *schnorring* (fundraising), as he wrote to one of Touro's earliest and wealthiest supporters, Leon Levy:

> The creative aspects of college administration are entrancing and fulfilling. But I feel like hell when I have to talk to my friends about financial matters. I suppose, however, that one cannot achieve heaven unless the ladder is planted on earth!

As a direct result of Dr. Lander's strong aversion to soliciting money, Touro College experienced a most unusual beginning. Casting about for well-funded allies, Lander connected with the Yeshivah of Flatbush, America's first coeducational elementary Jewish day school founded in 1927. As the school grew, so did its ability to offer ongoing Jewish education to its constituents. A high school was launched in 1950 and, beginning in the 1960s, the school operated a Midrasha—a program, aimed at college-aged graduates of its high school, with evening courses in Judaic studies. Students enrolled at Brooklyn College, or other area colleges during the day, were able, in this way, to continue their Jewish learning activities.

By 1969, there was already a history involving Dr. Lander and the Yeshivah of Flatbush, so he was not surprised when he was contacted by its newly elected Vice President, Dr. Leon Reich. A successful optometrist, and the father of young children enrolled at the school, Reich was calling Dr. Lander for help. Contentious school board elections at the Yeshivah of Flattbush had resulted in a loss of financial support, and the board was considering the elimination of Midrasha.

Through their meetings, Lander and Reich agreed to work together towards establishing a new school in the mold of Lander's overarching vision. Plans were made to move ahead and contact the New York sanctioning body in order to obtain a charter.

In March 1969, in what may be considered the first official act establishing Touro College, Leon Reich initiated contact with the State Education Department in order to obtain a state charter. Needing a name for the new school, Reich quickly came up with one and filed the application on behalf of "The Hebrew College of Brooklyn." But this name seemed entirely too limiting an appellation for Dr. Lander's grand image of his future school. Lander convened a meeting of his inner circle at the Harvard Club to discuss the matter of what to call the new college.

Seated with his confidants around a heavy, oaken table, situated in the plush and paneled facility founded by and for Harvard graduates, the irony of the moment was not lost on Bernard Lander. For it was Harvard University whose president, in the 1920s had openly proclaimed an enrollment quota limiting the number of Jews allowed to enter the hallowed, ivy-covered halls of America's oldest college. And today, here sat the man most directly responsible for the legislation that had rendered such quotas illegal, making his plans to create his own school that would someday, he imagined, rival the stature of Harvard. It was indeed an auspicious place to begin.

The men seated around the table with Reich and Lander included Arthur Schneier, rabbi of the Park East Synagogue in Manhattan and Michael Nisselson, a key fundraiser at Yeshiva College. Lander had enlisted them to brainstorm and come up with a suitable name for his new Jewish liberal arts college. "New College" was considered, but a phone call elicited the information that the name already was taken. A suggestion to name the school in honor of Israel's first chief rabbi, Yitzchak HaLevi Herzog, was an idea with a good deal of merit that would reflect the school's commitment to scholarship, Jewish observance, and modernity. Using the name, however, would require permission from the family, and that might lead to complications. Naming the school after Abraham Isaac Kook, the first Ashkenazi chief rabbi of British Mandate Palestine and a towering figure in the Jewish world both in Israel and the Diaspora, seemed appropriate, but there was some apprehension that students would be referred to as "Kookies." When Nisselson suggested "Touro," the response was positive.

Reverend Isaac Touro, a Sephardic Jew whose family had settled in Holland and included many scholars, was invited to Colonial America to serve as one of the spiritual leaders of the Newport, Rhode Island Jewish community. He was a close friend of Ezra Stiles, soon to become president of Yale College, and tutored him in Hebrew. Stiles was so enamored with the Hebrew language that he attempted to introduce it as a required subject at Yale. Yale's herald crest bears a Hebrew inscription to this day (*Urim v' Tummim* meaning Light and Truth; see Exodus, 28:30) due to the influence of Isaac Touro.

In 1790, the synagogue's warden, Moses Seixas, wrote to President George Washington, expressing his support for Washington's administration and extending the congregation's good wishes. Washington sent a letter in response, which read in part:

> … the Government of the United States … gives to bigotry no sanction, to persecution no assistance. … May the children of the Stock of Abraham, who dwell in this land, continue to merit and enjoy the good will of the other Inhabitants; while every one shall sit in safety under his own vine and fig tree, and there shall be none to make him afraid. May the father of all mercies scatter light and not darkness in our paths, and make us all in our several vocations useful here, and in his own due time and way everlastingly happy.

> — Geo. Washington, President
> The United States of America

Isaac's second son, Judah Touro, made a fortune as a merchant in New Orleans. A hard worker, Judah Touro avoided ostentation. He fought under the command of Andrew Jackson in the War of 1812 and was severely wounded in battle. As a transplanted Northerner in the Deep South, Judah Touro was averse to slavery. He frequently purchased slaves in order to set them free and would then establish them in business.

During Judah Touro's later years, he fully dedicated himself to the Jewish traditions of his youth. He founded Congregation Nefuzoth Yehuda and built its synagogue, religious school, and cemetery. His philanthropy supported civic causes including Massachusetts General Hospital, which his older brother had helped found, the Bunker Hill Monument in

Boston, and the public library in Newport. He established a library and a hospital, the Touro Infirmary, in New Orleans among his many other philanthropic endeavors. Judah Touro left $10,000 in his will for the up-keep of the Jewish cemetery and the synagogue in Newport that bears his family's name to this day. It was designated a National Historic Site by the U.S. government in 1946.

Judah Touro never married, and he dedicated the bulk of his vast for-tune to support Jewish life, providing for Jews in the Holy Land, as well as for congregations and benevolent organizations across the United States. He provided funds to Moses Montefiore to help establish Yemin Moshe, the first Jewish neighborhood outside the Old City walls in Jerusalem. Because Judah Touro had no descendents, the name had the advantage that it was in the public domain and unhampered by any family naming rights. If a future philanthropist were to offer a large gift to have the col-lege renamed, that opportunity would remain open. Importantly, and as Dr. Lander pointed out, the Touro name would reflect the new college's commitment to Jewish heritage as well as service to the nation at large—ideals upon which the future college was to be built.

The name met with immediate and universal approval by the group. And thus, beneath the crest of the nation's oldest educational institution—that of Harvard University bearing the motto "Lux et Veritas," Light and Truth—Touro College was born. The "light," in this case, was at the end of a far distant tunnel and the "truth" was that the really difficult work was about to begin.

CHAPTER THIRTEEN

First Steps

All beginnings are difficult.
— *Mekhilta, Exodus, chap. 19*

D eciding upon a name for the new college was a trivial effort compared to the challenges that now lay ahead for Dr. Lander and his dedicated crew of supporters. The immediate hurdle they now encountered was obtaining a state charter. In this quest, Dr. Lander was faced with an unusual dilemma. On the one hand, Touro College was to represent a radical departure from the prevailing direction of Jewish higher education. This was its raison d'être. In order to respond to the threats to Jewish survival represented by mainstream American college campuses, Touro was envisioned as a network of Jewish-sponsored schools, providing a program of comprehensive studies while emphasizing religious values and a sense of *Yiddishkeit*. At the same time, the new college could not deviate too widely from the established academic norms for fear of being denied the charter it needed to operate.

As the process of obtaining a charter moved deliberately and gradually forward, Dr. Lander set out to draft a wide-ranging statement of goals and principles that would articulate Touro's mission and serve as the new school's guiding roadmap. Both idealistic and pragmatic, these principles sought to articulate the objectives that had prompted the creation of the school while, at the same time, they were designed to address a host of practical issues.

Simply put, the overarching goal of Touro College would be to combine an education of excellence in the liberal arts and sciences with an integrated and intensive program of Jewish studies.

To foster such an environment, Dr. Lander firmly believed it necessary to avoid the impersonal nature of most large universities. Hence, Touro would be a small college with a faculty populated by instructors genuinely intent on teaching and guiding students, rather than those focused mainly on research and publishing. As Dr. Lander put it:

"Touro College would be home to a distinguished faculty involved with a limited number of able students."

In response to the question of exactly who would qualify as such "able students," it was determined that Touro would serve both those who had undergone twelve years of Judaic education as well as others who had received none—plus all levels in between. This was a moral issue in Dr. Lander's eyes. He unequivocally believed that the Jewish community has an equal responsibility to serve all students, regardless of their educational backgrounds. Touro would be marked by open doors and by open minds.

In terms of curriculum, each student would be required to pursue a program that included Torah, Talmud, Hebrew language, ethics, and philosophy. Graduates would be fluent in Hebrew and emerge with a solid grounding in their Jewish heritage. A year of study in Israel was foreseen as a key component of several of the planned degree programs.

As this "Statement of Objectives" evolved over the summer months of 1970, it became clear that what was being fashioned was not merely a blueprint for a single New York school but rather a model upon which to base a national, and perhaps an international, network of colleges.

The charter application borrowed heavily from this mission statement, including the following high-minded passage:

> The proposed Touro College is dedicated to provide its students with the opportunity to acquire an education in the liberal arts and sciences that embodies the concept that the values of Judaism have an especially meaningful relevance to the general culture of Western civilization. Its hope is to achieve the goal set by Moses Maimonides of the intellectual and moral perfection of the individual.

As Dr. Lander laid down the new school's lofty principles, and as the quest for a charter continued on its course, more down-to-earth issues were also being dealt with. Primary among these was the fundamental question of where to house the new school. Dr. Lander put out the word among his inner circle that he was seeking an affordable building that could house Touro's classrooms and offices. In late July, his phone rang.

"I was walking down Club Row on 44th Street and spotted a For Sale sign," said the familiar voice on the other end. "The sign read 'Government Surplus Property,' and I wrote down the phone number. I think you should take a look."

Dr. Lander visited the site that turned out to be a twelve-story structure, originally built to house the Yale Club. It looked ideal. He phoned the real estate agent and explained his situation, but the reply he received was anything but encouraging.

"We've had several serious inquiries about that building, Dr. Lander," said the agent. "Both Columbia and CUNY have expressed an interest. They're both looking for additional administrative office space. Your school doesn't even exist yet. So, with all due respect, I don't think you're in a position to compete here."

Instead of being deterred by this obstacle, Bernard Lander was spurred into action.

"Who actually handles the decision-making about the sale of this building?" he asked the realtor.

"Well, the client is the Office of Surplus Property Utilization," she replied.

"That's part of H.E.W. (Dept. of Health, Education and Welfare), isn't it?" said Lander.

Within two days, Dr. Lander was in Washington, meeting face to face with the director of the Surplus Property Utilization office—a gentleman who turned out to be a Reform Jew and who appeared to be sympathetic to the new school's mission as patiently and passionately explained to him by Dr. Lander.

"I will do what I can to help Touro get the building," he promised, "but you must make contact with the appropriate political leaders here in Washington and win yourself some support." In other words, if Lander wanted this building, he would have to pull some strings and push some buttons.

Lander turned to his old friend from Mizrachi, Matityahu Adler, the vice president of Bar Ilan University.

"I need your help, Mati," he explained. "No one understands Washington politics better than you. How do I get this accomplished?"

Adler directed Lander to Eddie Adams, a powerful beltway political consultant. Once again, fate stepped in when Lander learned that the Adams family, originally known as the Orienlichters, also hailed from Sieniawa. Adams clearly remembered Bernard Lander's parents from his childhood in New York and so the *lansman* (countryman) connection was sealed. As an adult, Adams had moved to Texas and worked as a newspaper publisher where he became a political ally of future president Lyndon Johnson. Throughout the 1960s, Adams had established serious political connections with countless Democratic leaders including the Kennedys.

"The first person you need to speak with is Emanuel Celler," Eddie Adams told Lander. Celler was the chairman of the powerful House Judiciary Committee and, at the time, the longest-serving member of the U.S. House of Representatives.

Celler and Bernard Lander soon became friends and the congressman was subsequently to serve as an active member of the Touro Board of Trustees and lifelong supporter of the school.

As Dr. Lander, with the help of Eddie Adams, was making the rounds in Washington, attempting to secure a permanent home for his new school, good news reached his ears. Touro had received its charter from the New York State Department of Education. A milestone had been achieved.

In a move designed to leverage one success against the fulcrum of another, Dr. Lander persuaded Edward Carr, the director of the New York Bureau of College Evaluation, to support his efforts in Washington. Carr wrote the following to the Office of Surplus Property:

> As you may know, the chartering of new institutions of higher education by the New York Board of Regents involves a careful screening process and takes place only when there is high promise of educational quality.... Confident in the promise of Touro College to achieve academic distinction, it is our hope that you will give favorable consideration to the application of Touro College.

A short time later, and based in large part upon this endorsement, the U.S. Office of Surplus Property recommended, not merely the sale of, but the actual gifting of, the 30 West 44th Street building to Touro College!

There remained, however, one more bureaucratic hurdle before Touro could receive the building. The gift had to be approved by the New York office of the Department of Health, Education and Welfare—part of the Republican Rockefeller administration. It was time for Dr. Lander to jump to the other side of the political aisle. For this mission he called upon his friend, Rabbi Ronnie Greenwald. Greenwald had been a political director of Richard Nixon's successful 1968 presidential campaign and was, at this point, serving within H.E.W. Greenwald went on to become perhaps the world's highest profile prisoner release negotiator, serving in this capacity in the administrations of five presidents. Greenwald's successes included securing the release of numerous Soviet-era Russian dissidents, including Natan Sharansky. His most notable failure was his long quest to secure a pardon for convicted spy, Jonathan Pollard. Fortunately, for the future of Touro College, Rabbi Greenwald succeeded in his mission to secure the needed signature, thereby entitling the nascent school to open its doors at 30 West 44th Street in midtown Manhattan in time for the fall semester of 1971.

The West 44th Street property, which was destined to serve as Touro's home for the next eighteen years, enjoyed an intriguing history. The ten-story Harvard Club, built in 1893, and the site of the 1969 meeting of founders who would select Touro College as the new school's name, stood only a few doors away. During its first decade, the Yalees were irked to witness their rivals towering over the area stables and one-story taverns. So, by 1902, the Sons of Eli had decided to erect a "bigger, better" twelve-story edifice that afforded them the ability to stand on their own roof and look down with relief on the neighboring Harvard Club.

The Yale Club's exterior was a blend of Beaux Arts and neo-classical styling and marked by a giant arch at the tenth floor level. The interior was replete with oak paneling, giant columns, chestnut pilasters and a two-story library. It stood as a sanctuary for Yale students and alumni until it was sold to the Federal government for wartime use in 1943. Uncle Sam moved out in 1969, and the building had remained vacant since then.

The building required extensive renovation before Touro could occupy the space. Even after the move, the building's grand stairwell was considered a fire hazard. Two manually operated elevators were installed that did not have the ability to respond to a push-button summons.

During the school's early years of operation, Dr. Bernard Lander, in his mid-fifties, could often be seen getting his exercise by scurrying up and down the staircase to fetch the elevator in behalf of a visitor or an older faculty member.

Although title to the West 44th Street building was granted free and clear, it became immediately apparent that funds would be needed for renovation before the school could open its doors. His quest for such funding again delivered Dr. Lander to the doorstep of Matityahu Adler. Adler reckoned that Lander could use the services of an angel investor—someone who not only possessed the means, but also the mettle to gamble on such an untested entity as Touro College. It would have to be a person who valued the school's core mission: that of combating the widespread assimilation taking place on the nation's campuses. Adler thought he knew just the man—a man with a number tattooed on his arm.

Eugene Hollander was a Hungarian Holocaust survivor who would play a pivotal role in both the establishment of Touro, as well as in an episode that would nearly devastate the new college. His core attitude about Jewish survival had been molded in the crucible of Auschwitz and other Nazi extermination camps. Hollander's story, as recounted in his memoir *From the Hell of the Holocaust; A Survivor's Story* (KTAV Publishing, 2001), is one of heroic struggle in the face of unimaginable horror. Coming from a prosperous and religiously observant Budapest family, Hollander was conscripted into one of the Hungarian Army's Jewish labor battalions. Running away, he returned to Budapest to rejoin his wife, Monica, just as the Hungarian fascists (the Arrow Cross) were being placed into power as the Third Reich's puppet regime. After witnessing the Danube flowing red with Jewish blood, Hollander was deported to Auschwitz, where he endured extreme psychic and physical suffering, pervasive terror, and the irrational brutality of the camps. Through a series of miracles amid the forced marches, he managed to cling to life through the end of the war, after which he regained his freedom, reunited with his wife, and launched a successful business career that would, in 1952, lead him to the United States.

Settling in New York, Hollander began investing in commercial real estate and then entered the nursing home business. Convinced that his life had been spared for a higher purpose, he devoted much of his time, energy, and talents to Jewish philanthropy. The lessons of the Shoah had been imprinted even more deeply into his psyche than the numbers tattooed upon his forearm. Hollander understood that the key to Jewish survival in a post-Holocaust world was strength, the strength to overcome both the threats posed by Israel's Arab enemies, as well as the threat of assimilation embodied in American modernity. This mindset made Hollander an ardent Zionist as well as a passionate rallier against the loss of Jewish identity through intermarriage. At the time Bernard Lander first met him, in 1970, Eugene Hollander was serving as treasurer of the American Friends of Bar Ilan University. He was also the president of an Eastside Manhattan Orthodox synagogue. Dr. Lander did not have a difficult time in enlisting Hollander's support for his dream of a network composed of Jewish colleges whose core mission so closely conformed to the man's deeply-rooted personal philosophy.

Emerging as more than merely a one-time funding source, needed to underwrite building renovations, Hollander immediately became a full partner in the establishment of Touro College. He began by taking out his checkbook every time money was needed for labor and materials on behalf of the building's transformation into a proper higher educational facility. Hollander's generosity removed an enormous burden from Dr. Lander's shoulders, freeing him to concentrate on the important work of planning the new school's curriculum, hiring staff and faculty, and, most importantly, recruiting students for the school's charter class.

As Hollander worked with the architects and engineers during the renovations of the West 44th Street building, he soon discovered that the scope of this job was an order of magnitude greater than what he had originally been led to believe. Hollander strongly advised Dr. Lander to secure financing from a conventional lender to underwrite the cost of completing the extensive renovations. Lander agreed to go into debt, but questioned whether the school would be regarded as credit worthy by any potential lender—given that it had yet to take in a single dollar of revenue. Lander's apprehensions were well-placed. Conventional financing was out of the question. Fortunately, Hollander again came to the rescue by agreeing to finance the project himself. Touro signed a note and began making payments to Hollander. These continued for a number of years until Hollander agreed, in an act of magnanimity, to forgive the debt and convert it into a charitable gift.

The critical importance of Eugene Hollander's generosity at this juncture cannot be overstated. Perhaps his most significant gift to the fledgling school was the removal of most financial concerns from Dr. Lander's agenda, thereby allowing Lander the time and freedom to develop the new school's vital academic program. It is ironic and unfortunate that Hollander's seminal role in the establishment of Touro College, as well as his support during the period that followed, was sadly overshadowed by his involvement in a series of scandals that would, in a few years, rock the young school (see following chapter) and threaten its survival.

The vision of Touro College, in the years prior to its opening, had always involved multiple campuses. An examination of Bernard Lander's earliest speeches and articles on the need to stem the tide of assimilation on our nation's campuses reveals that he consistently referred to a "network" or a "chain" of schools, wherein each would provide an Ivy League-style liberal arts education alongside an intensive Jewish curriculum. The idea behind such a network was that it would reduce the need for students to venture far from their home communities since it had been shown that most such students seldom returned. Building schools near major Jewish population centers would reduce the drainage of serious committed Jews from these communities flowing into New York. Now the time had come to fulfill this long-deferred dream and the challenging question quickly arose of "how do you create a network?" Opening one school was hard enough, but setting up multiple campuses on day one was clearly beyond the reach of even Lander's most ambitious aspirations.

The focus now would be to open a single college that would, by its very success, serve as a template for other schools that would soon follow suit. Thus, the network that Lander had envisioned, would evolve. The question of from where to draw students remained paramount during these planning stages. Dr. Lander had imagined that Touro would position itself as an alternative to the prestigious Ivy League schools that attracted the best and brightest Jewish college applicants from across the nation. Touro would offer the same high quality education as Brown, Cornell, or other top tier schools, but with one critical difference. At Touro, students would not be expected to lose their commitment to Jewish observance. On the contrary, by integrating an intensive program of Jewish studies—albeit one with fewer required hours than at Yeshiva College—a student's devotion to Judaism would be enhanced and elevated as the result of a Touro education.

In an attempt to narrow the focus—at least initially—of exactly who would be served by the new school, Dr. Lander, in consultation with the other founders, laid out an early recruitment plan aimed at establishing the viability of the new venture. The first decision reached dealt with gender. Lander decided that Touro, at least at the outset, would be a school for men. A women's division would be added as quickly as feasible (and it was). Touro's initial recruitment efforts then would target academically capable young men graduating from area Jewish high schools who might be considering attending Ivy League colleges.

The decision against opening its doors as a coed college did not sit well with Dr. Leon Reich and the rest of the leadership at the Yeshivah of Flatbush High School and soon led to a parting of the ways between Touro and one of its earliest supporters. But this rift did not entirely end Touro's relationship with Yeshivah of Flatbush. For many of its early years, Touro attracted Flatbush graduates through its doors, where they attained a world-class education and graduated as loyal, committed Jews.

Secondly, at Dr. Lander's suggestion, Dr. Reich had purchased the property directly across the street from the Flatbush Yeshivah building and managed to get it zoned for use as an educational facility. These lots were eventually sold to Touro College and became the site of Touro's very first campus construction project, making it the first step in Dr. Lander's dream of building a network of schools that would eventually stretch around the world.

As Eugene Hollander, who would become the first chairman of Touro's Board of Trustees, oversaw the metamorphosis of the Yale Club on West 44th Street into the college's new home, Dr. Lander remained busy assembling the new school's administrative staff. In October 1970, a mere eleven months before the scheduled opening of the school, Lander recruited George Cohen to serve as its first dean. Dr. Lander had first come to know Cohen during the year Lander had spent living in the dormitory at Yeshiva College's Talmudical Academy. Rounding out this trio of high school friends was Joseph Kaminetsky, who would go on to found the network of Torah Umesorah day schools across North America.

Cohen, the youngest of the three, looked up to Kaminetsky and Lander as his surrogate older brothers. The relationship endured over the years as Cohen earned his degree in philosophy and then joined the faculty at both Columbia and Long Island Universities. Moving from teaching to administration, Cohen next took a position with the New York State Department of Education. It was in this capacity that he and Bernard Lander would cross paths frequently during the 1960s. By the end of the decade, Cohen found himself serving as VP of Academic Affairs at newly opened Sangamon State University in Springfield, Illinois. As Dr. Lander began the task of fleshing out Touro's administrative staff and faculty, he decided to contact Cohen. Lander soon realized that Cohen was highly experienced in developing academic programs, arranging class schedules, and designing a college catalog along with many of the other tasks with which Lander was so busily involved. He decided he could use Cohen's help and invited him to come back east to work on developing Touro's unique academic program. Cohen accepted and quickly set to work putting all the pieces in place in time for the new school's slated opening.

It was a daunting task that immersed both men into sixteen-hour days of non-stop administrative creativity. After spending all day in their Manhattan office, the two men would retire to Lander's dining room table in Forest Hills and continue working until the wee hours.

Two of the earliest administrators to join the Touro team were Jerome Witkin and Max Celnik, both of whom Lander had known from his years at Yeshiva University. Witkin had served as an admissions officer and was charged by Lander with identifying the steps needed to attract and recruit top quality students to Touro—and then implementing them. Celnik was a librarian and, over the years at Touro, became somewhat legendary for his uncanny ability to make any requested book appear almost magically. Libraries were an important asset for any college and were scrutinized by the state's educational accreditation agencies. Celnik was able to impress not only the state inspectors but also students and parents with the extensive library he was able to maintain—and on a shoestring budget, no less. During his prior life with NCR (National Cash Register), Celnik was instrumental in the development and promotion of Microfiche technology that placed books and periodicals onto microscopic film that could be viewed on proprietary projection equipment. Although mostly supplanted by digital technology, Microfiche is still in use in many libraries throughout the world today.

In addition to assembling a capable administrative staff, Lander understood the need to field an active and dedicated board of trustees to offer necessary guidance to the new school. In addition to Hollander, who served as its chairman, Lander invited fellow academics Dr. Jacob Mosak, a United Nations economist; Dr. Shalom Hirschman, a research professor in the field of infectious diseases; and Gilbert Ginsberg, a law professor at George Washington University, to accept a charter seat on the newly formed board. This original Board of Trustees provided advice and oversight in such areas as the defining of Touro's academic objectives, laying out its core curriculum and concentrations, establishing grading policies, and developing its academic advisory system.

As the core curriculum took shape in the hands of the administration and board, it included a two-year humanities sequence that began with an introduction to world cultures as reflected in major works of Western thought. A great books component that included literature, history, and philosophy was integrated with instruction in creative writing and speech. Credit requirements in both core and elective areas were defined as part of the school's various degree opportunities.

Members of the board and administration were clear that Touro's curriculum would be unique due to its Jewish studies component. Bernard Lander had successfully imbued both with his commitment to upholding the obligation of Torah study "day and night." This personal belief was translated and institutionalized as part of Touro's DNA. The school's nascent leadership understood completely that Touro was being established to counter the disturbing pattern of students graduating yeshiva high schools and then being forced to place their Jewish studies on hold for four years during college. A portion of each and every day at Touro, they decreed, would be devoted to expanding a student's Torah knowledge.

A key component of Dr. Lander's "open door" policy for Touro was the ability to provide a Jewish studies education for any student, regardless of that student's level of expertise upon arrival. To this end, Jewish Studies courses were to be offered at varying stages of advancement in order to match them with students who held differing levels of proficiency.

The role of academic advisor was also specified during these early days. The advisor's role was to formulate an academic game plan together with each student, setting goals, and establishing milestones. During his junior year, the student, working with his advisor, was required to design a major research project to be completed and written up as a senior thesis the following year. In this effort, students were encouraged not to compete with one another, but rather between the student himself and his own "aspirations and abilities."

Grades, in the traditional sense, were deemed as irrelevant. At the end of each semester each student would receive either a Pass or an Honor, if he had distinguished himself in some way during his studies. Failures were not recorded in a student's grade record. He simply would not receive the course credit.

The all-important question of hiring a faculty was one that consumed Dr. Lander's energies and strained the well-stretched budget of the embryonic school. He elected to hire the minimum number of full-time instructors as required by the accreditation agencies and rely primarily on adjunct faculty, drawn from among the most distinguished professors teaching in and around the New York area. Lander also called upon his years in academia and contacted retired professors, many of whom had been put out to pasture against their own wishes. Some of these venerated instructors were at the height of their careers when their employment was cut short. Lander also sought out professors who, via their personal moral fortitude, would act as role models and mentors in behalf of Touro's students. Lander understood the vulnerabilities and impressionable status of college students. He firmly believed that a teacher taught lessons beyond the classroom and the lecture hall, lessons that were transmitted via the personal conduct of the instructor. While not all members of Touro's initial faculty line-up were observant Jews, no one who was likely to bring a negative cast to Judaism would be countenanced. While the overly casual wardrobe of a candidate for a professorship might be of some concern, it was his nihilism, and not his lack of a necktie, that would cost him the job.

Once assembled, Touro's first faculty represented an impressive panoply of academic prowess. Maurice Wohlgelernter was named chairman of the English and humanities department; Henry Wolf, the former director of mathematics for NASA's Apollo moon missions, headed the math department; and Nathan Reich was enlisted to head up social sciences and economics. These department heads were joined by other distinguished faculty such as Howard Adelson from City University; Isadore Danishefsky, biochemistry professor at New York Medical College; Louis Heller, vice president of the International Linguistic Society; Alvin Radkowsky, from the U.S. Nuclear Propulsion Division; and Michael Wyschogrod, professor of philosophy at Baruch College.

The final step in preparing the college for its opening day of classes was a bureaucratic one. In addition to receiving its charter from the state of New York, the college had to be accredited in order to grant degrees. Accreditation of colleges and universities is handled through regional rather than state agencies. It fell to the Middle States Commission on Higher Education to determine if Touro College had met all applicable standards and would therefore be permitted to grant baccalaureate degrees to its graduates.

The accreditation process was—and still remains—based on a comprehensive peer review system that calls for an in-depth self-study that is then validated by visiting academicians from other schools in the region. The visitors examine facilities, visit libraries, interview faculty and students, and determine if standards of quality are, in fact, being met.

Touro initially received what was called "Correspondent Status" from Middle States, a first step towards accreditation. This designation would allow the school to open its doors on a trial basis. Once the school became operational, the inspection team would visit the campus (or in this case, the school's single building) and make its determinations. The school would not be eligible for full accreditation until it had graduated its first class. Middle States assigned Dr. Henry R. Winkler, the senior vice president for academic affairs at Rutgers University, to serve as a consultant and work with Touro to help it achieve full accreditation.

With all the pieces assembled, the time had come to begin enrolling students for the school's first class year. In the spring of 1971, Dr. Lander, with George Cohen and Jerome Witkin and a few key faculty members, fanned out across the New York area to begin recruiting students. Their efforts succeeded in gaining the attention of the *New York Times*, which wrote favorably about the city's newest "… unique Jewish school." The team made the rounds of Orthodox synagogues and high schools.

Parlor meetings where parents of graduating high school senior boys were invited to learn about the many advantages Touro had to offer were organized as the campaign moved into high gear. A graduate student was hired to work within National Council of Synagogue Youth chapters and recruit students from among their ranks. Three points were stressed repeatedly as the recruitment campaign made its way across New York: an outstanding faculty, a limited number of students, and a supportive Jewish atmosphere were the sell points that proved convincing and compelling to a critical number of parents who agreed to enroll their sons at the newly formed college.

While most parents and students contacted by the recruitment team did not care to gamble on a brand new school that was still awaiting its accreditation, a sufficient number of others failed to be dissuaded by such considerations and thereby allowed for the school to begin its operations on schedule. And so, on the thirteenth day of September 1971 (the twenty-third day of Elul of the Jewish calendar year 5731), Bernard Lander's dream of a college that would embody the principles he so cherished and that would serve to secure the eternal future of the Jewish people, became a reality as Touro College—an exciting new experiment in Jewish higher education—opened its doors for the first time, and thirty-five young men entered through them.

CHAPTER FOURTEEN

Building and Believing

> A time to plant ... a time to build.
> —*Kohelet (Ecclesiastes) 3: 2–3*

As any student of Torah will agree, the role of the doorpost in Jewish tradition is a significant and lofty one. It was there, as recounted in the Book of Exodus, that the Children of Israel placed the blood of the paschal lamb so that the Angel of the Lord would "pass over" their homes as it visited death upon the Egyptian firstborn. In fact, the Hebrew word *mezuzah* actually means "doorpost." The meaning has evolved to refer to the bit of parchment inscribed with the words of the *Shema* that is kept scrolled and affixed to Jewish entryways to this day. This is done in compliance with the twice-told Deuteronomy directive commanding Jews to keep G-d's word before their eyes, bound to their hearts, and, according to Judaism's central affirmation of monotheism, "posted on the doorposts of your house."

With a great deal of anticipation and a bit of flourish, it was board chairman Eugene Hollander who was afforded the honor of affixing the first *mezuzah* on the main entrance doorway of the Touro College building on West 44th Street. Bernard Lander stood at his side wearing a broad smile as he watched Hollander complete the ritual and thereby mark the precise moment that Lander's long-deferred dream became a tangible reality. Hollander's welcoming words were brief, and his Eastern European accent lent poignancy to their meaning as he addressed the members of the incoming class:

> We promise you a kosher school. Here you will not find promiscuity. You will not find the drugs and political turmoil that exist at other colleges. Here you will not find the nihilism nor the negativity about Judaism that drains the life of our people.

141

Here you will find learning and *Yiddishkeit*. And this will make you not only wise, but also strong.

Twenty-five of the young men who entered en route to their first classes that day came from the metropolitan New York area. The remaining ten arrived from other east coast communities, Missouri, Michigan, and one from Canada. Most had attended yeshiva high schools of one sort or another, but a large group came from public high schools. The level of Jewish academic accomplishment among this group was diverse. Some were already advanced scholars while a few had only a passing knowledge of the *Shabbos Siddur* (the Sabbath prayer book).

The yeshiva-educated students at first bristled at the core sequence of humanities requirements. This attitude soon dissipated as they discovered and became excited by a world of new ideas unfolding before them. Most later admitted that they were pleased that they had been required to study the humanities since they would not have opted for such courses had they been offered as electives. The growing sense of camaraderie as this group worked its way through the great works of Western thought was palpable and taken as an encouraging sign by the new school's faculty.

Like any new venture, Touro College fine-tuned its operations during its first year. For example, students complained that the innovative Honors/Pass/No Credit grading system would be viewed askance by prospective employers upon graduation. The system was scrapped and a standard letter grade program adopted. It became obvious, almost at once, that some sort of remedial or introductory Hebrew and Jewish studies classes needed to be offered in order to supplement those students arriving without a yeshiva background. This, too, was soon put into practice.

While Bernard Lander served as Touro's chief administrative officer during those early days, his efforts to build support for the new school required frequent travel to communities outside of New York. He would appear at parlor meetings arranged to introduce Touro to parents of college-bound Jewish students. Lander's message would invariably hit on his unflinching mantra of depicting Touro as "a bulwark against the tide of assimilation."

"I am here tonight primarily to explain that if you elect to send your child to a typical American college, you are behaving irresponsibly. The chances of that student returning home to you after four years as a committed Jew are less than one in four." Lander would support his claims with solid statistical data that served to bolster his case—and persuade his audience.

"So where should responsible parents send a child if they wish to avoid this risk? I am here to inform you that Touro College is the answer. It will provide your child with an outstanding grounding in the humanities, prepare him for a future career, and preserve and enhance his commitment and understanding of Jewish teachings and traditions. If you wish to guide your child down a path that will pressure him to abandon Judaism and accept intermarriage, then you should send him to Michigan or Kent State. But, if you are the responsible parents I believe you are, you will point your son towards Touro. When he returns to you after four years he will continue to place a value upon his heritage, I promise you. There is nothing more important that you can do for the sake of your family's future and for the ongoing viability and vitality of our people."

While Dr. Lander was off persuading parents and enlisting future students, the day-to-day administrative activities of the school were being handled by George Cohen. Dean Cohen would carry out the preliminary interviews for new faculty members, for example, but no one was offered a position without first being personally approved by Dr. Lander.

In the ensuing years, the seeds planted by Dr. Lander took root and Touro began to grow rapidly. By its third year, more than 200 courses were being offered under the tutelage of 80 full- and part-time faculty members. Because of this expansion, the student-teacher ratio remained quite low (5.4 students per instructor), affording pupils the personal attention that Dr. Lander believed was so essential an ingredient in an effective college education. This precept extended beyond the classroom. Bernard Lander believed in providing an environment that would facilitate meaningful relationships between distinguished faculty members and students. Those relationships, he felt, were the key to enabling students to realize their full academic potential. Unquestionably, an environment imbued with such meaningful mentoring relationships was successfully brought into being during the early years of Touro College.

As Dr. Lander observed his teaching principles permeate and animate the academic milieu of Touro, he was forced to witness this fruition amid less-than-ideal physical conditions. Renovations to the building were necessarily delayed when severe structural flaws were discovered. Financing improvements through traditional lenders became problematic because of restrictions based on the U.S. government's gifting of the building. The surroundings increasingly took on the feeling of a derelict edifice or, some opined, the look of ancient ruins. Students would often be forced to wear surplus WWII army uniforms —left behind from when the U.S. Army occupied the building—in order to protect their clothing from falling plaster and debris. Yet, such hardships did not seem to diminish the students' esprit de corps. For example, when the nearby Harvard Club was undergoing a remodeling and pitched out an old hand-carved conference table, a contingent of Touroites rescued the ornate piece and hauled it up the rickety stairs to help furnish their crumbling library.

After a particularly nasty incident involving a burst water pipe that forced Max Celnik, Touro's legendary librarian, to protect his precious volumes with an umbrella, the entire school was forced to move to the Brotherhood-in-Action building, a few blocks to the north, while sorely needed structural work was finally initiated. While the flooring was reinforced and a steel stairway installed, the improvements did nothing to enhance the overall appearance of the building.

A major overhaul did take place in 1975, in preparation for Touro's first commencement exercises. This included the addition of a student lounge, improved laboratories, better lighting, and new modern elevators. Although this effort resulted in some level of improvement, the fact remained that Touro was housed in a seventy-five-year old building that had seen better days. Bringing it back to its original glory was entirely too expensive a proposition for the young, cash-strapped school.

Yet despite their less-than-gracious surroundings, the Touro students managed to create a vibrant and exciting college atmosphere. There was a student newspaper and an elected government council that ran social functions and organized intramural athletics. *Rosh Chodesh* (first day of the new Hebrew month) and *Yomim Tovim* (holiday events) were highlighted by the appearance of such noted figures as Rabbis Shlomo Carlebach, Meir Kahane, and Nachman Bulman, the renowned spokesman for Agudath Israel and Haredi Judaism. Since only ten members of the school's first year class were from out-of-town, the college did not, at first, become involved in student housing. But as it grew, and as Dr. Lander's proselytizing efforts bore fruit, more non-New Yorkers began to fill Touro's class rosters. Dormitory housing was often arranged in nearby apartment buildings and even hotels.

With inevitable growing pains, and under decidedly unglamorous working conditions, Dr. Lander and the school's administration took pride in the reputation Touro was garnering. After only a few formative years, Touro was becoming known as a home for serious academics in a small college framework delivered in a kosher, albeit spartan, environment. Not surprisingly, the school continued to attract a growing contingent of motivated students seeking the benefits of a quality liberal arts education without being asked to abandon their Judaism as the price of admission.

But this "small college," cloistered image—this "Jewish Amherst," as one of Touro's sobriquets proclaimed—did not sit well with Bernard Lander. From his earliest days, Lander was not one to think small. He did not view Touro as the culmination of his vision. Quite the contrary. He regarded the school as a template, a prototype to be replicated on campuses across America. Lander's grand vision involved taking the fight against assimilation to the frontlines—into the nation's heartland where Jewish life was being decimated by the forces at work on most college campuses. And this vision did not stop at the water's edge. Lander dreamed of building a multi-national university system that would certainly involve a major presence in Israel. He saw the Israel experience as an integral component of an American Jewish college student's proper education.

Neither was Dr. Lander's vision for the future of Touro restricted to benefiting only Jewish students. He envisioned the school operating law, medical and other professional schools that would deliver premier degree programs to all who qualified. Such expansion would enhance the standing of Touro and make it a more attractive option for Jewish students as they and their parents investigated where to enroll. In other words, the "ivory tower" syndrome that had come to characterize the small liberal arts colleges that dotted America's eastern seaboard was the antithesis of what Dr. Lander sought to achieve with Touro College. While it may have appeared to be just such a school to a casual observer, from the very beginning Touro was designed to extend its reach far beyond the traditional ivy-covered walls.

A key component of Bernard Lander's strategy in building Touro into a world-class "Great American College" was the assembling of a stellar Board of Trustees. He understood from his years at Yeshiva that a dynamic board sets the tone and establishes the long-range goals of any college or university. He successfully sought out board members who had achieved success in their own lives in order to leverage their expertise in behalf of the school. He recruited trustees who could assist with the school's fiscal planning and who had the means to contribute financially. To attract the caliber of leadership he was seeking, Lander appealed to each one's commitment to the preservation of Jewish life in America. Just as he had been doing with prospective parents, Lander laid out his case without rancor or alarm. He would explain repeatedly about the unprecedented threat that American Jewry now faced. Supporting synagogues and Jewish secular organizations was important, but the real battleground for the soul of American Judaism was on the college campus.

In so doing, Lander succeeded in motivating a core cadre of trustees to invest their time, toil, and treasure into Touro College. To a man, they believed in the school's educational mission and were able to witness the positive results with every graduating class.

As noted, Dr. Lander tapped Eugene Hollander to serve as the chairman of Touro's board. Hollander's street savvy business acumen had impressed Lander, and the man was a natural leader. The fact that Hollander was a generous philanthropist and did not hesitate to show his support for Touro through tangible donations also contributed to his desirability for this pivotal role.

In addition to Hollander, Touro's charter board of trustees included Dr. Shalom Hirschman, Gilbert Ginsberg, and Jacob Mosak. These men were invited because of their strong academic credentials. Lander also enlisted his former Yeshiva College classmate and good friend Moses Feuerstein. Feuerstein and Lander had served together for many years in leadership positions within the Orthodox Union. In addition to earning his MBA at Harvard, Feuerstein came from a wealthy family and had enjoyed a long track record of communal leadership and philanthropy.

Congressman Emanuel Celler accepted a seat on the board and suggested that Dr. Lander offer a similar position to his law partner, Milton Weisman. Weisman served with distinction for many years, including a long stint as chairman of the board's executive committee.

Another luminary Dr. Lander succeeded in attracting to the board was a near legendary figure in the home mortgage industry, Max Karl from Milwaukee. Karl had founded the Mortgage Guaranty Insurance Corporation (MGIC) that, to this day, remains the nation's largest home mortgage lender.

Once this core group was assembled, Dr. Lander continued to reach out to other notables whose presence would add luster and leadership experience to the board. In a stunning coup, he succeeded in enlisting Jacob Fuchsberg, a well-known New York trial attorney and politician. Fuchsberg was recognized as the first attorney in America to win a million dollar jury verdict for his client. In the early 1970s, Fuchsberg had been elected to the New York Court of Appeals. In addition to sitting on Touro's board, Fuchsberg also served as a trustee of New York University (NYU). He resigned from the bench in May 1983 but continued to serve as a Touro trustee where he assisted in the establishment of the Touro Law School. The law school was eventually named in his honor and is known today as the Touro College Jacob D. Fuchsberg Law Center.

Another outstanding addition to the early board was Leon Levy, a pioneer in the mutual fund industry who was responsible for the success of Wall Street securities giant, Oppenheimer & Co. Added to this heavy hitter line-up was Moses Hornstein, founder of Horn Construction. Hornstein joined Marvyn Carton, Edward Ginsberg, Harry Starr, Martin Barel, Roy Titus, Herman Gross, Jacob Goodstein, and Jack Roland on a panel composed of the cream of American industry, finance, law, and academics.

Added to this potent mix was a contingent of politicos. In addition to Congressman Celler, Dr. Lander also persuaded Assemblyman Stanley Steingut, along with Governor Nelson Rockefeller's chief political fundraiser, Samuel Hausman, to sign on board. This trend of inviting public figures to sit on the board was accelerated after Michael Nisselson became Touro's director of community and governmental relations. Nisselson urged Dr. Lander to seek out and enlist more well-known public servants whose names would add prestige to the fledgling college. This initiative netted board seats for New York State Attorney General Louis J. Lefkowitz, United States Senator Jacob Javits, State Controller Arthur Levitt, and New York City's newly elected mayor Abraham Beame, who became a trustee in late 1973.

Within two years of opening its doors, Bernard Lander had succeeded in fielding one of the most powerful and prominent boards of any institution of higher education in America. Naturally, creating such a strong concentration of high profile figures was bound to attract attention. In fact, the *New York Times* noted in early 1974 that "... the composition of Touro's board of trustees would seem to assure the college of getting attention for almost anything it proposed." But as Dr. Lander was soon to learn, such attention is not always desirable.

Perhaps the most notable individual to sit on Touro's early board was a figure who Lander selected hoping to cement the binational nature of Touro's future. Oved Ben Ami, the founder and mayor of Netanya, became Dr. Lander's partner in the attempt to establish a Touro campus in Israel. A glimpse at Ben Ami's long list of accomplishments reads like a primer in the history of Zionism. An incredibly enterprising pioneer, he founded the Boy Scouts movement in Israel and the Maccabi Sports Organization, not to mention the city of Herzliya. He almost single-handedly gave birth to the Israeli diamond-cutting industry before serving in the Haganah and being imprisoned by the British in 1947 for smuggling illegal immigrants across Netanya's beaches. Ben Ami founded the *Maariv* daily newspaper, for which he wrote for decades. His educational credentials included seats on the boards of Hebrew University, the Weizmann Institute, Tel Aviv University, and the University of Haifa.

Dr. Lander viewed Ben Ami's role on Touro's board as "serving as a link between Touro here and in Israel." At an early board meeting, Ben Ami announced that the city of Netanya had made a gift of twenty-five acres to Touro College for the purpose of constructing a college campus. Despite this act of largesse and the surrounding publicity it generated, Touro was unsuccessful in raising the capital necessary for such an ambitious project. Nevertheless, the dream of a binational university, with one foot in the United States and another planted in Israel, remained strong in the hearts of Dr. Lander and many of the other trustees he had called upon to guide Touro College towards its destiny. Today the *Machon Lander* school in Jerusalem is one of several programs that have fulfilled this dream of a true Israeli-American institution of higher learning.

The role that destiny played not only in the development of Touro College, but also in the shaping of Bernard Lander, the man, was at times quite powerful. A cursory look at the career arc of most successful individuals will typically reveal a series of clearly defined inflection points—places where the road diverged and a choice as to which path to follow had to be made. Accordingly, such critical inflection points appear at key moments in Dr. Lander's life journey. The decision to remain or depart from Yeshiva was the most salient of these to date. Yet, there was another, even more defining moment that occurred during the first year of Touro's operation. It placed Dr. Lander into an intriguing situation where he was required to choose between his dedication to Jewish education and the serious opportunity of acquiring vast wealth. The road leading up to this crossroads moment began in, of all places, Communist China. The choice he faced would test the very fabric of Bernard Lander's commitment to his lifelong dream.

Throughout the years that Bernard Lander served on the administration of Yeshiva University, he, and his brother Nathan, continued to assist their father in his wholesale textile business. The Lander family understood that most of the materials that David Lander imported were produced in Red China, sold to European dealers who, in turn, marked up the goods and sold them to American distributors. This two-stage process was necessitated by the fact that the United States did not enjoy diplomatic relations with the Maoist regime, which had controlled the People's Republic since 1949. Hence, no direct trade or commerce was permitted. Canada, on the other hand, enjoyed full diplomatic ties with China, and when Bernard Lander learned through a friend, in the mid-1960s, that the head of the Chinese textile industry would be visiting Ottawa, Lander decided to meet him.

Somehow Lander managed to get an audience with the Chinese official and immediately proposed that American buyers, such as his father, be permitted to buy Chinese-made fabrics directly. The response was disappointing. "American money has a bad smell to it," the Chinese official told him derisively. Lander returned to New York convinced that his mission had been a failure. But he was wrong.

In a few years, because of a thaw initiated by a Chinese–American ping pong match and Nixon and Kissinger's overtures, economic opportunities began to gradually surface. Evidently the Chinese were starting to overcome the foul odor they associated with the U.S. dollar. For the first time since the communist takeover, the government extended invitations to attend the giant and venerated Canton Trade Fair to a few select American businesses. As a result of the contact made by Bernard several years earlier in Ottawa, David Lander now found himself among this select group. Already in his eighties, David was not up to making the long journey, and he passed his invitation on to Bernard, who, despite the fact that he was deeply involved in Touro's first year of operations, decided that this was a once-in-lifetime opportunity and accepted the invitation.

Once at the Canton Fair, Dr. Lander was besieged by Chinese manufacturers, all hungry for direct trade with the United States. He soon realized that he was standing at a unique juncture in global economic history. China was about to open its gates to the West and the ensuing opportunities would make fortunes for those Americans lucky enough, and wise enough, to take advantage of this fortuitous situation. Dr. Lander felt as though it was 1849, and he had just spotted a nugget of gold in a California river.

Lander was wise enough to understand that if he were to exploit the tempting opportunities that now lay before him, he would need to abandon his grand designs for Touro College and devote himself full-time to operating his father's business. The evidence that Lander had correctly assessed the true worth of this Chinese gambit is confirmed by the fact that other textile distributor colleagues who accompanied him to Canton that year all went on to profit greatly and amass major fortunes selling wholesale Chinese fabrics to the American market.

Bernard Lander, with no small degree of difficulty, opted to let this truly golden opportunity pass him by and chose to instead return to 44th Street and his newly opened Jewish college where he would spend the remainder of his days. Did Dr. Lander ever look back with regret on the road not taken? If so, he never spoke of it to friends or family. Yet, it is a rare man indeed who does not, from time to time, recollect such past opportunities and whisper to himself: "What if?"

As Touro's inaugural class was completing its third year of matriculation, the issue of accreditation became of paramount importance. Middle States, the regional accreditation organization, had assigned Dr. Henry R. Winkler of Rutgers University to serve as a consultant in order to work with Touro as it prepared for accreditation. In May 1974 Dr. Winkler conducted an in-depth evaluation tour of Touro College. He was impressed with what he saw. His report commented frequently on the "high morale" he found among both students and faculty. Based on this visit, he recommended that Touro plan for an accreditation evaluation at the end of the following academic year to coincide with Touro's first graduating class. Dr. Lander took pride in the recommendation and saw it correctly as a tribute to Touro's leadership.

The opening of Touro's fourth year of operation was marked by a wide-ranging flurry of diverse activity as the school went into high gear in pursuit of its academic mission. A women's division was opening its doors, for example, while, at the same time, Touro was launching a school of general studies to serve the underprivileged community of New York. A law school, modeled on Yale University, staffed with former Yale law professors, was being planned to open the following fall. Planning was also underway to launch a medical school the year after that in conjunction with Long Island Jewish Hospital. The cover of Touro's undergraduate newspaper, *The Independent,* that fall featured a cartoon depicting Bernard Lander placing miniature school buildings on a map of the United States. Lander had made no secret of his grand designs for the future and in that frenetic fall of 1974, it appeared that he was well on his way towards realizing his dream of building a great Jewish university. But alas, there were storm clouds gathering on the horizon.

As Bernard Lander flew into his office in early September 1974, he was propelled by the ever-mounting momentum that was now being generated at Touro. What he saw on the front page of the *New York Times* on his desk that day stopped him dead in his tracks. It was a sensational article by a noted crusading reporter, John L. Hess, about widespread abuse in the local nursing home industry. The article, the result of months of undercover investigation by the Times, was to be the first in a series of more than 200 exposé pieces that would run for months in both the paper and on local news programs and would eventually result in multiple indictments against major New York nursing home operators. Featured at the top of the list of those standing accused of nursing home abuse was the name of Touro chairman, Eugene Hollander.

Hollander was accused, at first by the newspaper and then by the District Attorney and Grand Jury, of submitting falsified payment claims to both Medicare and Medicaid. Hess provided evidence that Hollander's nursing homes were providing a minimum level of care but charging the government the maximum allowable reimbursement rates. Although the overpayments Hollander enjoyed represented a small slice of the total millions that were fraudulently obtained, and were far smaller than those overpayments received by the other operators, his name was the one mentioned most often in the news reports. This was in some part due to his status as president of the Metropolitan Nursing Home Association. Oddly, Hollander's role as board chairman of Touro, "a small Jewish men's college," was also announced repeatedly by the media. Why *this* association, singled out by Hess from among Hollander's many other civic and philanthropic activities, was given such prominence can only be regarded as pandering to his readers' anti-Semitic sentiments.

As the scandal heated up, Hess and the *Times* continued to play upon Hollander's association with Touro and the prominent names who had accepted seats on the new college's board of trustees. Hess even took the unprecedented step of contacting each of the other board members and asking how they felt about serving on a board headed by a scoundrel like Hollander. The calls proved effective as, one by one, the high-profile board members lined up to submit their resignations. All the politicians resigned first. U.S. Senator Jacob Javits; Louis Lefkowitz, the state attorney general; and Mayor Abraham Beame, all disappeared like the clouds in the sky when blown away by a strong wind. Finally, with a heavy heart, Dr. Lander was forced to accept Eugene Hollander's resignation as well. The leadership of Touro College had been effectively excoriated.

Eugene Hollander was convicted of fraud and embezzlement and sentenced to prison. Not surprisingly, the fallout from this unparalleled crisis was far-reaching for Touro. Even though Touro had no involvement whatsoever in the actions of its chairman, the guilt by association was profound, and Dr. Lander's "great American university" now stood tainted in the eyes of many. The Long Island Jewish-Hillside Medical Center withdrew from the joint medical school venture whose planning was well underway. After that, Samuel Wang canceled his pledged gift to underwrite the founding of the "Samuel H. Wang School of Law." "I do not wish to see my good name sullied," he wrote to the remaining board members, "by an association with Touro College." Plans for Touro's Law School were placed on indefinite hold.

As Bernard Lander surveyed the extensive damage incurred by Touro College in the wake of the New York nursing home scandal, he did not indulge in any sort of illusions. Growth would be curtailed as fundraising sources dried up and philanthropists scattered. It was a monumental setback on the road to the dream that seemed just months before to be so solidly on track. The irony, of course, was that Touro's only crime was perhaps placing too much faith in a leader with impugned integrity. But as for Lander, he was never a man to bear grudges gladly. Lander could never forget the encouragement and generosity afforded by Eugene Hollander in the early days that provided the essential financial springboard for the creation of Touro College. Despite all the revelations and in spite of the massive damage invoked by Hollander's actions, Dr. Lander continued to remain on good terms with the man for the rest of his life. In fact, for over thirty years following Hollander's death, his widow could expect a regular phone call greeting from Bernard Lander, wishing her a "Good Shabbos" every week and a "Good Yontof" on every Jewish holiday.

In the final analysis, Dr. Lander understood that the crisis would eventually pass, but the mission of the school must endure. He believed with every shred of his character that Touro would recover its good name and that the initiatives that were now being deferred would eventually be reignited. He was, as it turns out, correct. Touro would recover and reassume its advancement on his envisioned blueprint for growth towards becoming a "great American university," but not before enduring yet more crises that would befall the school in the turbulent years ahead.

CHAPTER FIFTEEN

Growth and Graduation

The true sign of intelligence is not knowledge but imagination.

—Albert Einstein

As a result of Bernard Lander's unwavering dedication and devotion to the mission of Touro College, the school did not deviate from its growth path during the 1974–75 academic year— despite the fallout it faced in the wake of the nursing home scandal. As Lander prepared for Touro's first commencement exercises in May 1975, his pride of accomplishment far outweighed any residual remorse about Eugene Hollander. Graduating seniors had, as a group, scored well on professional school entrance exams, and many had been accepted into top-flight medical, law, and dentistry programs. Lander also looked with pride on the new degree programs that had recently been launched, including the physician assistant program, the School of Law, and a women's division. A look at the development of each of these sheds light on how Dr. Lander's character helped to shape the expansion of Touro College. A case in point is the Physician Assistant, or PA, program.

Although widespread today, in the early 1970s, nurse practitioners and PAs were unknown in the medical field. There were certainly no plans for a school devoted to PA training in the original academic outline drafted by Dr. Lander, Dean George Cohen, and others. In fact, it was not until Dr. Lander received a visitor, shortly after Touro opened its doors in 1971, that he learned the meaning of the term "physician assistant."

Dr. Lander always prided himself on having an open-door policy, and it was at this point that Shlomo Twersky walked through that open door to discuss a new type of health care professional. Twersky was the son of the Chernobyler Rebbe, Rabbi Yaakov Yisrael Twersky, of Borough Park.

Lander was impressed with the passion and enthusiasm that young Twersky displayed and gave him a full hearing.

"A PA is a medical professional somewhere between a doctor and a nurse," Twersky explained. "The concept started at Duke five years ago, and today PAs are being certified by the AMA. But they need to be trained. Trained at a Jewish school."

Lander was intrigued. Twersky went on to expand on his vision that involved a corps of Hasidic PAs, who would be trained to deliver health care to underserved religious neighborhoods.

"But who will fund it?" Lander asked.

"The Bruner Foundation has major funding available for programs that succeed in providing health care to underserved areas. I've spoken to their program director, Edith Friedman, and she is very encouraging."

Twersky went on to explain that, as part of his quest, he had initially contacted Yeshiva University's Albert Einstein School of Medicine. But, he explained, the administrators did not offer him a very warm reception.

"They offered me a finder's fee if I was successful in getting the grant from Bruner," Twersky said, "but they had no interest in serving the Hasidic community." This setback had not dimmed Twersky's optimism. "I know that if there was a PA program that incorporated Jewish law and teachings, I could recruit many capable young men from our community."

Lander was impressed. He paused a moment and then announced: "Go for it! Get trained yourself as a PA and then come back to Touro and run the program." Shlomo Twersky did exactly that. As Twersky was completing his studies, Dr. Lander recruited his own friend Dr. Samuel Korman to serve as medical director of the new program. Dr. Korman was a cancer specialist at Kingsbrook Jewish Medical Center in Brooklyn and, after signing onboard with Touro, he was able to arrange for clinical rotations and additional classroom space at Kingsbrook in behalf of Touro's new PA program.

Lander's initiative, originating as it did from a request made by Shlomo Twersky, met some resistance from Touro's board. They expressed concern that Touro was not yet ready to enter the health care arena and that such an expansion was premature and might dilute the school's academic focus. But Lander would hear none of it. He correctly viewed the PA program as the school's first step into the health professions that would someday result in a Touro School of Medicine. The PA program would share teaching staff with the existing undergraduate science program. Lander believed that with Twersky's recruitment efforts, the PA program would become a profit center for the school. He was proven correct on this count in rather short order.

But there was yet another overarching reason that Dr. Lander so enthusiastically embraced the development of a PA school at Touro. He was heartened by Twersky's vision of young Hasidic men training for productive careers in health care. Twersky's vision dovetailed perfectly into Lander's deep-seated belief in "Torah and Parnassah" that lay at the core of his passion for Touro College.

Upon his joining the Touro faculty, Twersky's first task was to work with George Cohen in drafting a grant proposal for presentation to the Bruner Foundation. Their efforts proved fruitful and garnered a substantial sum for the fledgling program to be used to defray startup expenses over the following three years. Once the grant was issued, Touro's board overwhelmingly approved the creation of the PA program.

Twersky next set to work with the new school's medical director, Samuel Korman, in devising a suitable curriculum, an effort that took Twersky and Korman back to Yeshiva's Einstein School of Medicine. They had arranged for a meeting with an Einstein professor who had developed an accelerated three-year medical curriculum. Twersky and Korman hoped to employ this never-used program as the core of the course schedule they were busy developing. Things, however, did not go smoothly at Einstein.

As Twersky and Korman walked in for their appointment, they soon discovered that they had arrived on the day of a university-wide faculty strike. Standing along the perimeter of a crowd in the building's lobby, the two witnessed Yeshiva president Samuel Belkin step to the microphone and proclaim: "I've just accepted your dean's resignation. Who's next?"

As they surmised, the professor with whom they had planned to meet was involved with other pressing priorities that day and was able to do no more than hand the two men a typed copy of his curriculum and wish them well.

After conducting an in-depth review, Twersky and Korman pared the program they were given down from thirty-six to twenty-three months with the first year devoted to general, medical, and social sciences. Year two covered clinical rotations that placed students into physicians' offices, hospitals, and clinics.

Envisioned initially as a program only for Hasidic young men, this restriction soon proved untenable. Twersky had planned to employ the services of a neighborhood community development group known as the Hasidic Corporation for Urban Concerns to handle recruitment, but it proved to be ineffective. Hence, the PA program was opened to the general public and launched during the fall semester of 1972. It was, and remains, a two-year senior program that earns graduates a bachelor of science degree with certification as a registered physician assistant. The program was accredited by the AMA as the school's first graduates appeared two years later. It would go on to serve as the cornerstone for Touro's School of Health Sciences and eventually lead to the acquisition of the New York School of Medicine in 2010. It is a testimony to Dr. Lander's vision and foresight that a program that arose from his dedication to the future of the Jewish people directly evolved into one that is today producing tomorrow's physicians for all Americans.

While Dr. Lander's plans to launch a PA program met with a less than enthusiastic reception among Touro board members, no such hesitation existed when it came to his plans to create a school of law. They fully supported his oft-expressed idea of building the nation's first Jewish law school—one that would incorporate legal traditions gleaned from the Talmud and Midrash into its degree program. Lander spoke of "a small school at the highest intellectual level" and envisioned an institution modeled after Yale, widely considered the nation's leading law school. Yale, with its small class size, public policy orientation, and tradition of preparing future governmental leaders, was exactly the type of law school Lander wished to create. Thus, he contacted and then enlisted the man best equipped to guide Touro's path towards this end, Eugene Rostow.

Eugene Victor Debs Rostow's socialist Jewish parents, having named him after the illustrious labor leader, bestowed names of beloved literary figures upon both of their other two sons. Eugene's brothers were Ralph Waldo Emerson Rostow and Walt Whitman Rostow, the latter of whom went on to serve as national security advisor to Presidents John F. Kennedy and Lyndon B. Johnson. Eugene Rostow was a prodigy in American law and served from 1955 to 1965 as the dean of Yale Law School, from which he had earned his LL.B. in 1937. He left Yale to join his brother in President Johnson's cabinet as Under Secretary of State for Foreign Affairs, the State Department's number three position. While serving at State, Rostow helped to draft UN Resolution 242 that dealt with the Israeli-Arab conflict in the wake of the Six Day War in 1967. With the ascension of the Nixon administration in 1969, Rostow left government and was teaching at Yale when contacted by Dr. Lander.

Rostow, widely considered at this point to be one of the finest legal minds in America, was two years older than Lander and held him in high regard. He was familiar with Lander's crusading efforts in the 1940s, designed to eliminate discriminatory quotas at Harvard and had himself led a similar campaign at Yale. Lander understood Rostow's liberal sensibilities and humanitarian concerns. He was aware, for example, of how Rostow had publicly condemned the U.S. internment of Japanese-Americans during World War II.

"Touro Law School will not only teach the law," Lander told him, "but it will also teach future lawyers to consider the moral, ethical, and social implications of the law." Rostow and Lander became friends, and together they enlisted the services of several of Yale's top retiring professors, including Myres S. McDougal, Harold D. Lasswell, and W. Michael Reisman. The group outlined a curriculum emphasizing a "social justice" policy orientation, which included innovative ongoing seminars that explored, among other topics, classic Jewish law. Under Rostow's leadership a proposed course of study for the new Touro School of Law was fashioned, and in November 1972, Touro's board of trustees unanimously agreed to petition the New York State Board of Regents to amend Touro's charter allowing the school to grant juris doctorates. With the support of Governor Rockefeller, the charter was officially amended on April 11, 1973, paving the way for the first new school of law to open its doors in New York City in more than fifty years.

As news of Touro's pending law school was spread by the public media and by the members of Touro's high-profile board, donors were soon enlisted who agreed to bestow their generosity, as well as their names, onto the new institution. Foremost among the donations was a major gift originating from Samuel H. Wang, a Jewish shipping magnate. In recognition of this magnanimous gift—which succeeded in generating several more substantial pledges in a bandwagon effect—the school would be dubbed The Samuel H. Wang School of Law. By September 1974 press releases were being issued, and four-color brochures had been printed by the thousands, all heralding the new Wang Law School. The message was a promising one:

> Touro's Law School will emphasize the Jewish legal experience as reflected by our prophetic teachings of social justice and our long legal tradition. To implement this objective, Touro will establish a Research Institute in Jewish Law in the Law School.

And then, along came the nursing home scandal.

Although the funding sources dried up and the brochures had to be discarded, the Touro Law School did, in fact, open its doors five years later. Today it is known as the Touro College Jacob D. Fuchsberg Law Center.

As Dr. Lander prepared for Touro's first commencement exercises, he could also look with pride to the women's division that had been successfully launched in the fall of 1974. Although Lander had, due to circumstance, initially opened Touro's doors exclusively to men, he immediately began formulating plans to operate a parallel women's school. To this end Lander again turned to the world of politics, successfully enlisting the services of Dr. David Luchins who, at the time, was working in the office of future U.S. Senator Daniel Patrick Moynihan. Luchins played a major role in recruiting the women's division's first class of sixty-four young students. He served as the school's associate dean for many years while continuing his association with Senator Moynihan, ultimately serving as the senator's senior advisor. Today Dr. Luchins is the chair of Touro's political science department, a position he has held since 1978.

Unlike the men's school, Touro's women's division attracted nearly three quarters of its inaugural class from outside the New York area. This fact was heartening to Dr. Lander, who always envisioned Touro as reaching out to the entire American Jewish community. Classes were conducted in rented space on the sixth and seventh floors of the Central Synagogue Community Building at 123 East 55th Street with dormitory housing arranged two miles away at the Esplanade Hotel near 74th Street. Given the proximity of the men's and women's divisions, the two schools were able to offer a common curriculum and share administrative services as well as classroom facilities at different times.

Today the school is known as the Lander College Mark and Anna Ruth Hasten Women's Division. It is situated in an elegant new glass and steel five-story complex at 227 West 60th Street in an educational and cultural corridor on Manhattan's Upper West Side. The building was a gift of the Hasten family, who became associated with Touro when Mark and Anna Ruth Hasten's daughter Monica was enrolled there as a student in the 1970s. The school bills itself as a "student centered institution where Jewish women can follow a rigorous academic program while continuing and deepening their Torah education and commitment" (see Chapter 20).

The pivotal 1974–75 school year also witnessed the inauguration of the Adult Program for Excellence or APEX, a program for disadvantaged adults. APEX included seminars on topics in the humanities and the sciences with an emphasis on relating these topics to real-life experiences encountered by adult students in everyday life. Each three-hour seminar, consisting of twelve to fifteen students, met once a week at the New York Theological Seminary on 49th Street and attracted students from the Latino and black communities. Adult students were able to earn class credit towards an associate degree while receiving further credit for "learning from life" experience. Many students, after completing the seminar program, went on to matriculate at Touro and receive bachelor's degrees in the humanities, social sciences, or business. Prospective students were recruited through social welfare agencies that were contacted by Dr. Joseph Mulholland, who had led similar extension programs at Queens College and Fordham University. Not only did the APEX program succeed in fulfilling Touro's mission of social responsibility, it also generated tuition revenue from various governmental social service agencies and thereby served as a profit center for the school.

As the accreditation process ran its course, Touro suffered another setback in its efforts to gain the imprimatur of the Middle States Commission. Although he would return five years later to help usher in the first class at the Touro School of Law, Dean George Cohen, a major and widely respected architect of the college's academic and administrative structure, turned in his resignation. This blow, coupled with the ongoing nursing home scandal, represented a difficult time for Touro and served to delay the accreditation process.

As Dr. Lander pulled faculty and administrators together to cooperate, he stressed the importance of completing the self-study survey requisitioned by Middle States. The study was, in fact, finished and finally submitted in January 1976. A seven-member Middle States team headed by Jerome Pollack, president of Fairleigh Dickinson University, visited Touro College at the beginning of March 1976. They came away highly impressed with what they found. Quoting from their report:

> Touro represents a return to the small liberal arts college of an earlier period. This very mission, which is shared at every level of administration, faculty and student body, is clearly the College's greatest strength and has led to an institution which is homogeneous in its commitment to its purpose. Flowing from this dedication are a faculty and student body, particularly in the liberal arts area, which have an intense loyalty to the school, an almost uniform high morale, and a devotion which manifests itself in a round-the-clock giving of time and energy.

This is not to say that the investigating team did not note certain flaws. Foremost was their observation that programs were overly diverse and needed to be more properly integrated. They also commented on the tenuous financial position of the school, noting its frequent cash flow issues. Yet, despite these negatives, in June 1976 Bernard Lander received a letter informing him that the Middle States Commission on Higher Education had voted to fully accredit Touro College; another critical milestone had been attained.

As Bernard Lander stood at the helm of Touro College during those early years, steering it through waters both choppy and smooth, his vision was consistently directed to the forefront and seldom to the aft. He took no specific joy in the vindication of his dreams—dreams that a few short years ago had been labeled as outlandish. Lander was far too occupied with building Touro College, piece by piece, to concern himself with how his success was being perceived by others—particularly by those in charge of his previous home, Yeshiva University.

However, by the mid-1970s, it appeared to many that YU was no longer the "only game in town," Dr. Lander went out of his way to dispel this notion. Starting before Touro had even opened its doors, Lander made it clear that his new school was not being founded to compete with Yeshiva. In an interview appearing in the March 1971 YU student newspaper, *The Commentator*, Dr. Lander emphatically stressed that he would be recruiting students who would not have opted to attend Yeshiva.

"We need multiple Jewish colleges to meet the needs of various types of students," he stated. He went on to explain, in the article and upon many later instances, that the YU approach was not for everyone.

"To enroll at YU, you must be willing to study in New York and dedicate yourself to a 9 to 3 schedule of Torah study. We are targeting the 75 percent of yeshiva high school graduates who would never consider YU and instead are winding up at secular colleges." Lander repeatedly made his case that for those three out of four graduates emerging from Jewish secondary schools who do not opt to go to YU, all the benefits of their Jewish education were being lost.

"We are offering an alternative to that 75 percent, for whom YU is not an option," he explained. "At Touro they will gain the education they seek, without losing the Judaism they need."

Dr. Lander was also quite selective about fundraising initiatives, purposely avoiding those institutions and individuals recognized as established YU supporters. Lander honestly believed that Touro and YU complemented each other. Those students seeking a more intensive Torah education—those training for the rabbinate, for example—would continue to enroll at YU. But those not so inclined, and who had been heretofore drawn to secular schools to obtain a college degree needed for meaningful employment in today's society, would be attracted to Touro. This worldview was apparently not shared by everyone.

A cursory examination of how YU responded to the advent of Touro College demonstrates clearly that its leadership did not accept Bernard Lander's vision of multiple Jewish colleges. Instead of viewing it as a complementary institution, they perceived Touro as a threat to YUs hegemony and on numerous occasions sought to undermine the interests of the new school.

In mid-1972, representatives sent by YU president Samuel Belkin, contacted Dr. Lander with an offer. He would be afforded a senior vice-presidential position, at an attractive salary well beyond what he had earned at the time he had left YU in 1969, *if* he would agree to abandon

Touro College. Lander rejected the offer without blinking an eye, stating forcefully that he had no intention of leaving Touro.

Yeshiva next attempted to lure Eugene Hollander away from Touro, offering him a position as treasurer of Yeshiva University's Board of Trustees. Later, during the course of the nursing home situation, several members of Touro's board of trustees received phone calls from YU representatives. The trustees listened as Dr. Lander's competence was impugned. They were told stories about his allegedly shoddy job performance during his fifteen years at Yeshiva and were told how this scandal would lead to the destruction of Touro.

Yeshiva stepped up its campaign against Touro when it appeared likely in 1974 that the newcomer would open its law school before YU did so itself. Touro had hosted an enormously successful fundraising dinner in October 1973 on behalf of its planned law school. When, a few weeks later, the Yom Kippur War erupted, plans for an opening were delayed for one year as America's Jewish philanthropic community turned its attention towards Israel. Just as that year was coming to a close, the Hollander nursing home scandal broke. Although he could not lay his hands on admissible evidence, Dr. Lander was nevertheless certain that Yeshiva representatives had used the nursing home scandal to persuade Samuel H. Wang to withdraw his pledge to found the law school. He also believed that YU had convinced Long Island Jewish Hospital to drop its plans to join forces with Touro in the development of a new medical school. In addition, at the time Touro sought to change its state charter to enable its granting of law degrees, it was reported to Dr. Lander that Yeshiva officials did their best to prevent the approval of the modification. Yeshiva's efforts succeeded in delaying the opening of both Touro's law school and its school of medicine. In the interim, Yeshiva launched its Cardozo School of Law in the fall of 1976.

A December 1974 piece in the *New York Times* reported on how a keen rivalry had developed between Yeshiva University and Touro College. The writer interviewed top officials at YU and in characterizing their attitudes about the new Jewish college, reported that they viewed it as "a brash intruder in a domain that Yeshiva formerly had to itself."

Dr. Lander reportedly told the writer, "Yeshiva is out to kill us!" Evidently the time of the "complementary" relationship with Yeshiva had passed and Lander, at this point, clearly viewed Yeshiva as a force to be reckoned with. For his part, Dr. Belkin merely told the *Times* reporter that he would "not dignify Touro's charges by responding."

Stricken with cancer, Samuel Belkin resigned his position as president in September 1975 and succumbed eight months later. Yeshiva's board chairman, Max Stern, was approached by Rabbi Joseph B. Soloveitchik, who suggested that the search committee consider Dr. Lander to serve as Belkin's successor. Stern reportedly felt that the opening of Touro College had complicated matters to the point that someone else needed to be found.

After a ten-month search, in August 1976, Rabbi Dr. Norman Lamm was appointed president of Yeshiva University. Lamm was the valedictorian of his Yeshiva College class in 1949 and counted Bernard Lander as one of his mentors and friends. After Lamm assumed the presidency, Lander suggested that the two meet in order to discuss the future association of the two schools. Lander took the initiative because he felt that Touro would be regarded as more of a collegial partner by the new administration and less in the role of a competing rival. Unfortunately, this was not to be the case.

At their initial meeting, Dr. Lander laid out a grand plan of separate institutions governed by a single board of trustees. The structure called for both schools to maintain a distinct identity, but to work together in meeting the needs of all qualified students. In subsequent meetings, Dr. Lander suggested changes that would position the State of Israel as a central construct of Yeshiva's mission. In addition, it soon became apparent that the association envisioned by Lander was merely a first step in his persistent dream of building a network of schools around the nation and the world. Dr. Lamm soon rejected both notions.

"If you want Harvard," Lamm maintained, "you come to Cambridge. If you want Yeshiva, you come to New York."

"But for each one that comes to New York, four stay home," Lander countered.

It was clear that the two men's concepts of an associated school remained vastly at odds. Dr. Lamm, expressing the sentiments of his school's leadership, saw Yeshiva more or less swallowing up the smaller newer entity and absorbing it into its existing framework. In this regard he extended to Dr. Lander the prospect of holding the honorary title of "chancellor" of the merged institution. The position carried an attractive salary, but no real responsibilities and no authority whatsoever. Apparently, Yeshiva failed to understand the mission of Touro College and Bernard Lander's inherent dedication to that mission. Discussions of an association between the two schools reached an impasse.

In the ensuing years Bernard Lander continued to meet opposition with *chesed* (kindness) in his dealings with Yeshiva University. One telling episode characterizing Lander's magnanimous approach occurred in 1978. At that time Touro had once again approached the New York State Department of Education for a modification of its charter that would allow it to offer a master's program in Jewish Studies. The approval process required that notification of Touro's request be sent to potentially competing programs in New York. In response, the agency received a letter from a senior Yeshiva University administrator urging the state to deny Touro's request, claiming that there was already a proliferation of less-than-ideal Jewish Studies programs in a time of declining enrollments. He referred to Touro's proposed program as being of "suspect quality," despite the fact that a cadre of distinguished scholars, already associated with Touro, had signed on to the program. In his closing, he condescendingly warned that Touro's "academic reputation would in no way be enhanced by offering a less-than-reputable M.A. degree in Jewish Studies." Despite the poison-pen letter, the state approved Touro's Jewish Studies program, where it has flourished over the ensuing decades.

By contrast, some three months later, Dr. Lander was asked by the same state agency to respond to a request submitted by Yeshiva University, enabling it to open a new program in accounting. Even though Touro was already operating such a program in addition to those in finance and business management, and recognizing that, if approved, Yeshiva's program represented a competitive threat, Dr. Lander responded without vindictiveness: "I am writing in response to your letter of March 15, concerning Yeshiva University's request to establish a program in accounting leading to the degree of Bachelor of Science. Touro College supports this request. We wish Yeshiva University well in its efforts."

Any animosities that may have arisen during this difficult period were never articulated by Dr. Lander during the remaining years of his life.

He remained, until his death, a loyal alumnus of Yeshiva. Although he obviously felt it could have done more, he repeatedly referred to Yeshiva over the years as "a fine school for the right student." While others may have harbored feelings of ill will, resentment, or envy directed at Bernard Lander and his success at creating a new Jewish institution of higher learning, such feelings were never reciprocated.

As the decade came to a close and the trauma of the nursing home scandal had run its course, it appeared that Dr. Lander would finally be able to pilot Touro College into some calmer, less turbulent waters. But, alas, more squalls were forming just over the horizon.

Dr. Bernard Lander over the years.

Bernard Lander's parents, David and
Goldie Lander, circa 1914.

Family Portrait ca. 1925
Left to right: Bernard, Hadassah, Nathan, David,
and Goldie Lander.

(Above) Rabbi Jacob Joseph school graduation.
Bernard Lander is the fourth from the
right in the center row.

(Left) 1928. Bar Mitzvah photo.

(Below) Rabbi Lander officiates at a wedding
while serving as first Rabbi of Beth Jacob Synagogue
in Baltimore, Maryland in the 1940s.

David and Goldie Lander, newlyweds.
Rabbi Bernard and Sarah Lander,
Rebbetzin Hinde Shragowitz, and
Rabbi Moses Joshua Shragowitz. November 1, 1948.

Sarah and Bernard Lander.
wedding portrait.
November 1, 1948.

Sarah & Bernard Lander
in 1963.

From left: Rabbi Hartwig Naftali Carlebach (second from left),
Rabbi Joseph Soloveitchik (third from right), and
Rabbi Dr. Bernard Lander. Circa 1960.

(Above) At the Hotel Roosevelt, NYC, on January 29, 1967. Dr. Lander being presented with a plaque by Brooklyn's Bobover Yeshiva B'nai Zion school recognizing his outstanding contributions to Torah Judaism in the U.S.A.

From left: Rabbi Bernard Berzon, Rabbi Elyas, Dr. Bernard Lander, and Rabbi Shlomo Halberstam, the Bobover Rebbe.

(Left) At the Kotel in Jerusalem with his parents in 1968. From left: David and Goldie Lander, Dr. Bernard Lander.

(Below) Dr. Lander receiving an honorary doctorate degree from Yeshiva University.

Presentation to Dr. Lander at Rabbinical Council of America Convention.

From the left: Rabbi Joseph Soloveitchik; Dr. Leon Stiskin; Dr. Lander;
YU president, Dr. Samuel Belkin.

With YU president, Dr. Samuel Belkin at YU
commencement, 1969.

Sarah Lander's parents, Rabbi and
Mrs. Shragowitz; Sarah Lander; and
Dr. Bernard Lander circa 1970.

Official photograph of Dr. Lander taken by Bachrach in the late 1960s just before the founding of Touro College.

At the podium during the mid-1960s.

From left: Dr. Bernard Lander; Dr. Leon Reich (with mustache, second left), then president of Yeshiva of Flatbush; Rabbi Emmanuel Gettinger (with beard, third left); Dr. George Cohen (with glasses, third from right), then Dean of Touro College; Max Celnik; Eugene Hollander (holding the hammer), then Chairman of the Touro College Board of Trustees. Fall 1971.

Rabbi Moshe Sherer, president, Agudath Israel of America; US Senator Jacob Javits; Dr. Bernard Lander in 1974.

Oct.-Nov. 1974 issue of *The Independent*, the Touro College student newspaper.

(Left) With Dr. David Luchins, Chair of Touro College's Political Science Department since 1978 and founding Dean of Touro's Lander College for Women in Manhattan; and former Vice President Hubert H. Humphrey circa 1975.

(Below) Dr. Lander (first right); Dr. Monty Penkower (second right, standing); Head of the Library, Max Celnik; and Dean Rosalind Berlow (seated) preparing for Middle States Reaccreditation visit in 1975.

From left: Dr. Shalom Hirschman, Dr. Mark Hasten, Max Karl, Jacob Fuchsberg, Dr. Bernard Lander, and Mordechai Hacohen.

With U.S. Senator
Al D'Amato (center).

From left to right:
Dr. Solomon Simonson,
Provost, Touro College;
Dr. Lander; President Reagan;
John Bainbridge, Dean of Touro
Law School; and Bruce K. Gould,
President of the Student
Bar Association.

Monica Hasten's graduation
circa 1980.

From left: Dean Stanley Boylan;
Dean Robert Goldschmidt; President Bernard Lander; Dr. Mark
Hasten, Monica Hasten.

(Left) Congratulating Dean Robert Goldschmidt after successful 1982 Middle States reaccreditation visit. In the president's office at 30 West 44th Street, New York.

Dr. Lander inscribing a Torah. Sept. 9, 1984.

(Top Left) Dr. Lander at his desk in the Empire State Building office, early 1990s.

With Sen. Daniel Patrick Moynihan at commencement exercises, 1991.

At the tomb of the Vilna Gaon in Vilnius, Lithuania. 1990.

At Soviet Mission to the UN, 1991 signing ceremony for opening of Touro College branch in Moscow.

From left: Mr. Ron Lauder; Mr. John Elghanyan, Touro Trustee; U.S. Ambassador Thomas Pickering; Dr. Bernard Lander; Mr. Albert Reichmann; Norman Allen, Trustee; Soviet Ambassador Yuri Vorontsov.

(Right) Traveling in Russia, 1991.

John Elghanayan,
Dr. Mark Hasten,
Dr. Lander circa 1990.

At Touro College 20th Anniversary Dinner in 1993.

From left: Mrs. Zissel Klurman, Mrs. Sarah Lander, President Bernard Lander, Rabbi Doniel Lander.

Dr. and Mrs. Bernard Lander before the 1993 Touro 20th Anniversary Dinner.

1993. On the dais at the 20th Anniversary Touro College dinner with Dean Robert Goldschmidt.

At post-commencement reception with Israeli Minister of the Interior, Yosef Burg in 1995.

(Above) With daughters Esther Greenfield and Hannah Lander at an office birthday party for Dr. Lander.

(Right) With son, Rabbi Doniel Lander.

With his children and brother at Dr. Lander's 80th birthday party in 1995.

From left: Mrs. Phyllis Lander, Rabbi Doniel Lander, Hannah Lander, Mrs. Esther Greenfield, Martin Greenfield, Debbie Waxman, Richard Waxman.

Seated: Bernard and Nathan Lander

In Jerusalem on Succot with lifelong friends, Eddie Steinberg and Eugene Gluck.

With brother, Nathan Lander.

At the Kotel. 1997.

With Israeli president Shimon Peres.

With Hannah Lander and President Bill Clinton.

Dr. Mark Hasten and Dr. Lander
visiting construction site for
Lander College for Men
in Queens.

With U.S. Senator Al D'Amato.

Welcoming the Middle States visiting team in March, 2004.

From left: Sister Mary Reap, Chair of the Middle States team; Dean Robert Goldschmidt, Chair of the Touro College Self-Study Steering Committee; Dr. Mark Hasten, Board Chairman; President Bernard Lander; Dr. Robin-Dasher Alston, Vice President Middle States Commission on Higher Education.

President Lander delivering address at 31st commencement exercises, May 29, 2005.

Front row: (from left) Devorah Ehrlich, then Dean of the Women's Division; Dr. Moshe Sokol, Dean of the Lander College for Men; Dr. Barry Bressler, Dean of Undergraduate Business; Dr. Nathan Lander; President Bernard Lander; Dean Stanley Boylan; Dean Robert Goldschmidt.

With his children at Dr. Lander's 90th birthday celebration held at the Lander College for Men in Queens, NY in June, 2005.

From left: Rabbi Doniel Lander, Deborah Waxman, Dr. Bernard Lander, Esther Greenfield, and Hannah Lander.

Dr. Mark Hasten, Chairman of the Touro Board of Trustees.

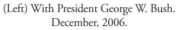

(Left) With President George W. Bush.
December, 2006.

(Right) Nathan and Bernard Lander.
Sept. 2005.

(Below Right)
From left: Rabbi Michael Hasten,
Dr. Lander, Anna Ruth and Dr. Mark
Hasten, Touro Chairman of the Board of
Trustees on April 30, 2007.

(Bottom) At the Lander College for Men,
Torah dedication ceremony on
May 20, 2007 with Dean Boylan and
Rabbi Doniel Lander.

Bernard Lander receiving a Sefer Torah from Chief Rabbi Lau and Dr. Mark Hasten at Touro's 36th Anniversary Dinner on April 30, 2007.

From left: Marty Oliner; Rabbi Lau; Dr. Lander; Dr. Mark Hasten.

From left: Dr. Joseph Weisberg, Dean of Touro College of Health Sciences; Dr. Antonia Coello Novello, New York State Commissioner of Health and former Surgeon General of the United States; Dr. Bernard Lander; and Rabbi Moshe D. Krupka, senior vice-president for college affairs, at School of Health Sciences commencement exercises. May 2006.

With Dr. Hart Hasten and Dr. Mark Hasten at Touro's 36th Anniversary Dinner on April 30, 2007.

(Above) With Dean Raful and US Senator Charles Schumer at Touro's Jacob D. Fuchsberg Law Center.

(Above Right) Chief Rabbi Lau paying tribute to Dr. Lander at Touro's 36th Anniversary Dinner on April 30, 2007.

(Right) Dr. Hasten at 36th Anniversary Dinner on April 30, 2007.

(Below) *From left*: Dean Jerome Miller, President Bernard Lander, Mayor Michael Bloomberg, Dean Robert Gold-schmidt, Chairman Mark Hasten, Roman Murashkovsky of Moscow University Touro.

At 2008 commencement exercises.

At Touro's 35th Commencement, May 24, 2009, from left: Dean Stanley Boylan; Dr. Mark Hasten, Board Chairman; President Bernard Lander; Dean Robert Goldschmidt.

Bernard Lander addressing the graduates at Touro College's 35th commencement exercises on May 24, 2009.

CHAPTER SIXTEEN

Trials and Turbulence

Happy is the man who withstands his trials.
                                           —*Exodus Rabbah 31:20*

Among the many lessons Bernard Lander learned in the wake of the Hollander nursing home scandal was a renewed determination to adhere to his own personal and professional convictions. As he witnessed high profile board members and philanthropists scatter, Lander became further convinced that Touro College must never become dependent upon the generosity of others for its survival. He began to implement measures that would allow the school's operating budget to be funded primarily by student fees and tuition payments. In this effort, he enlisted Touro stalwart Moses Hornstein and encouraged him to accept the chairmanship of the board of trustees, which he did in 1975. Together the two men embarked on a critical transition period that saw fundraising revenue fall from covering 63 percent of the school's operating budget in 1975 to only 10 percent three years later.

Ironically, it was Lander's same stringent commitment to his convictions that led to an eventual falling out between the two men. As part of Touro's drive to decrease its dependency on fundraising revenue, the school had sold a donated building on Park Avenue South for a sum payable over several years. Recognizing the college's immediate need for cash flow to fund its operations, Hornstein generously agreed to lend the school the funds needed to pay off all its current debts. In exchange he took a position against the note held on the Park Avenue building sale, resulting in Touro's ability to receive the full payment immediately—while Hornstein would assume the wait. Bolstered by the warm reception he enjoyed as a result of this act—which actually only cost him the time value of the money he had lent—Hornstein decided to act again in a move he correctly believed would financially benefit the school.

Hornstein informed Dr. Lander and the board that he intended to purchase an eleven-story building, the Bond Clothing Store at 372 Fifth Avenue, and donate the facility outright to Touro for use as classrooms and a library for both its men's and women's divisions. Besides placing an attractive asset on the school's balance sheet, the magnanimous gift would have a major impact on reducing Touro's operating costs. The benefits were manifold. By placing both divisions under one roof, students could share a common library, administrative and other overhead expenses would be consolidated, and professors—many of whom taught at both divisions— would save countless hours of travel time. Moses Hornstein saw the gift as a major step towards achieving Touro's financial independence. However, Bernard Lander saw things differently.

Lander regarded the proposed gift as a step towards something he refused to countenance: a coeducational college. Just as he had fought against the move of Stern College for Women to Washington Heights during his years at Yeshiva, Lander was adamant in his view that it would be inappropriate for Touro to be a coed college. His position puzzled not only Hornstein but others, who observed that "Touro was not Yeshiva" in that the former attracted many non-Orthodox students for whom coed classrooms were not an issue. But Lander argued that Touro's first students were Orthodox and it was still actively recruiting them. Establishing a coed program would be deemed offensive by such observant students, as well as by the families of prospective Orthodox enrollees. As a result, enrollment levels would decline, and Touro would suffer.

Lander recalled how he had split with some of the school's early sup-porters over this same issue. The Hollander affair had clearly hardened him, and he was not about to compromise now—even if it meant passing up a generous show of support from the chairman of the board. The chair-man was equally as adamant, however. Hornstein made a compelling case before the board: "If Touro is not prepared to move ahead with the estab-lishment of a shared facility, such as the Bond building, it has no chance of financial survival. If this gift is not accepted for the purpose specified, I intend to move that Touro cease operations and its assets be sold!"

The decision was left to the board, and while Hornstein enjoyed wide support among Touro's trustees, when the showdown arrived,

Dr. Lander prevailed, and the gift was rejected. Not surprisingly, Moses Hornstein did not carry out his threat and instead submitted his resignation. Touro again found itself facing yet another leadership crisis that would persist until October 1977, when Max Karl would be elected as the board's new chairman.

How the impact of these mounting travails weighed upon Bernard Lander's psyche may be somewhat glimpsed in a letter written to his friend, Dr. Samuel R. Weiss, shortly after the Hornstein resignation:

> Our survival in the midst of all the reverses that have beset us is a minor miracle. To this we must add the continued and systematic attacks by Yeshiva University … who have made overt efforts to induce our board members to resign … and to vote to close Touro College. All this has caused me great anguish and difficulties.

A further indication of Lander's mindset during this turbulent period is revealed in a response he sent to a staff member who had written him with a litany of complaints:

> We are going through difficult days and we are experiencing all the pains of growth. If I were to leave town for even one day, it seems, the fire engines would need specially built water towers to douse all the flames and remove the incendiary bombs that are flying around here!

As in the past, Bernard Lander turned to his wife as the stress of Touro's mounting troubles took their toll. Lander poured out his heart, anguishing over not only the material, but also the spiritual damage that was being inflicted. Somehow, the noble mission of building America's foremost Jewish institution of higher learning had turned a dark corner. Sarah consoled him with her wisdom and wit: "How silly we were, Bernie," she would say with a smile. "Just think; we could have been making a fortune importing goods from China."

But it was not within Bernard Lander's character to become depressed. At his lowest moments of despair, Sarah would remind him of Touro's core mission and of the hundreds of Jewish students sitting in their classrooms right now. Where would they go if Touro closed its doors? Where would they get the tools to build their lives in a positive direction without giving up their Judaism? Strengthened by Sarah's faith in him—as well as his own faith in G-d—Lander would redouble his inner commitment and push on.

Eventually the fallout from the Bond building affair and the loss of supporters like Hollander and Hornstein diminished as Dr. Lander pursued his efforts to decrease the school's reliance on fundraising dollars. Driven not only by his own reticence when it came to "*schnorring*" for money, Lander also believed that a school governed mainly by its largest donors was an invitation to corruption. Simply because a man was in a financial position to make a large philanthropic gift did not necessarily make him an expert in the management of a college. Lander strove to fill the empty board seats with individuals who were knowledgeable in the field of education, regardless of their level of generosity towards Touro. Word eventually reached Dr. Lander that Touro was reputed to now have "the cheapest board seat" of any college or university in the country. Hearing that remark brought a rare smile to his lips.

It was during this period that Bernard Lander began to cling more fervently to another of his founding principles. He became even more outspoken when describing his vision of a multicampus university that would encompass an American college presence in Israel and a law school. Although, by 1979, Touro was finally able to achieve a balanced budget—due primarily to the revenue generated by its growing School of General Studies—Lander was not about to turn inwards and embrace "consolidation," as more prudent heads were advising him to do. In particular, it was Robert Kirkwood, the director of the Middle States Association of Schools and Colleges, who pressed Lander to toe a more conservative line.

Kirkwood and his team conducted an evaluation of Touro College in late 1978 as part of the school's accreditation reevaluation process. While highly impressed with Touro's academic programs and student services, not to mention the excellent morale of both students and faculty, the report cautioned against President Lander's penchant for embarking on new ventures without first securing adequate financing. The report noted "the sharp imprint of its founder and current president; the institution is an outgrowth of his vision." Kirkland observed Lander's hand in nearly all the day-to-day decision making at Touro and cautioned about the risks of micromanagement. "Touro has come a long way in a short time," the report concluded. "The formative period of institutional growth seems to have been quite successful. The present consolidation period, however, dictates a delegation of responsibility." Delegating responsibility was never one of Bernard Lander's strong suits.

Lander was in no way inclined to lead Touro into a period of consolidation, which he interpreted to mean "dormancy." Despite Middle States' counsel that the opening of the law school be deferred until funding sources could be secured, Lander made no secret of the fact that he was pushing ahead with its planning. To underscore its seriousness about the cautionary advice, Middle States placed the question of Touro's accreditation status on hold. Instead of causing him to put on the brakes, on the contrary, the Middle States report seemed to spur Bernard Lander into a renewed frenzy of activity.

In addition to creating a new Touro school of law, Lander was busy expanding the evening programs for yeshiva and seminary students in Brooklyn, inaugurating a master's degree program in Jewish Studies, designing a medical school program with Israel's Technion University, and launching Touro's "Israel Option" program for undergraduate study in Israel. Amazingly, each of these new programs was successfully initiated and are all thriving today. In perhaps the most audacious repudiation of Middle States' advice to slow down its growth, Touro College opened its School of Law in the fall of 1980.

Judging by the following excerpt from a 1980 departure letter written to him by Richard Sawyer, who served as Dean of Planning and Review during this period, Dr. Lander clearly infused those who worked around him and under him with the same profound passion he brought to each challenge:

> Dear Bernie:
> You drive me crazy! You turned me from a shy, introverted, scholarly and utterly refined person into a raving lunatic during four of the nuttiest years that I have every spent in my life. … You are truly the most unforgettable man whom I have ever known. I was always torn between the conflicting desires of wanting to hug you as a friend and with wanting to go after you with an ax.

The reality of the emerging situation was hardly as humorous as Dean Sawyer's letter might suggest. As the evaluation process dragged on, it was clear that Touro was in real jeopardy of losing its vital accreditation. As Kirkwood observed Lander launching one new project before the prior one had gotten off the ground, he seriously entertained the denial of Touro's accreditation on the grounds of fiscal irresponsibility. A determining visit from the Middle States team was scheduled for May 1982. Touro was instructed to conduct a rigorous self-study evaluation in preparation for the visit. Dr. Lander entrusted this all-important task to one of the most loyal, ardent, and assiduous members of his administrative team, Dean Robert Goldschmidt.

Robert Goldschmidt arrived to Touro as an assistant professor of political science in 1974. He worked with the first Middle States evaluation visit in 1975 that resulted in Touro's successfully receiving its accreditation. He had also conducted the requisite self-study prior to the accreditation committee's 1978 visit. At this juncture, Goldschmidt was afforded the title "Special Liaison to the Middle States Association," and as such, he soon fielded a team to implement the current self-study requirement. Tall and debonair, Goldschmidt took pride in the intensive depth of his team's work, often going well beyond the peer review parameters requested by Middle States. When the evaluation team arrived for its visit, Goldschmidt's group was ready as they and senior Touro administrators met with the visitors at a hotel icebreaker on Sunday, May 2.

The Touro contingent expected a collegial get-acquainted session, but it turned out to be something quite different. By the terse greetings and chilly attitudes displayed by the visitation team, Goldschmidt quickly sensed that this was not going to be any ordinary evaluation session. The Middle States team was headed by Earland I. Carlson, former president of Westminster Presbyterian College. Carlson's pronounced animus towards Dr. Lander had clearly colored the attitudes of the other team members. Goldschmidt and his associates left the "first contact" meeting deeply disturbed. The evaluation team let it be known, through their private comments, that they were operating under a mandate from Robert Kirkwood to deny accreditation to Touro College. Kirkwood was reportedly annoyed by Dr. Lander's disregard of the committee's prior recommendations that the school consolidate and conduct its finances in a more fiscally responsible manner. As Goldschmidt reported all this to Dr. Lander, the alarming and unthinkable possibility that Touro might lose its accreditation entered the realm of reality.

As was customary, the visiting team members conducted their in-depth investigations on the following Monday, Tuesday, and Wednesday mornings. They spoke with students, interviewed faculty, toured the facilities, reviewed financial records, and questioned administrative staff at all levels. The first inkling of the committee's thinking was revealed on Wednesday afternoon as they delivered a preliminary verbal exit report to the school. Essentially, the committee heaped praise upon the high quality of Touro's programming and was highly positive in all its comments about the school's operation. But then a barrage of criticism ensued. As compared to colleges and universities with massive endowment funds and multi-million dollar fundraising budgets, Touro's financial profile looked appallingly anemic. The evaluation team saw little evidence of sound fiscal planning and repeatedly decried the school's "hand to mouth" financial status. Part of the Middle States mandate, Carlson explained, was to assure a freshman's parents that the school at which their child had just enrolled would still be financially solvent when graduation time rolled around. They could not, in good conscience, provide such an endorsement in Touro's case.

The Touro team members remained quite anxious following the verbal report, but Dr. Lander reassured them that Touro had presented itself honestly and well. The matter, he believed, was now in G-d's hands, and the time had come to pray.

The written report from the evaluation committee, containing the all-important recommendations, took several disquieting weeks to arrive. It began by lavishing praise on Touro's excellent programs and the outstanding job it was doing in meeting its educational objectives in all areas. The report quoted an African-American student directly: "I'm going to be a sergeant in the Army. I would have been a pot-smoking bum if it wasn't for Touro." The report extolled both the women's and men's liberal arts divisions that were ranked as "Excellent." The new law school was moving along on track, it was noted, and the school of general studies was providing measurable results in improving the lives of underprivileged students. The newly established M.A. program in Jewish Studies earned high praise. At the conclusion of the glowing report, the evaluation committee stated that "The chief limitation Touro faces is its financial status ..." The report's final paragraph concludes with

> Touro College has made substantial progress in the first decade of its history, a tribute in great part to the vision and leadership of its founding president. Now the institution's key challenges are to put in place a system of financial management that is both timely and accurate, demonstrate financial viability, and secure permanent facilities, while ensuring that the quality of its educational programs remains at a high level.

Goldschmidt's apprehension about the committee chairman, Earland Carlson, had evidently been misplaced. According to one member of the evaluation team, Dr. Marvin Farbstein, who years later joined Touro's administration, Carlson joined Farbstein in defending the school and speaking up against the denial of accreditation that was initially favored by a majority of the team's members.

On June 25, 1982, Middle States reaccredited Touro College for the maximum allowable period of ten years. While the reaccreditation process provided its share of nerve-racking moments during the waning days of a tension-filled era, Dr. Lander preferred to regard the experience as a new school's rite of passage, comparing it on at least one occasion with freshman hazing, noting that it is not the most pleasant experience but is intended to promote solidarity and build character. Touro's reaccreditation marked a sort of bookend for the college's first whirlwind decade—a decade that had witnessed both struggle and scandal; had seen both the elevated expectations of new birth alongside the disheartenment of dreams deferred; and, most significantly, had defined the period wherein Bernard Lander had, at long last, reclaimed his destiny.

CHAPTER SEVENTEEN

Compassion and Controversy

If I am not for myself, who will be? But if I am only for
myself, then what am I? And if not now, when?
—*Pirkei Avot (Ethics of the Fathers) 1:14*

These sagacious words, often referred to as the "Hillel Principle,"
have defined the Jewish devotion to social justice for centuries.
Bernard Lander had, over the course of his career, viewed himself as a proponent and an exponent of this philosophical stance. He was
determined, from the days of the school's earliest inception, to lead Touro College under the banner of social responsibility. Notwithstanding
Dr. Lander's special commitment to serving the needs of his own people,
he never wavered in his belief that as an Orthodox Jew, motivated by the
traditions of social justice enunciated by the Prophets, he must do all
he could in behalf of the underprivileged. It was that commitment that
had characterized his thirty-year career as a sociologist and his ongoing
involvement in the civil rights movement. He continually fought to see
that Touro College was anchored on a foundation of service to both
the Jewish and the wider American community. But the road to social
justice is never a smooth one. Several times, Lander's devotion to this
cause led to bitter controversy that tested and tore at the fabric of the
institution he had founded.

By the mid-1970s, Dr. Lander had already launched the APEX (Adult
Program for Excellence) continuing education program for disadvantaged
adults and was striving to obtain permission for the program to offer associate degrees. Just as Touro was emerging from the havoc inflicted by the
nursing home crisis, an opportunity arose that Lander felt could expand
Touro's level of assistance to the underserved senior community. He had
always felt that much of the programming available for senior citizens was
condescending and of a trivial or recreational nature. He believed that

many older Americans were fully capable of engaging in meaningful intellectual activity and solid academic endeavor. Evidently the New York State Board of Regents felt the same way. They announced that seniors enrolled in continuing education programs would be eligible for government support through the Tuition Assistance Program (TAP).

Dr. Lander turned to another trusted friend, Rabbi Abraham Besdin, and asked him to create a college-level program aimed at retired adults who had never attended college. Besdin agreed and modeled a program based on a similar one in place at Adelphi University. The Retired Adult Program (RAP) was launched and was soon catering to a cadre of alert, interested adults who relished the intellectual stimulation they had been denied when they were younger. Adult students demonstrated a dedication to learning unrivaled among Touro's college-aged pupils. Stories of how they trudged to remote community centers in the middle of crippling snowstorms abounded. Near-perfect class attendance was the rule. Relying upon a faculty composed of both existing Touro professors plus those newly hired specifically for the RAP, the program offered courses in the humanities and Jewish studies as well as a science survey course. The evaluation of the program after its first year by one of the subscribing senior centers ranked it as a stunning success:

> The first year of college courses for retired people has been completed successfully. I want to give credit for this marvelous feat to Touro College and its staff. The warmth, the understanding, and the patience that the professors displayed were qualities difficult to find in teachers and those who work with seniors. They motivated our members in their quest for knowledge and made the people in our classes feel that they are still vibrant and still able to function in the mainstream of life.

Most of the enrollees took advantage of the funding available through the state TAP and through a similar federal program to meet the costs of their tuition. This entitled them to pursue a degree at no out-of-pocket expense. Many of those ineligible for government subvention were granted subsidies directly by Touro. Naturally, as word spread of the "free degree" opportunity, the program grew rapidly. During its first year the RAP enrolled more than 400 students at 22 locations around the metropolitan

New York City area. That number grew to 750 enrollees by the following year. In addition to the benefit enjoyed by hundreds of New Yorkers of all faiths who were able, for the first time, to pursue their college ambitions, Touro College, as the provider of these services, was enjoying a revenue boost that helped to offset the loss of fundraising income in the wake of the Hollander nursing home crisis.

Spurred by the broad success of RAP, Dr. Lander branched out and initiated another adult education program in conjunction with the New York Association for New Americans (NYANA), a constituent agency of the New York Jewish Federation. As growing numbers of well-educated immigrants from the Soviet Union arrived to New York, the need for a retraining program became paramount. Touro began offering English language classes and then developed a more comprehensive program called the Educational Program for the Advancement of New Americans (EPANA). EPANA offered a three-track program in a four-semester humanities sequence, which emphasized American history, Western Civilization, and the English language. It also included courses in Jewish heritage, along with career-oriented training in computer science and accounting. Instructors reported their joy at working with such intellectually and academically advanced students who characterized the wave of Russian immigrants of that period. EPANA students also qualified for TAP money from the state, and thus, as with RAP, the 300-plus newly-enrolled Russian students represented a sizable new-found revenue stream for Touro.

By the late 1970s, Touro's Division of General Studies, which encompassed the APEX, the RAP and the EPANA programs had become the financial engine that was driving the continued operation of the school. Touro was operating in the black for the first time—and with only ten percent of its expenses being covered by fundraising revenue.

Recognizing that Touro's growth must be met by an appropriate expansion of its facilities, Dr. Lander cast his eye towards three buildings that had been abandoned by Finch College when it closed its doors a few years earlier. Lander negotiated a purchase of the buildings, located on the Upper East Side on 77th and 78th Streets, from the State Dormitory Authority. A newly enacted state law required that Touro undergo a financial audit prior to closing the deal. Two young auditors from a new agency, the Higher Education Services Corporation (HESC), created by

Governor Hugh Carey to administer college financial aid programs, spent a week scouring Touro's financial records. The head of the new agency, Eileen Dickinson, had publicly decried the use of state money to pay for adult tuition grants. "The State of New York has an obligation to educate its young people prior to their entry into the work force. We have no similar obligation to pay for the advanced degrees of grown adults who are able to pay their own way," she declared. The young auditors arrived at Touro's administrative offices from Albany with an agenda set by Ms. Dickinson—and they meant to fulfill it.

Even before the auditors' report was presented to Touro, the HESC and Dickinson—keen to make political hay—leaked many of its damaging findings to the press. Touro was accused of "recruiting unqualified students—some allegedly enlisted from nursing homes—and enrolling them in dubious programs just to get financial aid payments from the state." The press leaks were tinged with an odor of anti-Semitism. The *New York Times* reported that "the ill-gotten profits Touro enjoyed by defrauding the State were plowed back into other school programs that were designed to attract young Jewish scholars through the college's doors."

Shocked and stunned by the news, Bernard Lander denied the charges and publicly denounced the HESC's qualifications to sit in judgment of the school's academic programs, as he vigorously defended the content of the coursework. The New York Board of Regents, which conducted its own investigation into the charges and found them to be groundless, deemed the faculty fully qualified and turned up no evidence of fraud, commending the program by reporting, "Students in the Retired Adult Program expressed great satisfaction that they had the opportunity to learn and to pursue collegiate level degrees." The matter had become a political hot potato and although Touro was essentially cleared, it had been tainted by the reports and the damage had been done. The deal to purchase the Finch buildings fell through once the selling party learned that Touro was under investigation for possible abuses of the state's tuition assistance program. It was later learned that Governor Carey, concerned about the potential political fallout, had personally instructed the Dormitory Administration to walk away from the transaction.

While admitting no intentional fraud, Dr. Lander stated that "some mistakes had been made" by modeling the RAP after the older Adelphi

University program. By using the Adelphi template, Touro was offering fewer class meetings in the RAP than it did for its standard undergraduate programs. Lander further admitted that it was possible that some of the senior students enrolled in the program were not entirely capable of performing college-level work. Lander emphatically insisted that these "less than qualified" students were not granted admission merely to obtain their state-subsidized tuition fees. "I didn't want to turn anyone away who had a genuine desire to learn and who now had the means to pay for that learning." Nevertheless, Lander was compelled to backtrack on the road paved with his good intentions and repay the state the amount noted by the auditors as the total received by Touro in payment for educational services rendered to questionably qualified senior students. The entrance qualifications for the program were made more stringent as prospective students were required to submit writing samples and provide other evidence of their suitability. But these measures failed to put out the flames.

Despite Touro's willingness to make all necessary corrections, the HESC zealously pressed on with its attack. Sensing an opportunity signaled by Touro's repayment of the RAP subsidies, Dickinson announced that the college should now repay *all* student aid funds received—including those directed to the APEX and EPANA programs. In an effort to bolster its case, the HESC issued a spurious claim that the programs in question had not been properly registered—a trivial technicality based on minor name changes some of the courses had undergone.

Infuriated by this groundless campaign being waged against Touro, and with his sense of justice offended, Lander responded vigorously. He lashed out, publicly accusing the state's HESC officials, and Dickinson in particular, of acting in an "improper, irresponsible, arbitrary, and illegal" fashion and berated them for singling out Touro for such "solitary scrutiny." He denounced the commission for trying to make Touro a public whipping boy, forced to endure unjustified punishment for the perceived abuses "they contend exist in the state's adult education programs." Lander solicited the aid of Richard Sawyer, Dean of Planning and Review, who agreed to put down his ax and stand at Lander's side during the battle. Together Lander and Sawyer enlisted the support of leading rabbis and other public figures as the controversy provided ample fodder for the local and statewide media.

Ultimately, Touro prevailed, but not until the issue reached the state legislature in Albany. In August 1981, special legislation was passed absolving Touro of any obligation to repay the amount demanded by the HESC. Perhaps even more gratifying than the legislative action was a personal visit made by Governor Hugh Carey to Bernard Lander's home during which the governor apologized for the unwarranted HESC attack and for his having scuttled the Finch building purchase.

At the same time that Dr. Lander was waging battle against the HESC, he and Richard Sawyer were busy streamlining and extending the entire General Studies curriculum. Again, Lander was eager to see the growing program reach out and fulfill Touro's social justice agenda. This objective was eventually achieved, but not before another bitter battle—a particularly harsh and heart-breaking conflict—had to be endured.

When Joseph Mulholland retired (the founder of APEX, the department's first program), his position was filled by an African-American educator, Jacquelyn Petersen, who had been managing an extension program at Fordham College. Once arrived at Touro, she was charged with developing a full-fledged curriculum aimed at students from the underserved black and Hispanic communities. Soon after Petersen came aboard, and as a sign of its growing importance, the program was renamed the School of General Studies or SGS.

SGS, established in the Touro College model of small classes and intimate interaction between student and instructor, attracted many of Touro's most illustrious professors who saw their work there as a fulfillment of their personal commitment to the Hillel Principle. These included Professor David Luchins, who has taught political science at SGS for over thirty years. He had served for many years as senior advisor to U.S. Senator Daniel Patrick Moynihan and, to this day, urges his students to become involved in community affairs and politics. Another was Dr. Lester Eckman, a Holocaust survivor, WWII partisan fighter, and author of nine books dealing with the lessons of the Holocaust, who taught regularly at SGS. His courses were among the most popular ever offered at the school. Since its founding, the SGS has been home to instructors who go beyond mere pedagogy and strive to make a real difference in the lives of their students. This altruistic atmosphere was duly noted by the Middle State evaluation team in its 1982 report:

There is significant evidence that this is a school with a mission, articulated not only by administrators, but also by faculty and students. They are convinced that they have a role in serving those adults, new Americans and minorities in particular, whose opportunities otherwise for higher education would be limited or nonexistent.

Dr. Lander rejected the growing trend, embraced by other schools of that era, to adopt an "open admissions" policy for SGS. Even though such a policy would have swelled its ranks and generated more tuition revenue, Lander felt that standards should not be callously pitched aside in the name of social expediency. Touro insisted on testing prospective candidates. Those who did not make the grade were advised to pursue remedial courses, offered at no charge to students demonstrating financial need. This policy emerged as an initial point of disagreement between Dr. Lander and the new SGS dean, Jackie Petersen.

Jacquelyn Petersen grew up in a southern black family. Her parents strongly stressed the value of education, and this atmosphere no doubt contributed to the fact that both she and her brother overcame substantial hurdles and earned doctorates. Dr. Petersen held Dr. Lander in great esteem, inspired by his sense of mission and his dedication to the underserved communities of New York. The two educators also shared an abiding commitment to their respective religions, and this fact formed a foundation of faith for their professional relationship. Petersen worked aggressively towards the mission of extending Touro's services to those in need. During her seven-year tenure, the number of minority students at Touro rose from 500 to 2,700.

Yet there was something troubling about Dr. Petersen's approach. Beginning during her earliest days at Touro, she would from time to time complain to Dr. Lander about the "racist mentality" of certain administrators and faculty members. Lander did not lend much credence to such complaints and rationalized Petersen's charges as the product of a disadvantaged upbringing.

Surveys conducted among SGS graduates provided measurable positive results and demonstrated that the school was achieving its targets in terms of improving the quality of life for those whom it served. As the good news accumulated, Dr. Petersen stepped up her campaign before the board for increased SGS funding in the face of other major Touro projects such as the new law school and the acquisition of new classroom buildings. Her persistence led to an acrimonious relationship with Touro's financial directors, George Affsa and Sidney Frankel. Petersen felt that since her school was generating substantial revenue, it should be entitled to greater support on the expense side of the ledger.

The crisis began in 1985 as SGS moved into its new quarters in Spanish Harlem. The school had negotiated a long-term lease for the first five stories of one of the Taino Towers, a public housing project that contained many floors of unoccupied commercial space. Touro had poured money into the property, building classrooms and renovating the building's 300-seat auditorium. Dr. Lander was particularly pleased by this foray into the greater community, since he had spent six years conducting sociological studies in the area when he was at the University of Notre Dame. He envisioned the Taino Towers as evolving into exactly the type of community service facility for which he had strongly advocated in the name of social stability back in the 1960s. As the SGS moved into its new home, it was renamed the School of Career and Urban Studies, while at the same time the new immigrant program was split off into the Division of New Americans.

Just as loyalty is often tested by distance, the move to Taino Towers represented a fundamental shift in the thinking of Dr. Petersen, who began to let others know that she believed her new School of Career and Urban Studies would be better off as an independent "black" institution, and not part of a "Jewish school." While the civil rights movement of the 1960s saw black and Jewish leaders linking arms and marching side by side in the streets of Selma and Oxford, the ensuing decades had borne witness to a growing rift between the two communities. Particularly when it came to issues like the Middle East and affirmative action, black leaders found themselves increasingly at odds with mainstream Jewish political thinking. Dr. Petersen, who found herself caught up in this tide, was heard to issue increasingly disparaging remarks about her relationship with the administrators at the school's main 44th Street campus, which she labeled "Fantasy Island."

Dr. Petersen informed Touro administrators that officials at the State Education Department had told her that she is a far more capable administrator than anyone else at Touro, and that she could do very well running a school on her own. By the end of 1985, Petersen ratcheted up the tenor and temerity of her rhetoric. She accused Dr. Lander of funneling publicly obtained funds to Israel, acting as a "front man" for real estate interests, and, in perhaps her most audacious claim, charging that Lander was "laundering money for the United States through Korea."

As classes convened for the 1985–86 school year, Dr. Lander received numerous reports advising him that Petersen planned to "take" the SCUS away from Touro and establish it as an independent college. While he never seriously entertained the possibility that such a thing could happen—how would she obtain a charter for a "stolen" college, for example?—he understood full well that she could do a great deal of damage simply by making such an outlandish attempt. Despite repeated invitations to address her legitimate concerns through face-to-face discussions, Dr. Lander met with very little success. By February 1985, Petersen was making public announcements in which she issued groundless and inflammatory accusations against the school. She accused Touro of stealing her students' financial aid money and exploiting her minority students by taking their tuition money and spending it on every program but hers. Finally, she accused Touro of being racist.

Dean Petersen had crossed the line, and her groundless and highly offensive demagoguery finally convinced Dr. Lander that she and her supporters had to be dismissed. On March 6, Lander asked Yitzchok Goldson to present her with a letter advising that she was being placed on "indefinite leave of absence." The letter instructed her to "refrain from entering any of Touro College's facilities until further notice." She and her associates were afforded the opportunity to collect their personal belongings, but she responded by declaring: "It's not necessary; I'll be back!"

Petersen's first action after her dismissal was to form a student steering committee and encourage it to stage a student strike, which was called for March 10 and lasted three weeks. In terms of achieving its objectives, the effort was a disaster. African-American faculty members remained steadfast and classes continued undisrupted. Her next move was to join with a few community activists and retain the services of a community activist attorney. Together, the attorney and steering committee issued press releases, attempting to create a "cause célèbre" but again met with little success.

A student delegation was sent to Albany to speak with Governor Cuomo and officials of the New York State Department of Education. Again, they encountered no real sympathy. Donald Nolan, the Deputy Commissioner for Higher Education, told the delegation that he personally had great respect for the fine character of Dr. Lander and the impressive work he had done. If they were dissatisfied with their situation at Touro, he suggested, they could switch to any of the other fine schools in the area, such as Medgar Evers College in Brooklyn.

Petersen's campaign did succeed in prompting the state's Higher Education Service Corporation (HESC) to once again place Touro under public scrutiny. Concurrent investigations were initiated by the New York Department of Education and the U.S. Department of Health, Education and Welfare. The upshot of all the inquiries was naught. Upon examination, none of the agencies could find any evidence corroborating Petersen's outlandish charges.

Despite being discredited by the investigating bodies, Petersen kept up her campaign and urged supporters to "keep the faith." Progress was being made, she told them, towards obtaining a charter for her independent School of Career and Urban Studies. In an act that characterized his magnanimity, Lander generously agreed to extend the semester to allow those students who had missed classes due to the "strike" to complete their course work. And finally, in an action that probably should have occurred much sooner, Petersen, along with thirteen administrators who signed on with her, were summarily fired. Furthermore, Touro initiated legal proceedings against the steering committee that, Lander learned, had used proprietary Touro contact information in their campaign to discredit the school. The steering committee soon collapsed, and the legal action was eventually dropped.

Although the Jackie Petersen affair did not cause Touro any long-term damage, either to its enrollment or to its reputation, it still must be regarded as a difficult trial for Bernard Lander. As a figure in the public eye, Lander, who had always been reluctant to engage in any public squabbles, preferred to settle disputes quietly and with the decorum befitting a serious academic institution. Nevertheless, this preference for "quiet diplomacy" did not in this instance, nor did it ever, translate into capitulation or appeasement. When Jackie Petersen pointed a slanderous finger at what she termed a "racist 44th Street establishment," Dr. Lander took up the gauntlet and met fire with fire. As his cherished Hillel Principle decreed, "If not now, when?"

CHAPTER EIGHTEEN

Torah and Parnassa

If there is no flour, there is no Torah; if there is no Torah, there is no flour.

—Pirkei Avot (Ethics of the Fathers) III:21

B y 1976, Touro College had established itself as a rapidly growing New York liberal arts school, yet it did not offer an in-depth
program of study to meet the needs of Torah-educated students
graduating from area high school yeshivas. Dr. Lander had long spoken
of establishing such a curriculum, so it was no surprise that when two of
Touro's most talented managers, library director Max Celnik and Robert
Goldschmidt, Dean of Students, came to Dr. Lander that year with an
implementation plan, he welcomed it with open arms.

"We need to be where the students are," Dean Goldschmidt said.
"We need to open a branch campus in Brooklyn to serve the *parnassa*
(livelihood) needs of our community."

"Right now, those that can are still taking evening classes at Brooklyn
College," explained Celnik, referring to the area's growing population of
yeshiva-educated Torah scholars. "But many of them are not going to college at all. They need an appropriate environment in which to continue
their studies." The discussion centered on practicalities and, after the two
had laid out their plan, Lander announced his decision: "If you two are
prepared to run it, I'm with you one hundred percent!"

The need for a school of higher education in Brooklyn had been filled
since 1930 by City University's Brooklyn College in Flatbush, affection-
ately known as "the Poor Man's Harvard." Students from such schools as
Yeshiva Torah Vodaath and Yeshiva Rabbi Chaim Berlin would continue
their Torah studies and enroll at night at Brooklyn College while earning
parnassa during the day to support their families. In addition to Torah
studies, such students would often enroll in secular classes that would assist

them in advancing their professional careers. Although such study was often eschewed by many of the heads of Brooklyn's yeshivas—they advocated a life strictly devoted to Torah with no outside influences—many young men seeking an acceptable balance of Torah and parnassa enrolled at Brooklyn College. But by the mid-1970s, powerful forces in American society were at work to upset that balance.

Nationwide student protests against the Vietnam War, rising racial empowerment, the women's liberation movement, and a push towards open enrollment policies were taking a heavy toll across the nation's campuses. Unlike Touro, Brooklyn College was by no means immune to such seismic forces. As the extreme libertinism of what was dubbed "the counterculture" infiltrated New York, Brooklyn College was no longer a suitable place for an observant Torah scholar to matriculate. Indeed, the atmosphere of the campus and curriculum requirements had become ferociously antithetical to Torah values and a religious lifestyle. Goldschmidt and Celnik explained that Touro could effectively step into this void and attract a sizable number of students by providing meaningful higher education degree programs in an appropriate, kosher environment. Dr. Lander agreed, and in the spring of 1977, the Flatbush Men's Evening Program was born. No one suspected the cloud of controversy this move would raise.

Classroom space was rented in the Sephardic High School on Avenue R as a charter class of nineteen young men began taking courses scheduled on Monday and Wednesday evenings, focusing mostly on business administration. A separate women's evening program followed in 1979, opening with ten students meeting on Tuesdays and Thursdays in the Young Israel building on Avenue K.

The role of how to present the humanities at the Flatbush programs was something of a challenge. Due to the "Torah Only" orientation of most of the area's yeshivas, Goldschmidt and Celnik could not merely replicate Touro's men's and women's programs being offered in Manhattan. Such courses, with their heavy immersion in the study of Western Civilization, would prove an anathema to the "Torah Only" partisans of Brooklyn. The Flatbush program had to be structured differently if Touro hoped to attract a requisite number of students. There was, for example, no focus on the humanities or any required courses in Western Civilization.

Instead core courses concentrated on fundamental writing skills, speech, quantitative skills, analytical reasoning, and information literacy as well as modern economics, political science, business, computer science, and education. In order to promote ongoing religious study, students choosing to continue their Torah education in yeshivas and seminaries in New York, Israel, or elsewhere received transfer credit for such training towards their respective degree programs at Touro.

The dawning of the Flatbush program represented a concrete example of an educational philosophy, developed by Dr. Lander and known as "the sociological method." In essence, this approach is founded on the desire to serve diverse populations with sensitivity to their specific needs. The sociological method calls for educators to deliver their services at the place where their students are located instead of the other way around. It also advocates a curriculum that allows students to maximize their educational opportunities within the constraints of their particular socio-economic situation. Despite this broadminded approach, or perhaps because of it, Dr. Lander and Touro soon came under attack due to the emergence of the Flatbush Evening Program.

The program's initial Avenue R location, across Ocean Parkway from a leading yeshiva (Mirrer Yeshiva), was chosen because of its accessibility. Nevertheless, it was perceived as an act of transgression by the yeshiva community, aimed at luring students away from their Torah studies into a college setting. Lander attempted to explain that the students Touro was serving would be attending college anyway, but with Touro on the scene, they were doing so in a proper kosher environment. But his words fell on deaf ears. The school was ultimately forced to move the following year into a less controversial venue at the PS 149 annex on the corner of Ocean Parkway and 18th Avenue.

The level of vocal opposition to Touro's Flatbush initiative intensified with the opening of the women's program. A war of letters was soon launched by one of the area's leading voices, who warned Touro not to set foot in Brooklyn. According to him, one of the major accomplishments of the postwar years in Brooklyn was the fact that today's area yeshivas "taught true, pure Torah" and had worked long years to "eliminate secular influences" from the lives of their students. Touro was now seeking to undo all of this, according to the leader of this vocal opposition movement.

In his letters to Dr. Lander and other Touro administrators, this outspoken opponent insisted that Touro "keep away from Brooklyn" in order to avoid "a confrontation between brothers." In a February 1979 letter, he wrote:

> We come to you with a plea not to open your planned women's branch in any part of Brooklyn. To date, our pleas asking you not to come to Brooklyn have been ignored by you. A lot of friction and heartache could have been avoided. Now, your opening of a women's program will result in our doing all in our power to prevent your being here. We will not be quiet and passive.

Although Dr. Lander had a clear aversion to confrontation, he was not one to be easily intimidated. He understood the basis of the opposition, yet he realized that Touro's evening program in Flatbush was gaining widespread community support by filling a real need for rigorous degree programs preparing students for careers and professional achievement. As Brooklyn College became a less attractive option for yeshiva-educated young men and women, they came to appreciate the professional approach they were being exposed to at Touro. These skills and competencies would enable them to earn a livelihood with dignity, sufficient to afford private day school education for their children and to meet the other significant day-to-day expenses of Orthodox living. Lander also succeeded in enlisting the support of many Orthodox community leaders who understood how the Flatbush program had been specifically designed to meet the needs of yeshiva students and seminary graduates. Nevertheless, there remained a hardcore element that rejected college education in any shape or form. It was members of this contingent who were prepared to resort to extreme methods—threats, slander, character assassination—in order to enforce their world view upon the Brooklyn Orthodox community.

Lander's opponents launched a vigorous and underhanded campaign in which they fed misrepresentations of his views to Torah leaders across the United States and in Israel. These leaders were urged, and often acquiesced, to issue statements forbidding contact with Touro College. A picket line was organized in front of Touro's Manhattan campus on West 44th Street, protesting Touro's foray into Brooklyn. The protests took a decidedly ugly turn as outrageous placards began appearing in Borough Park and Flatbush in Brooklyn, as well as in Dr. Lander's home neighborhood of Forest Hills in Queens. The placards declared it a *mitzvah* (a divine commandment) for someone to murder Bernard Lander—even if the deed were done on the holiest day imaginable, a Yom Kippur that falls on the Sabbath!

The extremism of Lander's enemies was openly displayed when they published "The Mission of Touro College," which they distributed in front of Brooklyn yeshivas and to prospective Touro students. This propaganda piece included excerpts, purportedly from Touro's actual mission statement, accompanied by photos of several of the risqué girlie shows near Times Square. The accompanying text read:

Touro's educational programs involve the formal study of the humanistic traditions of Western Civilization as a preparation for life." The text went on to state: "With its location a mere 2 blocks from 42nd Street, students are able to take field trips and see everything first hand.

It is unknown whether anyone was actually taken in by this forgery, but its very existence demonstrates the lengths to which the culture clash surrounding Touro's entry into Brooklyn had by this point extended. The following episode is yet another instance that also demonstrates how Dr. Lander chose to deal with this sort of heated opposition.

As the storm of controversy raged over Touro's presence in Flatbush, Dr. Lander received an invitation in the summer from a rabbinic school principal to meet in upstate New York to discuss the Flatbush situation. Lander was aware that the invitation originated from an opponent, but since he was proposing a rational discussion of the matter, Lander felt compelled to accept the invitation. He was accompanied by Dean Robert Goldschmidt and the newly appointed Dean of Faculties, Dr. Stanley Boylan. The group hoped to clarify Touro's true intentions in Flatbush and to dispel the barrage of untruths that had been unleashed about the school and about Dr. Lander.

Shortly after the meeting began in the first floor conference room of the principal's office, their host suddenly excused himself and left the room, leaving Lander, Boylan, and Goldschmidt behind. The trio soon noticed a contingent of Orthodox men congregating outside the door of the office. Soon the crowd was so large that the three men realized that their way out of the office was completely blocked. Dr. Lander quickly understood what was happening.

"Our host is assembling a *Bet Din* (a rabbinical court). He obviously lured us here in order to put us on trial. If we step outside this room, we are certain to be attacked." Although he was speaking figuratively, a *Bet Din* did have the authority to perform an act of censure, known as *cherem* (excommunication) that would essentially attempt to exclude Dr. Lander and Touro from the Orthodox Jewish community. Lander approached one of the large leaded-glass windows, opened it, and led the others out of the room, through the hedges, and into their waiting car. Dean Boylan would later comment: "If you put an obstacle in his way, he will find a way around it."

Despite the heavy barrage of personal attacks against him launched by those intent upon keeping a "college" from operating in Brooklyn, Bernard Lander pushed ahead—driven by his conviction that the Flatbush program was meeting the practical needs of yeshiva students. The continued growth of the program over the ensuing years vindicated his position, and its expansion is a testimony to Lander's vision and commitment to the guiding principle of "Torah and Parnassa."

As enrollment swelled, Touro was required to move its classes into a series of ever-larger public schools. In 1986, the program settled into the Shulamith High School building where, for the first time, it was able to offer science, premedical, and predental courses. By the beginning of the 1990s, the Flatbush program was serving more than 600 students and once again found itself in need of more space. Dr. Lander understood the importance of the Flatbush program and went before the Board with a fervent request.

The school had recently sold its original office building on West 44th Street, and the proceeds were intended to pay down some of Touro's outstanding long-term debt. Lander petitioned the Board to instead direct those proceeds towards the construction of a 90,000 square foot new facility that would serve as a permanent home for Touro's Flatbush operations. The Board agreed, and in 1995 the new facility, containing state-of-the-art science and computer labs, an extensive library, ample office space, and thirty classrooms, opened its doors at Avenue J and East 16th Street. The move from shared facilities to the newly dedicated building allowed for classes to be held at any time of day and for a significant expansion of the curriculum. While the men's division continued holding classes in the evening hours, many new afternoon classes were soon being offered as part of the women's program.

By 2007, Touro Flatbush was flourishing with an enrollment exceeding 1,100 students and, once again, found itself short of space. The school today has flowed over into rented classroom facilities at the nearby Yeshiva of Flatbush school. Due to the pluck and persistence of Dr. Lander, the school has won the hearts and minds of most of the Orthodox community. In fact, many of the children and grandchildren of the program's most vocal opponents have attended and graduated from Touro in Flatbush.

Contributing to the overall success of Touro Flatbush is an adherence to Dr. Lander's "sociological method" principles. For example, one might expect a school building operated under a religious banner to contain a place of worship. Yet the Flatbush facility contains no *beis medrash* (prayer and study hall). Observant students and faculty members wishing to conduct daily prayers in the building do so in the hallway or main lobby. This is not an oversight; rather, the omission of a prayer room is due to Dr. Lander's sensitivity to the prevailing community attitudes. The demarcation between college study and religious study must be kept clear. The existence of a *beis medrash* might lead some to regard Touro in Flatbush as a yeshiva, and thus would offend certain students and their families. Dr. Lander was committed to clearly delineating the boundary between college—even one supportive of Torah values—and the yeshivas.

Another example of Dr. Lander's "sociological method" at work at the Flatbush facility is the "Open Curtain" program that serves young Russian women who have completed high school in their homeland and now wish to expand their education as they grow towards becoming Jewish wives and mothers. Recognizing that no such higher education facility, aimed specifically at Jewish women, yet exists in Russia—and with the encouragement and support of Rabbi Shmuel Kamenetsky of the Yeshiva of Philadelphia—Open Curtain facilitates the granting of visas that allow these women to enter the United States to enroll into a specially tailored program at the Flatbush campus, a program that effectively meets the educational aspirations and social needs of these young Russian women. In an act of extreme generosity, Dr. Lander convinced the Touro

Board to grant full tuition scholarships for all Open Curtain enrollees who demonstrate need.

Under Dr. Lander's watchful guidance, the Flatbush program has provided thousands of yeshiva students and seminary graduates with the professional competencies and credentials, and thereby the means, to support their families with dignity. While most heads of Brooklyn yeshivas are not willing to publicly endorse any college program, most do, in fact, quietly support Touro's Flatbush school and counsel those of their students who wish to learn marketable skills to enroll there. The satisfaction of seeing former enemies sending their children and grandchildren to the school represented a vindication of Dr. Lander's vision and brought him a great sense of gratification. The following excerpt from a letter written to him by a former staunch opponent is a case in point:

> Through the years Touro College has become a way of life in our family. My son-in-law, daughter, and oldest son are all graduates of Touro. … You have been instrumental in creating an ideal environment in which yeshiva students can obtain professional training while, at the same time, they can pursue full-time yeshiva studies. I cannot praise the school too highly for the implementation of a program long lacking in our community.

By 2010, Touro in Flatbush had graduated more than 6,000 students, who are now pursuing careers as doctors or lawyers, educators, CPAs, business entrepreneurs, therapists, social workers, and counseling psychologists. Their achievements have enriched not only the personal lives of their families but also the larger Jewish community.

The success of the Flatbush program and its eventual acceptance by the Orthodox community spurred Dr. Lander to go even further in reaching out to underserved Jewish communities. In 1988 he undertook the challenge of providing college-level education to the mostly disenfranchised Hasidic population. Members of the Hasidic community generally would not consider attending college. Dr. Lander believed that Touro was uniquely positioned to reach out to the Hasidim by offering specially designed courses that would be conducted with sensitivity to their particular cultural needs.

"They have the needed intellectual skills, but they have been loathe to attend college because of cultural considerations," Dr. Lander explained in his 1988 Touro College Master Plan.

Working with the New Square Hasidic community, Touro introduced a groundbreaking initiative in 1989 with the somewhat oxymoronic name of The Guided Independent Study Program. Dr. Lander sought out a true innovator to head the GISP and succeeded in recruiting Jerome Miller, who had conceived and developed programs for nontraditional students at other universities. Miller's challenges were substantial. For example, there was the question of language. Despite being born in the United States, Hasidim spoke primarily Yiddish. English was considered a second language and was not fully mastered by most of the young men Miller was required to educate. Given that most of the textbooks and coursework were in English, this deficiency represented a serious obstacle. To meet this challenge and other similar deficiencies, Miller instituted an independent one-on-one mentoring program. These "mentorials" proved successful and permitted students to complete their course requirements and carry out the requisite independent research into specialized areas of interest. Traditional classroom sessions were only held on a limited basis that kept the program in compliance with the State Department of Education re-quirements for certification.

The program was well received, and so, in the following year, Dr. Lander decided to push on into the predominantly Hasidic communities located in Borough Park and Williamsburg. Before opening the doors, Dr. Lander managed to enlist the support of COJO, the community social service umbrella organization. This endorsement helped greatly to boost enrollment levels. Despite the handicaps he faced because of his students' lack of a regular American-style education, Professor Miller established rigorous academic standards. A number of enrollees found the program too difficult, given their limited knowledge base and poor English verbal skills and, as a result, enrollment leveled off at about 300 students. Touro eventually found itself concentrating on the Borough Park neighborhood and no longer operates in Williamsburg.

Within one year, the GISP was renamed as "The School for Lifelong Education" or SLE and has, for the past twenty-some years, been educat-ing young Hasidic men and women—as well as other adult learners—and preparing them to function effectively in today's society. Mentoring is still in use and has proven to be an effective tool in overcoming the deficien-cies in the students' past education. It is this practice, coupled with Miller's introduction of learning collaboratives that encourage student interaction, that have largely contributed to the ongoing success of the SLE.

By 1998, the Hasidic program was poised for more growth when a junior college, operating in Borough Park, closed its doors. Dr. Lander saw this as an opportunity to strengthen Touro's presence and obtained board approval to open a second program focusing on career and professional studies. Named *Machon L'Parnasa* (Institute for Professional Studies), the program offers classes that strive to bring Hasidic students up to speed and thereby enable them to enter Touro's senior colleges. Enrollees at *Machon L'Parnasa* are most often men and women in their late twenties or early thirties who have growing families and feel the need to learn marketable skills in order to support them. The school offers a balanced program that permits students to carry out their many commitments while, at the same time, effectively prepares them to perform college level work. The results speak for themselves. Hasidic students emerging from *Machon L'Parnassa* often end up at the top of their classes once they begin their studies and successfully earn the advanced degrees they need to find meaningful and gainful employment.

A seminal moment took place at the first *Machon* graduation ceremony. One member of the charter graduating class took to the podium and announced to family, faculty, and friends, "I started my new job last month. A job that is only possible because of the training I have received here at *Machon L'Parnasa*." He then removed a check from his pocket and held it up high. "This is my first paycheck," he proclaimed proudly. "Not just my first paycheck on this job, but this is the *first* money I have ever earned in my entire life. For that opportunity I thank the faculty and staff of this program and Touro College."

Meeting the educational needs of the religious community has been a passion of Dr. Lander's that persisted throughout his life. In 2008, he was the pivotal force that brought into existence an undergraduate nursing curriculum that, unlike any other similar program, follows the Jewish calendar. By offering clinical rotations on Sunday instead of Saturday, and by suspending classes on Jewish holidays, the program provides career opportunities, especially for observant women, in a field that would have been nearly impossible to enter in the past. Today, for the first time, Orthodox women are able to dedicate themselves to a life of healing without forfeiting their dedication to a life of Torah. This reality represents the most concrete implementation of Dr. Lander's vision of "Torah and Parnassa."

The countervailing threads of ancient Jewish history and the modern State of Israel have been deeply woven into the fabric of Touro College. This is due, in large part, to Bernard Lander's strong Zionist sentiments, along with his unflinching vision of a school that would serve Jews wherever they might be—in the Diaspora or in Eretz Yisroel. Today, one of Israel's most prestigious postgraduate institutes of higher learning, *Machon Lander*, bears his name. How this evolved is a tale that exemplifies the manner in which Dr. Lander, time and again, and despite enormous hardships and setbacks, witnessed the fulfillment of his original academic vision.

For the fifteen years prior to the founding of Touro College, Dr. Lander, as head of the Bernard Revel Graduate School at Yeshiva University, devoted himself to the advancement of Jewish studies. It was this legacy and his love of this field of study that he brought with him as his personal contribution to the academic arsenal he assembled when starting Touro. While he wished to quickly establish an advanced graduate degree program, similar to the one he ran at YU, circumstances intervened, and Touro was limited, during the 1970s, to offering only an undergraduate major in Jewish studies. The courses, delving into Jewish history, culture, and civilization, proved highly popular, and throughout the turbulent years described in earlier chapters, Lander often sought to leverage the momentum of these courses into a valid graduate-level program. Doing so would signal Touro's first master's degree program, and Lander could conceive of no better discipline in which to first grant advanced degrees than in his area of expertise, Jewish Studies. The opportunity to act arrived in 1977.

New York's Herzliah Jewish Teachers' Institute, or HJTS, was founded in 1918 and by the late seventies had trained more than 1,200 students to serve as Jewish scholars, community lay leaders, and other non-clergy positions in the Jewish world. Dr. Lander had heard that the school was floundering—suffering from low enrollment and faculty desertions—so he was not surprised on receiving a call for help from Dr. Jacob Katzman, the school's president.

Lander quickly understood that by merging HJTS's faculty into Touro's, an advanced degree program in Jewish Studies could be brought into being. Absorbing HJTS would enable Touro to win approval for a master's level program. In addition, the merger would bring to Touro one of the finest and most extensive Jewish text libraries in America—more than 25,000 volumes in Hebrew, Yiddish, and English.

On June 21, 1979, Touro's Board of Trustees approved Dr. Lander's proposal to merge with HJTS. The Graduate School of Jewish Studies was launched shortly thereafter. Dr. Katzman was granted a seat on the Touro board and brought with him an innovative outreach program called "The Jewish People's University of the Air." The JPUA provided twenty-seven college-level courses taught by leading professors in Jewish studies through weekly radio broadcasts on National Public Radio. This prototypical "distance learning" program helped to put Touro on the map as more than 90 colleges, 350 community organizations, as well as the United States military began offering JPUA courses. Two of the courses were even translated into Spanish for use in Latin America.

Dr. Lander went to work, enthusiastically fielding a distinguished team of academic luminaries to build the new graduate school. The curriculum would be designed by Dr. Moshe Sokol, an expert in the area of Jewish philosophy. Dr. Michael Shmidman, a Harvard-educated professor of medieval Jewish history, would serve as dean. Both men would go on to teach at the school as well. Classes started during the fall semester of 1981 with the new school's stated mission to provide "advanced students with a deeper understanding of the roots of contemporary Judaism and Jewish communal life in the history, literature, and thought of the Jewish people over the last millennium."

As the Graduate School of Jewish Studies gained traction and began to receive national recognition, Dr. Lander pushed for another of his life-long goals: that of creating a true binational college. He enlisted Dr. Shmidman in behalf of an initiative aimed at opening a graduate branch campus in Israel. With the aid of Dr. Carmi Horowitz, a Harvard colleague who was teaching at Ben Gurion University in the Negev, Dr. Shmidman led a trial summer program in 1986 with classes held on the campus of Michlalah Jerusalem College in the Bayit Vegan section of Jerusalem.

The success of the Israel graduate program is one of the shining achievements in Bernard Lander's professional career. From the most humble beginnings as an experimental binational summer graduate program, the school soon began a cycle of growth that has not abated to this day. Offering courses with the permission of Israel's Board of Higher Education, the program began to attract first dozens and soon hundreds of students each year. This growth was the direct result of the highly focused attention and devotion that Dr. Lander lavished on the school. Constantly channeling substantial amounts of Touro's limited funds into the program, Lander succeeded in attracting world-class, award-winning academics to the school.

Most of the enrollees at Touro's Graduate School of Jewish Studies Jerusalem campus were college and high school level educators who earned continuing education and graduate degree credits that translated into higher pay scale advancement opportunities. Much of the faculty was composed of adjunct professors "borrowed" from Hebrew University and other Israeli campuses. Many reported that they enjoyed their work more at Touro than at their "home" institutions because of the high intellectual and motivational level of the students.

By 1999, the Israeli branch of Touro's graduate Jewish studies program enjoyed an enrollment of more than 400 students. It had grown to become the largest master's degree program in Jewish studies in the world and enjoyed a global reputation as one of the most academically advanced institutions of its kind anywhere.

Israel's Council of Higher Education, the sanctioning agency responsible for the nation's higher learning accreditation, took note and determined that Touro's Israel program could no longer continue as a branch program. It had to become an independent Israeli institution. Soon after, the graduate school was spun off and, in 2004, was renamed "The Machon Lander Graduate School of Jewish Studies." Machon Lander continues to embody the spirit and life force of its namesake and is well-poised to do so for generations to come.

CHAPTER NINETEEN

Going Global

Raise your eyes and look out from where you are:
northward, southward, eastward, and westward.
—*Bereishit (Genesis) 13:14*

There was nothing the slightest bit provincial about Bernard Lander. Since his visit to the Canton Trade Fair, shortly after Richard Nixon's historic trip to China in 1972 (as recounted in Chapter 14), he had strode often across the global stage. Although he had closed the door to exploiting the China opening in the context of his family's fabric business, Lander nevertheless understood that opportunities were also being generated in his chosen field of education. After the death of Mao Zedung in 1976, Chinese leadership was anxious to modernize its economy and thereby enable it to compete in international markets. Its first step was education, and it acted quickly to fill the need for Western-style business training. Dr. Lander recognized that Touro's strong business curriculum, its location in New York City—the focal point of the global economy—and its record of successfully teaching American business practices to ESL (English as a Second Language) students left it perfectly poised to meet this emerging need.

In pursuit of this opportunity, Dr. Lander began contacting major Chinese universities in 1981, proposing the establishment of a new School of International Business and Management to be headquarted in New York that would provide advanced training management techniques and courses in the laws of international trade as well as in an assortment of languages and cultures. In 1982, along with his friend, former U.S. Congressman Lester Wolff, Dr. Lander founded the Pacific Community Institute (PCI), which they hoped would serve as a precursor towards the creation of the new school. PCI served as a forum for the discussion of economic and political issues between the United

States and China. The PCI also sponsored student exchange programs designed to groom future business leaders as well as a series of conferences that were held in South Korea and Taiwan as Touro strove to enhance its reputation in Asia.

In June 1988, Bernard Lander traveled to Beijing where he concluded an agreement with China's International Trade Research Institute for the establishment of a new management training program to be located in New York. The initiative failed to get off the ground, however, due primarily to cost considerations. Costs also posed an obstacle for plans, advocated by members of the U.S. House and Senate who sat on PCI's Congressional Advisory Board, for Touro to build a series of branch business colleges in China, Singapore, Thailand, Taiwan, and the Philippines. Although he, too, supported the concept, Dr. Lander could not justify the costs of such an enormous investment in light of the many other demands for funding being placed on the school's budget by programs closer to Touro's central mission. Instead, he worked to bolster PCI student exchange programs that succeeded in bringing hundreds of Asian students through the doors of Touro's New York facilities during the 1990s.

Although the initiative did not result in the establishment of a hoped-for Touro presence in China as the country pursued a more Westernized economy, this was not to be the outcome in Russia. The difference was most likely due to the fact that after World War II, the U.S.S.R. contained roughly half of the world's Jewish population. Prohibited for generations from practicing the rituals of their faith, Soviet Jews did not, however, assimilate into obscurity as did other ethnic and indigenous people swallowed by Soviet society. This fact—some would call it a miracle—was due to a long-standing anti-Semitic aspect of the Russian psyche that influenced the Kremlin's internal policies. This antipathy towards the Jew accounted for Stalin's decision to declare Judaism to be a nationality, distinct from all the geographic designations—such as Georgian or Azerbaijani—to be permanently recorded on Line 5 of every Soviet citizen's identity booklet. Hence, millions of Soviet-era Jews grew up knowing nothing about Judaism other than it was a mark of shame permanently stamped on their lives and that it condemned them to a second-class existence, barred from the best universities and professions by the Line 5 designation of "Ivrai." This curse turned into a blessing when the Soviet Union fell, and it became clear that the establishment of "Ivrai" as a reviled nationality had the unintended consequence of preserving the Soviet Jewish population more or less intact. Stalin, who sought to isolate and separate the Jew from Soviet life, instead succeeded in rescuing half the world's Jewish population from the abyss of history. No one understood this phenomenon better than Bernard Lander.

By 1988, when Gorbachev's policies of Glasnost and Perestroika were in full swing, Dr. Lander wrote to his friend and financial supporter, Albert Reichmann:

> The reports from Russia describe a resurgence of religious identification among many elements of Russian Jewry. Thus, there is the possibility of bringing back to Yiddishkeit, the grandchildren of Gedolai Yisraoel who have been forcibly estranged from our people. It is a modern miracle that after 70 years of atheism, the spark of Torah identity shines so brightly.

The letter to Albert Reichmann, the eldest of Toronto's Reichmann brothers and founder of the Olympia & York real estate empire, was intended to generate enthusiasm for the rebuilding of Eastern European Jewry, long devastated by the ravages of Nazi and Soviet oppression over the course of the twentieth century. Lander was not only successful in enlisting the financial support of Reichmann for this initiative, but also that of several other high-profile Jewish philanthropists, including Ronald Lauder, former U.S. ambassador to Austria and heir to the Estée Lauder cosmetic fortune. Lander made a strong case:

> We are currently working with China to create a Graduate School of International Business that will no doubt appeal to the current Russian leadership. In addition, Touro, in New York, has been working with Russian-speaking Jewish students since 1976. We understand how to effectively re-introduce them to their Jewish heritage and to American culture at the same time.

The strategy employed by Dr. Lander in pursuing the Eastern European opening was highly emblematic of his overall professional philosophy. He sought to deliver a Jewish Studies program, incorporating serious Biblical and Talmudic components, to a Judaically-starved

Russia under the banner of Business Administration. He succeeded in winning high-powered converts to this cause. His partners were inspired by Lander's dream of bringing new life to what had once been the center of Jewish scholarship and culture for centuries. Lander and his well-heeled partners were keenly aware of Israeli philosopher, Emil Facken-heim's Eleventh Commandment: "Thou shalt not deliver unto Hitler a posthumous victory."

The International Board that Lander had assembled to spearhead this initiative contained more than financially powerful players. Another key participant was Rabbi Ronnie Greenwald, who had assisted Dr. Lander in securing Touro's original building on 44th Street years before (see Chapter 13). Greenwald had spent years behind the Iron Curtain, most notably working to secure the release of Soviet refusenik Natan Sharansky. In 1989, Greenwald informed Dr. Lander that Lithuanian officials in Vilna were seeking to establish ties to American educational institutions. Early feelers were extended, and Lander's suggestion of instituting a Jewish Studies program in Vilna met with a positive response. One of his contacts, the deputy mayor of Kovno, suggested that a trip to Lithuania might be productive.

Visiting the Soviet Union was still a complex matter for an American in 1989, but Dr. Lander, at age seventy-four, was a seasoned traveler and anxious to hit the road towards Jewish renewal. He arranged for a four-day visit to Lithuania with a one-day stop in Moscow on the way back. Finally the visas and reservations were in order, and Dr. Lander, along with Dean Stanley Boylan, embarked on what turned out to be a most challenging and memorable sojourn. Bad weather in New York delayed their departure and caused them to miss their train connection in Vienna that was to deliver them to Warsaw. Dr. Lander, armed with a determined charm and a formal letter of introduction from U.S. Senator Daniel Patrick Moynihan, managed to arrange air passage from Vienna to Budapest and then on to Warsaw. Once there, they retained the services of a Polish taxi driver for the twelve-hour trip to Vilna. The entry point to the U.S.S.R. was at Brisk, and this circuitous route caused the group to pass through countless Polish and Lithuanian villages that had once been home to the world's largest Jewish population and stood then, in 1989, as bleak, grey industrial backwaters—stark testimony to the drab and faithless Soviet way of life. It is easy to imagine how Dr. Lander and Dean Boylan must have felt as they toured this cultural wasteland, carrying out the specific mission of resurrecting Yiddishkeit in the region. The idyllic images of yeshivas and saintly rabbis, etched on to the collective Jewish memory, surely must have guided their steps.

After crossing into Lithuania at 1:00 AM, their path became more treacherous. They discovered that their Polish driver was unable to read the Russian / Cyrillic road signs, and the party soon became lost. Fortunately, Dean Boylan's rudimentary Russian skills saved the day. After running out of diesel fuel in a remote rural area, the crew arrived in Vilna after filling their tank at a farmhouse and spending thirty-five hours in transit. Taking only the time required to shower and change clothes at their hotel, Lander and Boylan went on to Kovno where they presented Dr. Lander's proposal for a Jewish studies program as part of a new classical liberal arts college. The discussions were fruitful and, in a few months, led to the drafting of a memorandum of understanding between Touro and the University of Vilnius that provided for the establishment of a department of Judaic studies at the university as well as a summer business education program in New York for professors and students.

Before departing for Moscow, the group met with Vilna's Jewish community leaders, who had kept the torch of Judaism burning over the long decades in a city that was once known as "the Jerusalem of Eastern Europe." They were shown the massive 500,000-volume archive of Judaica, collected by the Nazis and being stored in the basement of a former church. The amazing collection contained a mountain of Yiddish literature but also a large number of sacred texts and priceless Torah correspondence. Rabbi Greenwald eventually succeeded in moving this treasure of Jewish heritage to New York, where it is today housed at the YIVO Institute for Jewish Research.

The final stop was one of remembrance and renewal at the ancient Jewish cemetery where the group admired the monument erected in tribute to the Vilna Gaon. Dr. Lander also paused at the graves of Rav Avraham Danzig, author of the *Chayei Adam*; and Avraham Ben Avraham, the former Count Valentine Potocki, convert and martyr to Judaism. At the grave of the Vilna Gaon, Dr. Lander solemnly promised to do all that he could do to rebuild Torah study in Eastern Europe and prayed to G-d for His blessing in this sacred task.

In Moscow, Dr. Lander and Dean Boylan were joined by the personal representative of the Reichmann family, Rabbi Shlomo Noah Mandel, whose presence helped to open doors to Soviet officials who sensed that cooperating in this educational enterprise would lead to better political relations with the United States. After their discussions, Rabbi Mandel led the group to the Choral Synagogue but found it closed for repairs. The group moved on to Red Square, where for probably the first time in the shadow of the Kremlin, *mincha* (afternoon) prayers were recited by the three men.

Their last stop before heading home was the newly opened *Mekor Chayim* yeshiva, whose very existence was a beacon of hope in the restoration of Jewish life in Russia. The group learned that opportunities for joint cooperation existed among Moscow institutions of higher learning and was encouraged to ardently pursue such initiatives by the school's head, Dr. Ze'ev Dashevsky. The group arrived home exhausted but fervently encouraged about the prospects for a Jewish renaissance in the Soviet Union. Dr. Lander was particularly intrigued by the idea suggested by Dr. Dashevsky about launching a new school in Moscow. Fortunately, he was not the only man in New York with just such a vision.

Dr. Roman Murashkovsky was one of Boris Yeltsin's best friends and his closest Jewish ally. After earning his degree from the Moscow Academy of Political Science and heading the Soviet Ministry of Gas and Oil, Murashkovsky and his wife, Renée Lekach, settled in New York during the early 1980s. Murashkovsky shared Yeltsin's desire to Westernize the teetering Soviet economy and, by the end of the decade, was knocking on leading university doors seeking a partner in establishing a U.S.-Soviet business school in Moscow. After receiving little encouragement from the trustees of Yale and Columbia, Murashkovsky reached Touro's doorstep, where he was met by Dr. Lander—freshly arrived from Russia and brimming with enthusiasm for the very concept Murashkovsky was pitching.

Dr. Lander explained, however, that his main concern was to rebuild Jewish life in the U.S.S.R. and that the school must include a vibrant Jewish studies program. Murashkovsky, who had become more familiar with his own Jewish heritage since moving to America, understood this condition and agreed without hesitation. Convincing the Soviet authorities was, of course, another matter entirely.

The question of why a communist regime, billing itself as "The Workers' Paradise" would need trade unions is a matter better left to chroniclers of twentieth-century political history. Suffice it to say that the membership of the U.S.S.R.'s massive umbrella trade union was greater than the entire population of the United States in 1950. Dr. Lander, with Murashkovsky's guidance, soon came to learn that the trade union organization represented a de facto government with powers akin to that of the Communist Party. It was with the heads of the trade unions that Dr. Lander embarked on a two-year negotiation path that would lead to the eventual establishment of an International School of Business and Management, a Touro branch campus located in Moscow.

On February 7, 1991, with the Soviet and U.S. Ambassadors to the U.N. looking on, Bernard Lander signed an agreement with the U.S.S.R.'s Association of Trade Unions establishing the first American-sponsored degree program in the Soviet Union. The implications of this historic event soon became evident when it was announced that the new International School of Business and Management, unlike Russian universities, would actually charge tuition. Of course, charging and collecting are two different issues. In order to allow students who could not begin to afford even the most modest tuition levels to enter the program, a vigorous promotional campaign was undertaken. Touro exploited the widespread belief among Russian companies that an American-style business education was needed by their newly emerging executive class. Renée Lekach convinced company after company to send their employees to the new school and to underwrite the tuition bill as a necessary expense to keep their company competitive. Renée managed to place a Touro infomercial, starring Dr. Lander, on prime time Russian television. The marketing push paid off. In a building belonging to the national labor union, a school teaching modern American management techniques opened its doors in the capital city of the U.S.S.R. The initial class of one hundred students was studded with the CEOs of many of the Soviet Union's forward-thinking commercial enterprises.

In the "President's Message" that appeared in the first publication issued by Touro's Moscow branch in 1991, Dr. Lander articulated the excitement of the period. At this point, in April, the Soviet Union had loosened its grip on the Warsaw Pact nations, the Berlin Wall had fallen, but the Soviet Union remained extant. Here is an excerpt:

The threat of a world war passed with the disintegration of the Iron Curtain. … The Moscow Branch of Touro College's pioneering International School of Business and Management is one girder in the bridge to a future of peace and prosperity for our citizens. It presents a remarkable opportunity for emerging leaders to be a part of a successful future. We invite you, the leaders of tomorrow, to grasp the opportunity by joining with us and by applying your fullest intellect and energies to acquiring the skills and technical abilities that are the basic tools for meaningful leadership in business, economics, marketing, and management. Touro College is proud to share in this historical adventure between our two great nations for a better tomorrow.

One of Dr. Lander's first acts upon establishing the school was to recruit Rabbi Dr. Simcha Fishbane to run the Jewish Studies Program in Moscow. A former Israeli Army chaplain, Dr. Fishbane set to work recruiting a number of the Western Jews who found themselves in Moscow. Plans were drawn up, and the program was set to begin offering classes in October, 1991, after the Jewish holidays. On August 18, Dr. Lander, Marvin Farbstein and Howard Glickstein, the dean of Touro's Law School, set off again for Moscow. This time their mission was to set the curriculum of the new Jewish Studies Program with Dr. Fishbane and to plan a summer law program with Dean Glickstein.

Lander, Farbstein, and Glickstein, arriving in Frankfurt to connect with their flight to Moscow, were greeted by unbelievable breaking news. The military had taken control of Moscow, and reports of a coup d'état had begun to circulate. Passengers were informed that the Moscow flight would be delayed by one hour to give passengers time to decide whether to turn back or not. Almost every passenger on their Moscow-bound flight declined to board and turned back or found alternate destinations. But, this was not to be the fate of the Touro trio.

"I have appointments in Moscow," pronounced Dr. Lander with just a touch of bravado. "We're going!" And so they did.

The three arrived in Moscow aboard the last plane to touch down from the West before commercial flights stopped running. At 7:00 AM the following morning, state-run television interrupted with a frantic announcement of a state emergency as the dreadful sight of tanks in the streets greeted Muscovites on their way to work. Soviet president Mikhail Gorbachev was confined to a dacha in the Crimea, and martial law had been declared by the military.

Although Lander's tenacity and his willingness to wade into what was a highly volatile situation were commendable, the result, not surprisingly, was much consternation back home. Lander's longtime secretary Ruth Schneider and Dean Boylan both recall frantically trying to reach Dr. Lander. They had arranged for Albert Reichmann to send a private plane to Moscow to evacuate the group and bring them to safety. After some intense anxiety and frustration, they finally got through to Lander by phone.

Dr. Lander, however, would not consider turning back. Actually, Lander and the others were excited by the fact that they were on hand to witness the drama of history unfolding before their eyes. It was like having front row seats at the French Revolution.

As the coup reached its climax, Lander and the others looked down from their hotel room balcony to the tanks and military half-tracks that had filled the streets below. They were confined to their rooms by the curfew that had been announced earlier. Glickstein gestured out the window and began expressing his frustration about sitting passively while history was being made out in the streets. Perhaps, he suggested in jest, they should head to Red Square to see what was taking place?

"You're right. How do we get there?" responded Lander. Eventually Howard Glickstein managed to convince Lander that he had been joking and that they would be risking their lives to go out on the street during a military curfew.

After a tense and sleepless night marked by rumor and counterrumor, the scenario began to take shape. The grim gray men who claimed to have seized power had called in the troops to take over the center of popular reform and resistance, the Russian White House, and to depose their leader, Boris Yeltsin. Yeltsin heroically urged his followers to stand their ground and not be dissuaded by the military might arrayed before them. Waving the flag of Russia, Yeltsin mounted a tank and commanded the soldiers not to fire on their own people. It was clear that the takeover could not succeed without significant bloodshed, and the plotters had committed themselves to a "bloodless coup." Once these realities became clear, both the KGB and the Red Army withdrew their support for the takeover regime, and the coup promptly fizzled.

None of these dynamics were immediately clear to the Touro trio confined to its hotel room as all three looked down to observe that the tanks and troops below had begun to move. Marvin Farbstein, who had spent considerable time in Moscow, realized that the troops were headed away from the city. A wave of relief washed over the men as they stood by the windows, watching life returning to normal in the streets below. In reality the trip had been quite productive, under the circumstances, and the opening of the new school was still set for the coming October. On the flight home, it was announced that the conservative coup had failed and that Gorbachev was free and returning to Moscow.

The next few months saw the rapid dissolution of the Union of Soviet Socialist Republics, an entity that over its seventy-plus-year lifespan had perhaps perpetrated more cumulative human misery than any regime in history. Boris Yeltsin replaced Mikhail Gorbachev and presided over the dismantling of the Warsaw Pact and the granting of autonomy to all of the former Soviet republics. The impact of such massive change upon the former Soviet Jewish community was profound. Held prisoner for generations, and denied the freedom to immigrate to their ancestral homeland in first Palestine and then Israel, many Jews viewed the fall of the Soviet Union as a divine act of liberation.

But what did such new freedom mean for Touro College and its plans to open a branch in Moscow? Dr. Lander astutely observed that the timing could not have been more perfect. While many Jews would certainly leave Russia, many more would stay behind and take advantage of the new religious and economic freedoms that were being forged. At the exact point in history when the Jews of Russia needed a place to learn about their heritage, here was Touro ready to open its doors. Dr. Lander saw the divine hand of G-d at work in all this and would comment about it quietly to those in whom he confided.

As Rosh Hashanah was being celebrated openly that fall in Moscow, Dr. Fishbane was busy posting flyers all around the city urging prospective students to attend an open house to learn about a new Touro College–sponsored Jewish Studies program. He considered the irony of his actions and realized that a mere three years earlier he could have easily been arrested by the KGB for this exercise in free speech. Dr. Fishbane had no way of estimating how many people might respond and was willing to start with twenty, or even fewer. He was shocked when more than 100 prospects showed up, all enthusiastic to exercise their newfound freedoms by rediscovering the heritage of their parents and grandparents.

After the open house, word spread quickly, and applications began to pour in. Somehow the issue of tuition fees was no longer much of an obstacle as the beginnings of a stable economy began to take root. In October 1991 the Touro College of Jewish Studies opened its doors. Many of the students had applied to immigrate to Israel and had enrolled in order to study Hebrew. Within eighteen months, enrollment levels in Touro's Jewish Studies program exceeded 500. This virtually overnight growth astounded everyone at Touro, including Dr. Lander, whose most optimistic expectations had been exceeded. A New York attorney, touring Moscow in 1993, wrote to Dr. Lander after visiting the school:

> I witnessed with my own eyes, classes filled with eager, motivated, and satisfied students participating amid lively discussions, questions, and an overall pursuit of knowledge and religious values. I met with a friendly staff of teachers, secretaries, and other faculty members and had an opportunity to talk to students. I must say that Touro College is a Jewish landmark in Moscow today. Amongst knowledgeable people, both Jewish and gentile, the name Touro College evinces admiration and great respect.

With the phenomenal success of the Jewish Studies program, it is easy to overlook the fact that it had ridden into Moscow on the coattails of Touro's International School of Business. It, too, was successful from day one, primarily because of a stellar faculty assembled by Renée Lekach. The school managed to keep its balance even amid the shifting sands of those early days. The flag of the Soviet Union was replaced in Moscow with the Russian flag on December 25, 1991, as the hammer, sickle, red star and other symbols of the Soviet era were relegated to museums and history books. Naturally, the Soviet-era Association of Trade Unions, Touro's erstwhile partner in the operation of the business school, ceased to exist, thus forcing the school to seek new quarters that it eventually secured in the summer of 1992. Having a stable permanent home entitled the International School of Business to be approved as a branch of Touro College by the Middle States Association. This approval provided Touro's Moscow branch with the ability to grant U.S. college degrees. Sanctioning by the Russian authorities soon followed as Touro College became the first foreign university to be licensed by the Russian Ministry of Higher Education on June 1, 1992.

Eventually, the Moscow branch of the International School of Business was spun off as an independent institution. Today, known as Moscow University–Touro, the school operates with reciprocal agreements in place with Touro College and offers both U.S. and Russian State undergraduate diplomas as well as a recently initiated Touro M.B.A. program. It enjoys a current enrollment of close to 300 undergraduate and 65 M.B.A. students.

As for the Jewish Studies program, conceived during that turbulent time? It is now known as the Lander Institute Moscow and has, since 1991, educated many of the top leaders of the Jewish community in both Russia and Israel. The Lander Institute forms the nucleus of the Dor Revi'i Jewish community in Moscow and currently includes a Jewish day school, a kosher grocery, and a *kollel* (an institute of Talmudic scholars).

The fall of the U.S.S.R. represented, at the same time, a source of turmoil and great opportunity for Dr. Lander's strategy of establishing schools across Eastern Europe. While the basic template remained the same—Touro would offer badly needed Western business training to emerging Eastern bloc economies while insisting that Jewish studies programs be established as well, quid pro quo—the dynamics had fundamentally shifted. As a result, the country that had initially drawn Dr. Lander into Eastern Europe, Lithuania was no longer an attractive venue despite its past prewar glory as the center of Jewish learning. Dr. Lander held the traditions of the past in high esteem, but he was, at the end of the day, a pragmatist. There simply were not enough Jews in Vilna to warrant the energy and resources required to establish a new Jewish studies program—not when so many more attractive communities were coming on line. Locations in Poland, Austria, Hungary, and Ukraine were scouted for suitability and opportunity. Sadly, while viable sites were identified, Dr. Lander was unable to muster the necessary financial backing among his potential partners to allow him to pursue the creation of these Eastern European schools.

The largest Jewish community in the world, outside of Israel and the United States, was in Paris at the beginning of this century. While a rising tide of anti-Semitism and Islamification has driven many Jews out of France, it remains home to a sizable population. Rabbi Dr. Robert Adout, who served as principal of a Jewish high school in Paris, realized a need for programs similar to Touro College's men's and women's divisions for observant students who were eager to dedicate part of their day to Jewish studies while enrolled in college. Dr. Adout shared Dr. Lander's concern for providing a supportive environment for religiously-committed students who wish to grow spiritually while pursuing the secular education needed to make a living.

Working on his own in Paris and financed solely by community funds, Dr. Adout set up a small undergraduate program in 2006. Once it was operational, Dr. Adout contacted Touro and asked if his school would qualify to become part of the Touro Europe family. Touro obtained approval from Middle States, and in 2008 the French school became affiliated with Touro as a branch campus. With American-style business courses being taught in English and Torah studies taught in Hebrew, the first class of students received an American undergraduate degree issued by Touro College at its commencement in 2010.

Under Dr. Lander's leadership, Touro has now opened programs in several European capitals. In each city, the objective has been to strengthen the local Jewish community by keeping its college-age youth at home in a framework where they continue to grow as Jews. As evidenced in Europe, new branches are not opened solely for business reasons. In order to qualify, Lander needed to be convinced that there was a real local need. Other considerations also came into play. Lander would not begin planning until he located a suitable individual with the appropriate academic and leadership credentials to operate the new program. Local community support was also a fundamental requirement. As evidenced in Lithuania and other locales, if the circumstances were not right, Dr. Lander would not move forward but would instead seek alternative ways of serving a Jewish population in need.

In the twenty-first century, it has become common for respected American universities to export their programs abroad. Dr. Lander's vision was far ahead of the pack when he pioneered international programs back in the 1980s. His concept of an integrated international business school combined with a vibrant and dynamic Jewish studies program has been proven successful in numerous European communities. But there is no reason why the template cannot continue to be replicated in other cities. It is a concept that has outlived him as new opportunities to export the "Lander Method" continue to come on line. Each such future school, even those established many years after his death, will bear the unmistakeable mark of the man from whose fertile mind and upright heart they first sprung.

CHAPTER TWENTY

Passing the Torch

The legacy of heroes is the memory of a great name and the inheritance of a great example.

—Benjamin Disraeli

In one of his life's proudest moments, Bernard Lander stood and observed his son, Doniel Lander, receive *semicha*, his rabbinic ordination. Doniel's true love had always been Torah education. Even as he completed his MBA studies at NYU, he was known to spend much of each day studying talmudic texts at Touro as part of Rabbi Menachem Genack's intensely focused *kollel* (study group). Doniel also would frequently teach at Touro's men's division and organize summer study programs as he pursued coursework toward a doctorate in finance. Eventually, he arrived at a career crossroads.

After weighing his options, Rabbi Doniel Lander informed his father of his intentions to dedicate his full energies to teaching Torah and that he would not be pursuing his doctorate. Whatever disappointment Bernard Lander may have felt at receiving such news was far overshadowed by his pride in his son's decision. But now that Doniel's course had been set, the question was how to most effectively implement his mission.

The senior Lander agreed with his son that a need existed in the Touro family of schools for a traditional advanced level yeshiva. Doniel's vision of such a rabbinical school imagined an institute that would embody and formalize the teaching principles of his mentor, Rabbi Joseph B. Soloveitchik, and expose R. Soloveitchik's "Brisker" approach of Talmudic study to a wider audience. The senior Lander encouraged his son's efforts to establish just such a school in the Queens area.

At the start of the 1983 school year, seventeen students filed into the basement of a Kew Gardens Hills neighborhood center in Queens to begin their advanced studies at the newly opened Yeshivas

Beis Dovid. The school's name was a tribute to Doniel Lander's late grandfather, David. It was soon learned that another similar school was already in existence under the same name and objected to Lander's usage. The name was changed to the Ohr Hachaim Institute for Advanced Studies.

The school quickly established itself and began attracting a growing number of qualified students interested in expanding their study of Talmud. The new yeshiva permitted learners to attend classes at Touro's Flatbush program two nights per week. During the early years of its existence, Ohr Hachaim moved from one synagogue basement to the next in the Kew Gardens Hills area as its expanding student body caused it to continually outgrow each venue. Eventually, the school settled in a refurbished private home that was later expanded as growth continued. By the early 1990s, the institution had become something more than an advanced yeshiva. It was, by this point, a vital Torah center serving the entire Kew Gardens Hills observant Jewish community. With new growth came increased revenue that permitted the school to purchase five adjacent homes that were eventually demolished to make way for the modern edifice that Touro erected for the school on the corner of Main Street and 71st Avenue. In 1996 the new building was dedicated in memory of Rabbi Doniel Lander's late and revered mother, Sarah Rivkah Lander—Dr. Bernard Lander's partner in life and in building Touro College, who had passed away one year earlier.

Today Ohr Hachaim enjoys an enrollment of more than 200 students and serves as home to a kollel of twenty advanced scholars. Under Rabbi Doniel Lander's leadership, the school has extended beyond its physical facilities and operates several model high school programs in the Queens and Monsey areas of New York. Also, a new classroom and dormitory facility for high school students opened its doors in 2007 next door to the Sarah Rivkah Lander building. Ohr Hachaim continues to serve its mission of strengthening Jewish life in the area as evidenced by the many school alumni, as well as others, who have chosen to settle in Kew Gardens Hills largely due to the presence of Ohr Hachaim. The school continues its growth path towards the future and today stands as a major component of the Lander Legacy—both that of Rabbi Dr. Bernard Lander and that of his son, Rabbi Doniel Lander.

Perhaps no other component of Touro College inspired and animated Bernard Lander more than the school's women's division. A staunch believer since his earliest days in maintaining the prohibition against studying Torah in a mixed gender environment, Dr. Lander believed just as fervently that the women's curricula and facilities must be on a par with that of the men—and even exceed them. Although the women's division moved its location six times during the first twenty years of its existence, Dr. Lander placed a special priority throughout those years in providing comfortable classroom and dormitory facilities at each venue. Working with Dr. David Luchins, its first director, Dr. Lander saw to it that the school's faculty and academic standing enjoyed the same level of excellence for which the Touro men's division had become well known.

Charged by Lander with assembling and maintaining a top-flight faculty, Dr. Luchins consulted with Rabbi Shimon Schwab and worked closely with Rabbi Joseph Elias, the head of New York's Rivka Breuer Teachers Seminary. Lander also enlisted the celebrated Jewish scholar, Rabbi Berel Wein, as well as his own rabbi, Joseph Grunblatt of the Queens Jewish Center, to teach regularly at Touro women's division. Under Dr. Lander's watchful eye and with the guidance of devoted faculty members, such as Rebbetzin Sara Freifeld, the school's dean for eight years, and Dr. Judith Bleich, who both acted as inspirational mentors and positive role models, as well as Rabbi Dr. Samuel Hoenig, long-time chair of Judaic Studies, the women's division has grown dramatically. Yet, despite such expansion, the division is still characterized by small class sizes and close, nurturing relationships between faculty and students. Dr. Lander would have wanted it no other way.

The single most exemplary event in the history of Touro's women's division to date is unquestionably the 2006 opening of its new home, not far from Lincoln Center on Manhattan's upper west side, between Amsterdam and West End Avenues. Built specifically for the Lander College for Women, at a cost of ten million dollars, the 48,000 square foot, five-story glass and steel building boasts modern classrooms, an impressive library, athletic facilities, and ample administrative office space. The building and the prime real estate upon which it sits was the munificent gift of a single donor family: current chairman of Touro's Board of Trustees, Dr. Mark Hasten and his wife Anna Ruth.

To fully understand the significance of this landmark gift, one must turn back the clock to those turbulent days in the mid-1970s as Touro College and Dr. Lander were emerging from the wake of the nursing home scandals. As has been recounted, many of Touro's high-profile board members had fled amid the flood of negative publicity. As a result, Dr. Lander's proactive efforts to rebuild the board took him on a search both far and wide, all the way to central Indiana.

Indiana was home to Monica Hasten, who was an exemplary student in Touro women's division and had first learned about the school during her frequent trips to New York City with her Indianapolis NCSY group. She had become acquainted with Dr. Lander and had often spoken to him about her family background and in particular about her father Mark Hasten's amazing life story. Through Monica, Dr. Lander learned that her father was a highly successful businessman involved in real estate development and banking, as well as a respected leader in the Jewish community. He learned how Mark had been forced to flee his boyhood home as the Nazis descended on eastern Poland, how he and his family had found sanctuary in Kazakhstan, and that he had then enlisted into the Polish Brigade of the Red Army. After the war, Mark was reunited with his family and, as he moved through a series of European DP camps, he became active in Betar, the Revisionist youth organization, as well as the underground Irgun movement under the leadership of Menachem Begin. On the day that Israel became a state in 1948, Mark found himself sailing to its shores aboard the ill-fated *Altalena*, arriving in time to join the IDF and see combat in Israel's War of Independence. Hasten eventually immigrated to the United States via Canada in the early 1950s, where he married, earned an engineering degree, and went to work for General Mills, a position that saw him originate such popular consumer snack products as Bugles and Pringles. In the 1960s he joined his younger brother, Hart Hasten, in the nursing home business before branching out into real estate and banking. Mark Hasten's extraordinary life saga is recounted in his stirring autobiography, *Mark My Words!* (Brotchin Books, 2003)

One afternoon in 1977, Mark Hasten picked up the phone in his office to accept a call from the president of his daughter's college:

"Mr. Hasten, this is Bernard Lander. I'm in Indianapolis, and I'd like very much to meet you since Monica has told me so much about you."

"Fine," he replied. "Come on over for dinner tonight." Dr. Lander accepted, and afterwards the two men discussed Hasten's extensive involvement with Jewish day school education in Indianapolis.

"That's what I wanted to talk to you about, Mark," Lander said. "I want you to do me a favor. Please don't say yes or no, just agree to think about it. I want you to become a member of our board at Touro." Dr. Lander explained that the current chairman of the board was a man named Max Karl from Milwaukee. Karl was familiar with Mark Hasten's story and had recommended to Dr. Lander that Hasten be invited to sit on the board.

Mark Hasten promised Dr. Lander that he would think it over. Lander proceeded to educate Hasten about how Touro College was founded and outlined the school's purpose and overall mission. Although Hasten might have regarded this invitation to serve on the board as an elaborate fundraising ploy, he soon learned otherwise. Lander did not solicit Hasten or even suggest that he make a donation. In fact not once during their entire thirty-three-year relationship did Lander or anyone else, ask for one dollar from Mark Hasten on behalf of Touro. The gift of the real estate upon which the new Lander School for Women was built originated entirely with Hasten.

As the evening wound down, Dr. Lander flattered his hostess, Mark's wife Anna Ruth, stating that his trip to Indianapolis was worthwhile if, for no other reason, than the opportunity to sample the fine chicken soup she had prepared.

"Any man who is so discerning as to select a wife capable of creating such an outstanding chicken soup," Lander joked, "clearly merits a seat on the board of Touro College." Hasten, not able to argue with such compelling gastronomic logic—and after consulting with the chef—agreed to accept the invitation.

Hasten has served on the Touro board ever since, frequently flying to meetings from his homes in Indiana and in Florida. In 1995, he was elected to succeed Max Karl as board chairman, a position he currently holds. Under his dynamic, hands-on leadership, Touro has continued to flourish and enjoy startling growth. Touro women's division, now known as the Lander College for Women—The Anna Ruth and Mark Hasten School, is a place where a student's commitment to Judaism is enhanced as she engages in her professional studies.

While not agreeing on everything, Mark Hasten and Bernard Lander, over the years, forged a deep-rooted friendship that persisted until Lander's death in 2010. Today, Dr. Hasten, who received an honorary doctorate from Touro in 2006, works closely with Touro president Dr. Alan Kadish and Lander College for Women dean Dr. Marian Stoltz-Loike toward fulfilling and promoting the school's ongoing growth that is a key component of the Lander Legacy.

Charles Darwin is said to have pointed out that it is not the strongest of the species that survives, but the most adaptable. The ability to appropriately adjust one's tactics while not abandoning the overall objective is a skill that was highly developed in the personal character of Bernard Lander. Perhaps no better example of this attribute exists than the case of Touro College's flagship men's division, today known as the Lander College for Men.

The 1980s was a time of struggle and challenge for all of Touro, but perhaps no area was harder hit than the men's program, which found itself uncomfortably housed in the West 44th Street building, crowded in with the School of General Studies, the Retired Adults program, the Law School, and the School of Health Sciences. Enrollment was declining, as were the average test scores of incoming freshmen. Despite the hardships, the school continued to offer an outstanding education at the hands of a highly dedicated staff. Unhappy with the school's declining fortunes, Dr. Lander decided to take action and secure a proper permanent home for this core division. He did not reckon on how long it would take him, however.

After an initial foray in 1985, which involved the purchase of a former Forest Hills tennis club, met with strong neighborhood resistance, the property was sold and was followed by an attempt to acquire a Staten Island campus from the State Dormitory Authority in 1991. This effort also met with eventual failure. In 1994 a suitable property was finally identified and acquired in the Kew Gardens Hills neighborhood of Queens. The planning, financing, and construction of the new facility would consume the next six years. By the time the men's division was set to move into its new quarters in 2000, Dr. Lander realized that much had changed in the Orthodox Jewish community that the school was originally built to serve.

When Touro opened its doors in 1971, it was regarded as a remedy for a chronic problem facing the observant Jewish community. Young men were emerging from traditional Jewish high schools and being shipped off to college campuses where they would, in most cases, abandon their Jewish identities in pursuit of a secular education. Dr. Lander's vision, embodied by Touro College, was to provide parents with an alternative, a place where their sons (and later daughters) could gain a true college education without sacrificing the values they had been raised with. But by the turn of the twenty-first century, Dr. Lander had to ask himself if such a remedy was still needed.

By 2000, most graduates of Jewish high schools went on to study for one or two years in yeshivas or seminaries in Israel, an experience that served to strengthen their identities as committed Jews. Returning home after such an experience, those wishing to continue their education would often live at home and commute to a nearby college. Attending a yeshiva during the day and taking college courses at night was another practical option. Others, who decided to live on campus, sought out those schools known for their vital Jewish student life and continued their Torah studies in a strong extracurricular environment. In other words, Touro was no longer the only alternative facing entering freshmen intent on preserving their orthodox way of life while advancing their education. To be sure, many college students were still divesting themselves of their Jewish heritage upon reaching college, but the vast majority were those emerging from less observant, more assimilated home environments.

Dr. Lander was highly aware of the shifting landscape into which the new men's division was to find its place, and he quickly brought his skills at innovation to bear. He understood that Touro men's division was facing the possibility of becoming irrelevant, or at the least, severely marginalized, if it continued in its current direction. Lander determined that the school was paying a heavy price for being neither fish nor fowl—neither adequately Torah intensive to compete with RIETS at YU nor sufficiently academically robust to compete with local and out-of-state colleges—and set out to chart a new course. It was based upon this decision that the Lander College for Men was reinvented as it finally established its permanent home in the Kew Gardens Hills section of Queens.

Dr. Lander was unequivocal as he articulated the defining purpose of the new Lander College for Men. In devising this new incarnation, he had reached into his own past as a Yeshiva student some seventy years earlier. He recalled how his school day was divided into general and Judaic studies and how well the two were integrated. He and the top-flight team he brought to the task set about creating a program of high level, intensive Torah studies combined with a strong afternoon college curriculum. Another guiding principle Lander incorporated from his own life was the powerful influence of faculty role models. He insisted that nothing contrary to Torah or Jewish Law was to be taught in any classroom of the new Lander College. He publicly announced at the time that the new school was designed to "serve someone who wants to achieve a high level of pre-professional education and also a high level of Jewish studies."

This was to be an institution built to serve "*Shulchan Aruch* Jews" as Dr. Lander put it (referring to the authoritative sixteenth century code of Jewish law authored by Rabbi Joseph Karo). "There will be no split between professors of Talmud and professors of English," he declared. To spearhead this approach, Lander recruited two highly respected rabbis, Rabbi Abba Bronspiegel and Rabbi Yehuda Parnes, to head the school's Beis Medrash program. Both men had earned highly burnished reputations while teaching in YU's RIETS program and had experienced ideological tensions with Yeshiva's president. With the addition of Rabbis Bronspiegel and Parnes to the faculty, it was evident to all that the school was clearly going to be a "*frum* (observant) college."

Dr. Lander turned to one of his most trusted and talented colleagues, noted scholar Dr. Moshe Sokol, to establish the college. Dr. Sokol was joined by Dr. Geoffrey Alderman, a distinguished Oxford-educated academician, who served as academic dean and was succeeded soon afterward in that position by Dr. Sokol. Dr. Lander directed them to recruit only the most highly qualified professors to fill all of the school's faculty positions. Working with Dr. Sokol, Dr. Lander established a core curriculum of courses in Jewish history, Western history, and literature, establishing a strong footing in the basic liberal arts. A focus on writing and speaking skills in the required core courses plus a computer science requirement ensured that all would graduate with marketable skills. Students were required to conduct intensive work in a major field of study in addition to enrolling in one course each in the sciences and in the liberal arts outside of their major area. And thus was created, under Dr. Lander's supervision, a balanced, rigorous academic environment that has persisted through today.

Dr. Lander devoted equal attention to the school's physical environment. He insisted on locating the school in a structure that would "promote academic and Jewish excellence in a personalized environment." This desire translated into the design of an attractive Beis Medrash, spacious libraries, modern classrooms, state-of-the-art laboratories, comfortable dormitories, and cozy dining and lounge areas. Today, the building's glass atrium and many open spaces provide an inviting, open, and airy atmosphere. The seven-acre campus, located in one of New York's most vibrant and attractive Jewish communities, boasts a full-sized soccer field and basketball and tennis courts, all of which host a wide range of intramural athletics. Dr. Lander called upon his brother, Nathan, to assist in coordinating academic policies and overseeing the establishment of the campus.

It perhaps can be said that Bernard Lander placed his highest aspirations into every fiber of the Lander College for Men in its Kew Gardens incarnation. By any conceivable measure, those expectations have been exceeded. The powerful combination of highly skilled faculty with positively motivated students has created a dynamic synergy that not even Lander could have imagined. With classrooms, dormitories, and the Beis Medrash all filled to capacity, the men's school stands as the defining embodiment of Lander's lifelong "pursuit of excellence." It is clearly the flagship component of the Lander Legacy.

There remains, however, one aspect of the Lander Legacy that, as of this writing, remains unfulfilled. Dr. Lander was a strong believer in educational diversity and an adherent of the Solomonic dictate "Educate a child according to his nature." The following episode illustrates Lander's philosophy on this question.

During the 1960s one of Dr. Lander's Forest Hills neighbors asked to speak with him.

"It's my son, Bernie," complained the neighbor. "He's seventeen, and he doesn't want to stay at the yeshiva. He wants to drop out." Lander asked if he could speak with the son, and a meeting was arranged.

After discussing the boy's feelings, Lander concluded that the boy did not have the inclination to sit and apply himself to the long hours of study required to succeed in a standard yeshiva environment. It was clear to Lander that he was not enjoying his studies. In fact, the process was turning him off and turning him away from Judaism. Lander recognized that sending this young man to a major college campus would quickly result in his wholesale abandonment of his Jewish upbringing. Lander looked the lad in the eye and asked him:

"Well, what DO you like to do?" The boy answered without a moment's hesitation:

"I like to take pictures."

"Well, if you enjoy taking pictures, then become a photographer!" Lander advised him. Although the boy's father was surprised and less than thrilled with Dr. Lander's counsel, he respected it and permitted his son to pursue his chosen career choice. Today, the young shutterbug is a respected commercial photographer … and a committed Jewish husband, father, and respected lay leader.

Dr. Lander expounded on the need for educational diversity late in his career when he wrote

> It is abundantly clear that multistrata religious educational programs must be developed if we are to meet the religious needs of our youth. Not everybody has the capacity or the drive to become a *Gadol B'Torah* (a great Torah scholar). Not everybody has the psychological makeup to sit a full day in the Bais Medrash. There is no purpose in increasing the thousands of children at risk through monolithic educational systems that are designed only for the elite. To do so is suicidal for the Jewish community and increasingly devastating for individual families.

While Dr. Lander was able to witness, to a certain extent, the creation of a multistrata, nonmonolithic approach within Touro's family of religious education programs, his dream of expanding this approach to the nonreligious population still waits to be fully realized. Those students, for example, who are seeking a full time, immersive Torah experience, may find it available at Ohr Hachaim, while those who opt to combine a full day of Jewish study with standard college courses in the evening can do so at Touro's Flatbush campus and in Queens. And those male students wishing to engage in serious Torah studies in an integrated environment with high quality academics are able to fulfill that agenda at Lander College for Men. But what about the student who does not possess the background, temperament, or the raw ability to simultaneously pursue a rigorous program in both Torah and academic studies?

As of this writing, Touro is on the road towards offering a less intensive college option. The beginnings of such outreach programs, such as the School for Lifelong Education, are taking shape at Touro branches opened in recent years. This unfinished aspect of the Lander Legacy will undoubtedly be realized, eventually, by those to whom Dr. Lander has passed the torch of his lifelong dream, the dream of a school system serving the entire Jewish American community, where all students, regardless of their orientation, may come and prepare for a successful life while at the same time expanding and enhancing their Torah knowledge and Jewish identity.

CHAPTER TWENTY-ONE

Building the Dream

Death is merely moving from one home to another. The
wise man will spend his main efforts in trying to make
his future home the more beautiful one.
   —*Rabbi Menachem Mendel Morgenstern of Tomashov*
                                   (the Kotzker Rebbe)

T he Reagan-era optimism that characterized the 1980s served
to infuse and ignite the zeitgeist at Touro College. The decade
opened with the establishment of a law school that attained full
accreditation as the decade came to a close. Those years also saw the
founding of Ohr Hachaim, the launching of a Jewish Studies master's
degree program in New York and Israel, and the birth of the School
for Lifelong Education. The law school's quest for full accreditation led
Bernard Lander towards Touro's first instance of property ownership. Up
until then, all of Touro's activities, both academic and administrative,
had been housed in leased premises. The nascent law school was located
in the West 44th Street building for its first two years, but this home
was deemed unsuitable by the New York Bar Association's accreditation
council. The search for new accommodations eventually led Dr. Lander
to a former junior high school building in the Long Island community
of Huntington. The building was purchased in 1982, and as a result, the
Law School was soon granted its provisional accreditation.

Touro's growing biomedical, physical and occupational therapy programs were also housed together with the law school in the Huntington
building, resulting in severe overcrowding. Seizing an opportunity, Dr.
Lander managed to secure a donation of several recently vacated buildings
at the Long Island Development Center in Dix Hills and immediately
transformed it into the campus of the School of Health Sciences. The law
school finally found itself in a proper home and now only lacked for an

adequate endowment fund before it could achieve full accreditation. Dr. Lander's apparent Midas touch in the realm of real estate development once again came to the rescue. He convinced the Touro board to sell the Seminole Tennis Club property it had acquired only three years earlier and proceeded to locate a buyer willing to pay three times Touro's original purchase price. By placing the proceeds into the law school's endowment fund, the Bar Association was assured of the school's long-term financial stability, and as a result, Touro's Jacob D. Fuchsberg Law Center finally received an absolute charter from the New York State Board of Regents in 1990. The law school's endowment fund would serve as a model some fifteen years later for the establishment of Touro's vital overall endowment fund.

Another major real estate transaction carried out by Dr. Lander at this time left Touro College fully poised for major growth in the 1990s. This was the sale of the school's first home at 30 West 44th Street. The transaction was complicated by the fact that, while Touro held title to the property, it had never actually purchased it. The building had been a gift from the United States federal government back in 1971, and the title carried many covenants and encumbrances regarding use of the property. Despite these hamstrings, Dr. Lander was able to interest the University of Pennsylvania in the building and tentatively accepted its offer.

The government restrictions required that any proceeds from the sale of the property be entirely directed into other campus buildings. It was Dr. Lander's plan, therefore, to use the sale proceeds to acquire the vacant real estate directly across the street from Yeshiva of Flatbush in Brooklyn and thereupon erect a five-story, 100,000 square foot facility to house its evening programs. After discovering the total cost of the property and construction, Dr. Lander returned to the negotiating table and explained to the University of Pennsylvania team that the price for the Manhattan building had gone up. He would need additional funding to build the replacement structure required by the government restrictions. After some back and forth, the University of Pennsylvania acquiesced, and the sale was consummated in the summer of 1989.

The ensuing decade was one of unparalleled growth driven by rising enrollment levels, emerging profit centers, and, at its core, the dynamic and driven leadership of Dr. Lander. Once the cash-strapped stepchild of

Jewish higher education, Touro College soon found itself in the enviable position of managing a cash surplus for the first four years of the decade.

After dedicating the new Flatbush facility, Dr. Lander next turned his attention to Touro's other men's and women's divisions. He soon learned that the Sunnyside Campus of the College of Staten Island was to be vacated. A sprawling forty-two-acre campus, with its seven buildings, was an ideal site for the fast-growing men's division. The negotiations did not bear fruit, however, and Dr. Lander's path next took him to the last sizable undeveloped tract of land available in Kew Gardens Hills. There was a good reason that this twelve-acre parcel remained undeveloped. It was a swamp.

Known as "Gutman's Swamp," the property was considered unsuitable for any sort of development under the prevailing wisdom. The landowners at the time had failed in their attempts at construction and now found themselves mired in another sort of swamp known as bankruptcy court. Amazingly, all of this failed to deter Dr. Lander, whose vision for the property included modern classrooms, athletic fields, and dormitories. He called upon several of his engineering contacts from his days as a consultant for the New York State Housing Commission, who explained how land reclamation could be effected at the site. Armed with these assurances, Dr. Lander convinced the Touro Board to authorize substantial funding to acquire the Kew Gardens Hills property. And, as described in the preceding chapter, the site became home to Lander College for Men.

But, as it often does, a shadow was about to fall across the sunny landscape of Touro's rapidly accelerating growth. In early 1991, Sarah Lander was diagnosed with the cancer that would end her life four years hence. While other women might have retreated from the world at such news, Sarah Lander continued her *chesed* (good works) activities as long as she was able. Bernard called upon all his resources among the medical community as he sought out new treatment options for his beloved life's partner. It can never be known, but many believed that his efforts succeeded in extending Sarah's life —a life that ultimately came to an end on January 22, 1995.

The impact of such a loss on Bernard Lander was profound. Returning to his office after the seven-day *shiva* mourning period, the seventy-nine-year old president was observed as being inconsolable and nearly comatose, sitting blankly at his desk, unable to overcome his deep sorrow. There was talk amongst the board members that perhaps the time had come for Bernard Lander to turn over the reins and retire. They were wrong.

Moving beyond his personal grief, not only at the loss of his dear wife, but also at the death of two close friends and associates, Touro Board chairman Max Karl and friend Harold Jacobs, Bernard Lander roared back to life at the conclusion of the *shloshim* thirty-day mourning period. He felt that while his own time might be approaching, he remained in this world for a reason. He still had work to do towards his mission of building Touro College, and these intimations of his own mortality had convinced him he'd better get to it quickly.

Back at the helm of the driving locomotive that was Touro College in the mid-1990s, Dr. Lander encountered some unexpected twists and turns that served to slow down—but not derail—the school's forward progress. The first was a surprise decision by the New York State Dormitory Authority to withhold approval of a planned bond issue. By the mid-1990s, Touro College was sitting on a large accumulated surplus. Rather than employ these funds to fuel its own growth, it made much better financial sense to leave the monies invested and look to borrowed sources of capital. As long as there was a positive spread between interest earned and interest paid, Touro, like many institutions, would rely upon publicly offered bond issues to underwrite its real estate acquisitions. Just as a renter interested in owning his own home merely needs to come up with the down payment, Touro likewise only had to commit a small portion of the purchase price of any acquisition from its own pockets. The building itself would serve as collateral with the interest payments to bondholders coming from the rent savings. In 1994, plans for a major bond issue were initiated through the state Dormitory Authority, which served as underwriter, vouching for the credit worthiness of the bond issuer.

Although Touro's credit ratings were triple-A, the state eventually announced that it would not grant approval for the bond issue. The reason was that word had reached the Dormitory Authority that Touro was to be the target of a broad-based federal government investigation. While the investigation failed to reveal any wrongdoing, the immediate impact was the cancellation of the pending bond issue by the Dormitory Authority.

Just as the shockwaves of this setback were being absorbed, Dr. Lander found himself facing another precarious situation. While Touro could, in the wake of the bond issue collapse, choose to fund its growth from its own surplus coffers, doing so was contingent upon enrollment levels at the very least remaining constant. However, this is not what happened. By 1994 the immigration levels of Jews from the former Soviet Union began to level off and then dramatically decline. The revenue surplus in which Touro had basked since the beginning of the decade was now starting to shrivel.

While the Board did slow down the pace of new construction during the mid-90s because of these factors, the prevailing cash crunch did not seem to deter Dr. Lander's impassioned enthusiasm for expanding the physical presence of Touro College. Persuading the Board to authorize major expenditures in 1997, Lander used the funds to purchase an expansive building in Bayshore, along Long Island's south shore, to house the rapidly growing School of Health Sciences. The following year, Lander heard of a parcel available in the neighboring community of Central Islip that was adjacent to a federal and state courthouse complex. Even though funds were not available at the time to build on the land, Lander convinced the board to approve the purchase as the future site of the Fuchsberg School of Law.

This frenetic pace of property acquisition did not mean that Bernard Lander was oblivious to the financial realities that Touro was facing. What it did mean, however, was that instead of retreating from these challenges, Lander opted to confront them head on.

At a meeting of Touro's trustees at the time, Dr. Lander projected that tuition revenue from the School of General Studies and the New Americans division would continue their downward direction. He advocated a course correction that would shift the school's focus toward proven profit centers, such as Touro's professional schools in health, education, and business. Following his lead, Touro's first medical school began operations in 1997 in California. It was at the same time that Touro was authorized to begin granting MBA degrees. Perhaps the most innovative and controversial initiative in this push was towards a newly emerging educational area that was, at that point, in its infancy: Distance Learning.

Bernard Lander's interest in using technology to expand a school's educational scope dated back to Touro's involvement with The Jewish People's University of the Air. That 1980s program, which conducted

Jewish Studies classes via National Public Radio broadcasts and distributed cassette tapes of its lectures, had been well received as a first tentative venture into the world of distance learning. The advent of the Internet, coupled with satellite technology, introduced bold new possibilities for expanding the teaching environment beyond Touro's physical classroom walls. Dr. Lander's bounding enthusiasm—highly surprising for a man in his eighties—for new high tech solutions, hardly met with universal approval among Touro's trustees and administrators. In fact, it was not until after Dr. Lander met Dr. Yoram Neumann, an Israeli educator with a strong background in American distance learning, that Lander was able to provide a concrete demonstration of his vision to the board.

Neumann, at Lander's behest, displayed the distance learning approaches he had developed at a California university to the trustees while, at the same time, pointing out their shortcomings.

"What is needed to make this work," Neumann explained, "is a semi-autonomous international distance learning university that is not hampered by the constraints of a bricks and mortar school."

Dr. Lander became inspired by Neumann's concept of an online university that "knew no bounds" and swung into action. He invited Neumann to meet with him and board chair Mark Hasten in order to lay out the start-up costs needed to launch the Internet school.

In 1998, Dr. Lander petitioned the board to allocate the startup capital that Dr. Neumann needed. By this time, Touro's financial position had become stronger due primarily to the dynamic partnership of Dr. Lander and Mark Hasten. Over the prior six years, Touro had acquired property, purchased without financing and a minimal number of gifts, that boasted a significant market value. Despite strongly voiced misgivings, the board was swayed by Lander's impassioned case and authorized the establishment of Touro University International. Licensure was applied for in California and soon granted.

Once the Internet school was up and running, Dr. Lander offered Dr. Neumann a suggestion based upon Lander's own experiences with the Jewish University of the Air. He recalled how the cassette tapes he had produced of classroom lectures were very popular with military personnel back in the 1980s. Neumann agreed to launch a military initiative that proved highly successful. As was the case thirty years earlier, soldiers move frequently and are unable to commit to a structured campus environment. At the same time they are encouraged by the military to bolster their education in order to qualify for promotion and greater benefits. Dr. Neumann was able to forge a highly successful partnership with the U.S. Army that saw it extensively promote Touro University International among the enlisted men in uniform and, more importantly, agree to underwrite a large portion of each soldier's tuition payments.

An even more salient example of Dr. Lander's eagerness to pursue grand designs in building Touro was the partial acquisition of the Mare Island facility near Vallejo, north of San Francisco. The U.S. government had established the facility under President Abraham Lincoln in order to establish a shipyard on the three-mile strip of land located in San Pablo Bay. More than 500 ships, including seventeen nuclear submarines, were built at the Mare Island Naval Shipyard. In 1999, when Dr. Lander learned from the dean of the Touro medical school that the Navy was about to decommission its Mare Island facility and donate the property to the City of Vallejo, he immediately seized upon the opportunity of acquiring a portion of it as the future home for the School of Osteopathy.

The property's forty-four acres would provide ample space, but it carried numerous complicating factors. For example, the facility included several architecturally significant buildings that were protected under historic preservation statutes, including a chapel built in 1901 containing a collection of twenty-nine Tiffany stained-glass windows, considered one of the finest collections in the world. Dr. Lander dealt with these wrinkles by appealing to the Vallejo civic leadership. He wrote to Mayor Gloria Exline:

> We seek to move our medical school to Mare Island and establish a full educational campus centered in the old naval cryptographic school. The city of Vallejo will be severely affected by the loss of 9,000 jobs when the naval base closes. Allowing us to open our medical school at the site would serve to greatly minimize that impact.

Exline embraced the concept and referred Dr. Lander to the Lennar Corporation, a real estate firm to whom Vallejo had turned over the Mare

Island property for the purpose of development. The city then issued a bond issue to finance the renovations. Lennar representatives informed Dr. Lander that they would part with the parcel in which he was interested for a sizeable sum.

On the advice of Mark Hasten, Touro opted to lease, rather than purchase the space needed to house its medical school. The ten-year lease carried an option that entitled Touro to buy the parcel "at market price" to be negotiated at the time. The plans were drawn up, and it became clear that a good deal of capital was required in order to finance the extensive renovations that would see the transformation of a naval base into a medical school—without demolishing a single historical treasure on the site. Touro accepted the indebtedness stipulated in the lease agreement as well as the cost of the renovations and set to work.

Another stroke of good fortune would bless this project in the years that lay ahead. At the conclusion of the ten-year term, Touro discovered that the property owner, the Lennar Corporation, was operating under Chapter 11 bankruptcy protection. Instead of Lennar, Mark Hasten found himself negotiating the sale of the property with the court-appointed receiver. He was able to negotiate a purchase price that proved to be an unbelievable bargain.

If the California obligations did not stretch Touro's credit-worthiness to the limit, a parallel financing deal through New York City surely would do so. The New York money was needed for the construction of the new Kew Gardens Hills campus and was being negotiated over the summer of 1999. With major funding initiatives going on simultaneously on both coasts, Touro suddenly found itself in a cash crunch. Summer's end—after several months of salaries being paid out and no tuition revenue coming in—is typically the tightest time of year for cash flow at educational institutions. It was at this juncture that both municipalities were evaluating Touro's ability to repay the monies raised by their respective bond issues. The situation was worrisome since any sign of financial weakness could torpedo not merely one, but both pending projects.

As a precaution, Dr. Lander brought in Touro's CFO, Mel Ness, to assemble realistic cash flow projections for the coming years based on current trends. The projections illustrated that Touro's financial position, while appearing temporarily tenuous, was actually quite strong and due to get stronger over time. The bonds were issued, and both the construction of the Lander College for Men and the Mare Island renovations were able to proceed on track.

The bond approvals, however, did not help alleviate Touro's cash crisis. The money raised could only be used for the specific projects they were intended to finance. Salaries and other expenses still had to be paid at a time when enrollment in Touro's programs aimed at minority and ethnic populations hit a ten-year low. At the same time the medical school was bleeding money, and the Internet school was under construction and yet to take in the first dollar. In an unprecedented move, Touro was reluctantly forced to delay monthly salaries during that tightly stretched summer of 1999. In addition to creating a severe hardship for its faculty and staff, this action placed Touro's accreditation from Middle States into jeopardy. If another pay cycle were to be delayed, Touro would be stripped of its ability to issue credible degrees.

The distasteful chore of borrowing from friends was left to Dr. Lander who convinced several trustees to issue short-term loans that would tide things over until revenues returned in the fall. Not surprisingly, these personal loans came with strings attached. Dr. Lander was required to agree to a full audit, with a focus on the salaries of the administrative staff. Dr. Jay Sexter, former president of Mercy College, was retained by the board and charged with the duty of bringing Touro's fiscal house into order. This prudent move helped to calm the jitters that any of Touro's lenders may have been experiencing after learning about Touro's inability to make its payroll.

Dr. Sexter was brought in to do what Bernard Lander could not bring himself to do and that was to fire an employee who was underperforming or whose job was no longer vital. Whenever the subject of laying off a member of Touro's administrative staff was broached, Dr. Lander's first question was "What will happen to his family?" It was this compassion to a fault that was perhaps Dr. Lander's greatest shortcoming as an administrator. He simply could not sacrifice a loyal employee at the altar of fiscal responsibility. But Dr. Sexter could. Within a few months, Sexter succeeded in saving Touro sizeable expenditures per year in administrative salaries by cutting back on nonessential staff. The cuts were carried out with minimal adverse effects upon the school's ongoing operations.

After reining in Touro's runaway expenses, Sexter next turned his attention to the various far-flung projects that Dr. Lander had underway. Perhaps the most painful of the ensuing cutbacks arrived when the board heeded Sexter's advice and cancelled Dr. Lander's plans to construct a new Touro campus in central Jerusalem. Lander was reluctantly forced to pull out of a joint venture with Yeshurun Synagogue, which went on to eventually erect an extraordinary edifice designed by noted Israeli architect, Ada Karmi-Melamede.

The new century brought new hope and a renewed vigor to Touro as the course corrections carried out by Dr. Sexter had their desired effect. The Internet school was launched and by 2001 had grown to 750 students. The College of Osteopathic Medicine and the College of Pharmacy were, by the same year, fully functional at the Mare Island facility and were both generating more than enough revenue to cover their operating costs. Enrollment levels at Touro's other schools began a meteoric rise during this period as well. The Graduate School of Education, for example, under the dynamic and visionary leadership of Dr. Anthony Polemeni, currently Vice-President of the Division of Graduate Studies, saw enrollment levels jump from a relative handful in 2001 to more than 6,000 students on two coasts by the end of the decade.

Touro's phenomenal growth was fueled during those years by the opening of a new medical school campus in Nevada, plus new schools of pharmacy, education, and health sciences in California, as well as an explosion in the enrollment at Touro University International (the Internet school) that reached nearly 8,000 students by 2007. Touro's overall enrollment level, which stood at 8,500 students at the beginning of the decade, rose to nearly 25,000. Dr. Lander was greatly heartened by the return of cash surpluses and vowed to use the funds to enhance the academic excellence of the Touro faculty. This promise is being kept today. Touro has succeeded, in recent years, in recruiting some of the finest academics in their respective fields by aggressively offering highly attractive salary and benefit packages.

In the decade before his death, Dr. Lander was blessed with a gift that few men are privileged to receive. He had lived long enough to witness his life's vision not only emerge, but to mature adequately and gain a level of stability that would guarantee the ongoing fulfillment of his dream for generations to come. While he may have wished to leave behind a school with a broader global footprint, he was nevertheless heartened by the momentum of growth during the century's first decade during which Touro launched undergraduate programs in Los Angeles, South Florida, and Paris, among others.

The rampant real estate dealing that characterized the 1990s also spilled over into the 2000s. In 2002, a 40 percent portion of the Kew Gardens Hills property was sold to a developer, turning a profit over what Touro paid for the entire parcel in 1993. Dr. Lander obtained board approval to direct these profits towards establishing Touro's first meaningful endowment fund, a fund that continued to grow as one successful real estate transaction followed another.

It was due to the combined real estate savvy of Dr. Lander and board chairman Mark Hasten that the new campus for the Lander College for Women arose in Manhattan, providing greatly enhanced space essentially at no cost to the school.

In 2002, Dr. Hasten was alerted to the availability of an attractive vacant property on New York's swanky Upper West Side. The lot had been the site of a button factory at 60th Street near Tenth Avenue. Dr. Hasten liked what he saw and felt it would make a fantastic new home for Touro's women's college. With the participation of another board member, Hasten put up the $250,000 needed to secure an option on the property. He shrewdly determined that if the building could be granted a zoning variance that would bestow full air rights to the owner, its value would be substantially enhanced. Hasten and a team of real estate attorneys set to work, and the variance was granted. Touro exercised the option and purchased the property for a sum that was partially funded through the sale of the school's former home on Lexington Avenue. The site was soon sold to a residential real estate developer with the stipulation that 44,000 square feet of any building they would construct at the site be given to Touro for use as a school for women. In 2006, the builder erected a gleaming fourteen-story edifice containing luxury high-rise condominiums—except for the first four floors that became home to the newly named Lander College for Women/The Anna Ruth and Mark Hasten School.

Mark Hasten converted the $250,000 sum gifted to the school for use as a down payment into the first installment of a $10 million donation from the Hasten family. This landmark gift is the largest every received in Touro's history.

The following year witnessed the payoff on the gamble Dr. Lander had taken when acquiring the Central Islip, Long Island property. The dramatic new 185,000 square foot law school building was completed with funds partially acquired through the first major fundraising campaign in Touro's history. Primarily because of Dr. Lander's long-standing aversion to fundraising and his principled belief that a school should be self-sustaining, Touro had never before embarked on a major campaign of this sort. Under the capable leadership of Dean Howard Glickstein, the campaign reached out successfully to alumni and to Long Island businesses, whose contributions earned them naming rights to various campus components in the magnificent new facility that today sits adjacent to several New York state and federal court buildings.

Perhaps the most ambitious example of the Lander/Hasten real estate juggernaut is Touro College's Nevada campus. Working with Jay Sexter, the duo sought to find a suitable home for its recently chartered Nevada medical school. Mark Hasten identified two newly constructed adjacent buildings, with a combined size of 310,000 square feet, situated on a 14-acre plot in the Las Vegas suburb of Henderson. The buildings had originally been built for warehouse space and contained characteristically high ceilings. Mark Hasten hit upon the idea of partitioning the space in the smaller of the two buildings into two separate floors. That way one building could be used for the medical school and the other leased out for warehouse storage. The rental income would provide sufficient cash flow to offset the interest payable on the note issued by G.E. Financial to Touro and used to purchase the entire property.

Working closely with local officials who were enthusiastic about the prestige and employment opportunities that Touro's presence would bring to their community, Touro was granted permission to convert the space that, at the end of the day, contained a total of 560,000 square feet in both buildings. The note was approved with much less difficulty than in prior years due to Touro's outstanding track record that had, by this time, earned the school a triple-A credit rating.

Dr. Lander never wavered in his concern about delivering educational opportunities to underserved areas and segments of society. It was this characteristic that provided the impetus behind his successful establishment of a Touro medical school and school of pharmacy at 125th Street in the Harlem section of Manhattan. The school, modeled after the Schools of Osteopathy and Pharmacy in Nevada and California, was built from scratch and held its first commencement exercises in 2011 for a graduating class of 122 newly minted physicians.

The term that perhaps best sums up the nature of Bernard Lander's character is that of a "realistic dreamer." Drawn from Ben-Gurion's well-known comment, "To be a realist in Israel it is necessary to believe in miracles," this prevailing mindset, which had for decades caused Touro to "rely upon a miracle" to meet its financial requirements, had now finally been left behind. This term had gained a special cachet among members of the Touro administration. The last name of the school's CFO, Mel Ness, is the Hebrew word for "miracle." So relying upon a "Ness" to save the school in times of financial crisis became an all-too-accurate double entendre.

Moving beyond such reliance, Touro had matured by the first decade of the twenty-first century into a formidable and steadfast center of higher learning, ready to take its place among the nation's foremost colleges and universities under the dynamic leadership of Touro's current president, Dr. Alan Kadish. Central to this new era of stability was the establishment of Touro's first meaningful endowment fund. The fund was established, among its other purposes, as a repository for permanent gifts, as a named beneficiary of insurance trusts, and as a mechanism for endowing chairs and professorships. The monies accumulated and placed into trust are today providing Touro with the financial strength needed to weather economic downturns, tuition revenue declines, and other unforeseeable difficult circumstances. Surplus funds generated by Touro's operational revenues that exceed its expenses are now regularly channeled into the endowment fund.

As the new endowment fund was being launched in 2005, Dr. Lander understood that to do so in an effective and meaningful way would require a substantial initial deposit. The most expedient way of generating that type of capital was through the sale of an asset and hence, the board began to consider the offers it had been receiving for one of Touro's newly developed and most rapidly growing divisions.

The fact was that Touro's distance-learning methods simply worked. Steadily increasing numbers of students each year were completing their assignments, participating in classes, and scoring well on exams as they deployed their own computers and teleconferencing satellite technology from their homes. By the 2003–04 academic year, Touro's online university generated considerable profits, and Dr. Neumann projected that if growth trends continued, profits would triple by the end of the decade. It was not an easy decision to place such a high potential asset on the auction block, but Dr. Lander and the board believed that doing so in order to establish a true endowment fund was the finest act they could perform in behalf of Touro's long-term future.

The sale was also complicated by questions involving state licensing and accreditation issues and, as a result, it took more than two years to close the deal. In October 2007, Touro University International, after having attracted six serious offers, was sold for a substantial sum, all of which was channeled directly into the endowment fund. This action immediately placed Touro among the top 300 schools in America in terms of assets held in reserve.

While the sale of Touro's successful online division was a bittersweet experience for Dr. Lander, he could not help but feel that his faith in the potential of distance learning had been vindicated. The numbers bore this out. The eventual sale of the Internet school had returned a 150-fold return on investment in less than eight years.

Such positive developments, which Dr. Lander hoped would serve to burnish Touro's reputation and academic standing, were sadly offset during this period by further public relations bombshells. In July of 2007 a New York City grand jury indicted ten people for their involvement in a scheme to create and sell fraudulent student transcripts in what was described in the press as a "Grades for Cash" scheme. Evidence showed that two Touro employees, over the course of a three month period in early 2007, made changes to student transcripts—for a fixed fee—by accessing the Touro computer server using their personal computers from home. District Attorney Robert Morgenthau's office reported how one student saw his overall grade point average rise from 1.23 to 3.63 overnight. His falsified transcript showed that he had received As and Bs in all five of his fall 2006 semester courses when, in fact, he had failed four of them.

Touro was once again rocked by this scandal as it mushroomed into prominence in the New York media. The fact that the crimes were discovered by an alert supervisor in Touro's Office of the Registrar, investigated by administrators, and then reported by Touro to the police, failed to mitigate the wave of negative publicity. Adding to the furor were unproven allegations that the "grades for cash" practice had been going on for four years prior to discovery. In the wake of the indictments, the New York State Department of Education, in a move intended to protect the public from unqualified individuals, conducted an extensive review of professional licenses that may have been based on fraudulently obtained credentials from Touro College. To Touro's credit, no fraudulently obtained licenses were found. Also, since it was Touro itself that discovered and promptly reported the crimes being perpetrated by its staff members, the school was neither exposed to decertification by Middle States, nor was Touro itself ever accused of any wrongdoing in the case by District Attorney Morgenthau, who later praised Touro's efforts.

The projects that Bernard Lander initiated during the final decade of his life, and whose development remain pending as of this writing, have a common touchstone attribute. They are all intended to enhance and expand Touro's permanent endowment fund. An excellent example is the ambitious plan put into motion for the 200 undeveloped acres adjacent to Touro University's 44 acre Mare Island campus in Vallejo. Alerted in 2006 to the fact that the plans for developing the north end of Mare Island were headed nowhere (due to Lennar Development having fallen into bankruptcy), Dr. Lander turned this bit of bad news into yet another vehicle of opportunity. Working closely with Mark Hasten, Dr. Lander rushed into the breach with far-reaching plans to erect a combined educational, residential, commercial, medical, and biotech facility on the sprawling tract to the north of Touro's current campus. In January 2007, Touro was granted exclusive rights to develop just such a project.

The plans called for the creation of a university village, using a similar community in nearby Berkeley as a template. The village would encompass student and faculty housing as well as an 80,000 square foot academic center. Positioned in the heart of the Bay Area's biotech corridor, plans for the North Mare Island project also laid out a 500,000 square foot office park that would lease space to nearby universities and biotech companies.

These ambitious plans that were to create the University Village and Health Science Research Campus at Mare Island carried a hefty price tag, a considerable portion of which was to be devoted to the acquisition of one of America's first heavy ion particle therapy cancer treatment centers. Dr. Lander's devotion to this project was evident in the final years of his life. He would often spur on the group working on the North Mare Island Research and Therapeutic center project with the message: "Hurry up. People are dying."

Sadly, because of the enormous costs involved and due to the financial meltdown that began in 2008, the board elected not to proceed with the project, and this most ambitious example of Bernard Lander's vision was destined not to become a part of the Lander Legacy.

Another large land parcel—252 acres this time—was acquired by Touro in 2006 in the Orange County town of Warwick, New York. Situated along scenic Blue Lake, next to Waywayanda State Park, the property was envisioned by Dr. Lander as the perfect spot for a new *kollel* community. It was intended to include a 60,000 square foot environmental studies campus along with single-family homes to house students and faculty. Mark Hasten played a leading role, both in acquiring the property, which was purchased in 2008, and also in the planning and development of what was to be Touro's Warwick campus. In 2010, the board decided that, given the prevailing precarious real estate market, it would be best to forego the project and place the property up for sale. It was sold the following year for a handsome profit and the money was earmarked to provide funds for a future Warwick-like endeavor.

Finally, in an acquisition that may be viewed as the realization of Dr. Lander's most ambitious and far-reaching dream, Touro succeeded during the summer of 2010 in merging with a medical school that will allow it to grant Medical Doctorate (M.D.) degrees. The New York Medical College, located in the hamlet of Valhalla, in Westchester County, New York, and owned by the Catholic Archdiocese of New York, has been training future physicians since before the American Civil War. As the largest medical school in the nation not affiliated with a major university, NYMC enjoyed a long tradition of excellence and was considered one of the most venerated medical schools in the United States. The purchase of NYMC was the culmination of a lengthy global effort spearheaded by Dr. Lander. The paperwork that finally culminated in the sale was being hammered out in late 2009 as Dr. Lander lay in his hospital bed during the final months of his life. During those moments when he was able to communicate, his first question was invariably "Did we close on the medical school yet?" The agreement was signed shortly before Dr. Lander's death in February, 2010. Although it required more than a year of hard work, Dr. Kadish completed the affiliation in May 2012 and New York Medical College became part of the Touro College and University System.

Yet even this major milestone in the saga of Touro's growth was not to be reached without its share of controversy. In an action that was precisely the type of student unrest that led to the founding of Touro College in the early 1970s, a vocal group of NYMC students initiated a protest against the proposed acquisition. The students cited concerns about the value of their medical degrees once they began being issued by a school whose officials had been accused of selling grades for cash. The student group launched an email campaign directed at the campus community and local media outlets in Valhalla in which they outlined their strong opposition to the negotiations that were underway between Touro and NYMC. "The most important of concerns revolve around Touro's current reputation and circulating rumors," said a fourth-year medical student and president of the school's Student Senate.

Not all students were opposed to the move, however. Many recognized that acquisition would strengthen the school's tenuous financial position and result in a more fiscally sound institution. One student, quoted in the media coverage, stated, "I'm in favor of the merger with Touro. There is a silent contingent that accepts the partnership as a financial necessity. Not all NYMC students are against the merger." Faculty, staff and board members also raised concerns. However, after Touro's mission and Dr. Lander's legacy were explained by Drs. Hasten and Kadish to the NYMC community, the majority embraced Touro's mission and ethos and supported the acquisition.

Touro officials expect more extensive benefits to emerge beyond mere financial stability. Bringing NYMS into the Touro family will enable the medical school to embrace many of the innovations in health education that Touro has pioneered. Among them is a technique inspired by one of Maimonides' teachings found in his medical treatise, *The Preservation of Youth*: "The physician should have both technical knowledge as well as an understanding of the patient's personality." Touro has succeeded in observing this advice through the practice of interdisciplinary collaboration—joint medical and allied health training—that will, when deployed at NYMS, educate both doctors and nurses at the same facility and thereby cultivate a caring atmosphere and improved patient outcomes.

The development of the Valhalla medical school acquisition during those years, coupled with Touro's ever-expanding presence in the associated health fields—it was educating more physician assistants than any school in America—greatly influenced the board as it sought to recruit a successor to Dr. Lander who would serve as Touro's next CEO. That search led to Dr. Alan H. Kadish.

The Touro Board could not have selected a more highly qualified president than Dr. Kadish, a renowned physician and educator who joined the Touro administration in 2009 as senior provost and chief operating officer. Prior to joining Touro, Dr. Kadish enjoyed a long association with Northwestern University's Feinberg School of Medicine in Evanston, Illinois, where he rose to the position of Associate Chief of Cardiology and Director of Clinical Trials at the Bluhm Cardiovascular Institute, the primary teaching affiliate for the Feinberg School. A dedicated clinical researcher and prolific writer, Dr. Kadish is the author of more than 250 peer-reviewed articles in the field of cardiology. Assuming the titles of CEO and President upon Dr. Lander's death in February 2010, cardiologist Kadish today serves as the "lev tov," or "good heart" of Touro College.

Working closely together with Dr. Kadish in guiding the future course of Touro is Rabbi Doniel Lander (see chapters 11 and 20), who has been appointed Chancellor of Touro College while continuing to serve as Rosh ha-Yeshiva of Yeshivas Ohr Hachaim, Mesivta Yesodei Yeshurun, and Mesivta Yesodei Yisroel. A brilliant Talmudic scholar and renowned rosh yeshiva who has masterfully trained a new generation of young rabbis and scholars, Rabbi Lander also plays a vital role in fortifying and shaping the mission and vision of Touro. As a highly respected *mara d'atra* (rabbinic authority), distinguished leader, and acclaimed educator, Rabbi Lander is uniquely qualified to perpetuate and further his father's legacy. Touro College and University System enjoys the attention and dedication of a chancellor and president united in strengthening a remarkable citadel of higher education in service to the Jewish people and humanity.

The stunning saga of growth chronicled in this chapter represents only a portion of the many varied activities and acquisitions in which Touro has been involved in recent years. While Dr. Lander, during the final decade of his life, was a "hands-on" manager of all of the school's far-flung activities, it was these projects in which he had the greatest level of personal involvement and spiritual investment. Slowed by age and severe vision impairment, Dr. Lander never suffered any diminution of his mental capabilities. More importantly, the passion that burned in his heart for the school he founded—and for the future of the Jewish people—never flickered or lost any of its extraordinary ferocity.

Indeed, it is Dr. Lander's phenomenal lifetime accomplishments on behalf of the physical and spiritual welfare of the Jewish people and the perpetuation and enhancement of Torah scholarship that served—in his own mind and heart—as the crowning glory of his legacy. The diverse institutions that comprise the Touro College and University System successfully meet the educational needs of students of multiple faiths, cultures, nationalities, and socio-economic backgrounds. Yet, at the forefront of Dr. Lander's consciousness and at the core of his soul, lay his intense concern for meeting the broad range of needs, from financial to spiritual, of *acheinu bnei Yisrael*—his fellow Jews.

Many successful men and women leave behind a legacy of achievement that may be measured in the size of their personal estates. Bernard Lander's legacy may certainly be viewed in this way by considering the current asset position of the college he founded or the total square footage of the facilities discussed in this chapter. But to do so would be missing the point. Instead, the Lander Legacy must be evaluated by how the man's lifework succeeded in perpetuating the ongoing welfare of the Jewish people and society in general. Secondly, one must consider the sustainability of the structures left in place that will serve to perpetuate the work accomplished during Dr. Lander's lifetime. On both counts—the establishing and the enduring—the Lander Legacy must be regarded as a remarkable and singular success.

CHAPTER TWENTY-TWO

Recollections and Respects (Epilogue)

A Jew needs roots; he must be deeply rooted in the experience and traditions of the past. The past for the Jew is always alive and relevant. It's that past that animates the present and inspires our future.

—*Rabbi Dr. Bernard Lander*

O n February 8, 2010 (25 Sh'vat 5770), Rabbi Dr. Bernard (Dov Berish) Lander, age ninety-four, passed away, surrounded by his loving family. And with the unyielding finality of this ordinary obituary statement, the singular saga of one of the most extraordinary Jewish leaders of our age came to a close. The narrative of Bernard Lander's life, as recounted in the chapters of this book, chronicles a journey of unparalleled accomplishment, single-minded determination, and deep piety and devotion to the welfare of *Klal Yisrael*. Yet, it requires more than a catalogue of events to gain a true understanding of a person's life.

In this, the final chapter, the reader will discover selected recollections, episodes, and incidents drawn from the rich panorama of Dr. Lander's life as articulated by those friends, family and colleagues who knew him and shared some of the more private moments of his life. It is hoped that through exposure to these more intimate glimpses, the reader will gain a fuller and more fulfilling understanding of the life of Bernard Lander.

The following passages are drawn from a variety of sources, including publications, personal interviews and eulogies delivered at the time of Dr. Lander's death. Many are excerpted from the outstanding book *Words of Inspiration—Divrei Hesped* (Touro College Press, 2011) edited by Dr. Michael A. Shmidman, Dean and Professor of Jewish History at Touro Graduate School of Jewish Studies. In this volume,

Dr. Shmidman has collected many of the emotional and eloquent eulogies and tributes delivered by Dr. Lander's family and colleagues at the time of his passing.

from an article by David Lichtenstein, in the *Jewish Star*. Published on February 27, 2010:

A year or so later Dr. Lander asked me to come up to his offices again. While we were talking a woman came into the office. She had previously been a member of the faculty but had resigned to fight cancer. "How are you doing?" He stood up and spoke to her in a loving and effusive manner; they spoke for several minutes.

"Dr. Lander, I know you've been carrying my insurance for the last year. Can you please keep paying for my medical?" she importuned. "I can't afford to lose it."

"Of course we'll keep it, as long as you need it," he said.

"Dr. Lander," the woman began to weep, "I'm so scared. I still have a daughter to marry off ..." The woman was shaking.

Dr. Lander said to her, "We must have faith. G-d in heaven is merciful. Many times in the past I thought that for Touro the end was near; but with faith, we persevered."

He began telling her about miracles he'd witnessed.

"When I began the school it was against all odds," he said. "All I had was a dream. Over a period of three years I was approved by New York State to open a college. It was against all odds. We had no funds. I had no Board of Trustees. I painstakingly put together a wonderful Board of Trustees. New York State Attorney General Louis Lefkowitz was on it. United States Senator Jacob Javits, State Comptroller Arthur Levitt, Mayor Abraham Beame, were some of the members on the board. This board was going to be my entryway to allow me to create what had been my dream, a Jewish college. The chairman of the board, a gentleman by the name of Eugene Hollander, a person with business acumen and leadership qualities who was also an extremely wealthy man, who had made his money in the nursing home industry." Lander went on and described the details of the 1974 nursing home scandal.

"I had spent the last four years building something that evaporated in front of my eyes. It would take me over five years to recover from this.

During that year of the nursing home scandal, the entire school's survival was at stake. But I had faith, and G-d helped, and look where we are today."

"Forward," he said. "We must march forward."

He continued telling stories where faith in G-d and persistence had guided him through. The woman listened quietly and then she sobbed, "I have faith, I just am fearful for my daughter." Dr. Lander began crying too. I sat there as they wept quietly together.

The last time I saw Dr. Lander was four weeks ago at Cornell Hospital. He lay in bed hooked up to an assortment of machines. Touro was about to have a board call to decide on a new undertaking, a new medical school. He insisted on chairing the call from his hospital room. His daughter Hannah and longtime aide Dr. Fishbane helped him out of bed and sat him in a chair.

The call lasted for around an hour. The entire board was on the call vigorously debating the pros and cons of proceeding with the new school. Before it came to a vote Dr. Lander raised his hand to signal to have his oxygen mask lifted. He wanted to say something. He leaned forward into the speakerphone. "Forward," he said. "We m ust march forward. Onward. Forever onward."

from an article, "Rabbi Dr. Bernard Lander Zt"l: Three Scenes," by Rabbi Simcha Weinberg, published in the February 9th, 2010 issue of *Reflections & Observations*:

I just returned from the funeral of Rabbi Dr. Bernard Lander. I share one of three memorable scenes of our interaction:

Scene I. (April 1984) Four Clergymen Learn About Teshuva: A priest, minister and imam—no, this is not a joke—joined me for the drive from Comstock New York to the Homowack in the Catskills for the New York State Department of Corrections Chaplains' Conference. One of the clergymen immediately fell into a drunken sleep as we began the long drive in a snowstorm. We were not friends and did not have anything to say to each other, so I turned on my tape deck. Dr. Lander was speaking about Teshuva—Repentance. He based his talk on Simon Wiesenthal's *The Sunflower*.

Dr. Lander was a spectacular speaker, and as he told the story about the concentration camp inmate summoned to absolve a dying

German soldier of his murderous sins, he held us all in the palm of his hand.

Could the inmate forgive the soldier for murdering babies? Did he have the right?

Somehow, the drunken passenger awoke and insisted that we start the tape from the beginning, which we did. No one in the car said a word as we listened to Dr. Lander speak of repentance and forgiveness, an issue with which we all struggled on a daily basis as we counseled convicted murderers, serial killers, rapists, and every imaginable type of violent criminal.

The tape finished, and the imam said, "Play it again." A priest, minister, imam, and yours truly, listened together to a rabbi's Teshuva lecture again, and then, yet again.

The imam, priest, and minister tried to convince the Albany official in charge of the conference to have a special session so that everyone could hear Dr. Lander. It didn't happen. When we returned to Comstock we immediately demanded an appointment with the superintendent to advocate that each of the corrections officers should have to listen to Dr. Lander's lecture. The "sup" laughed us out of his office.

by Dr. Simcha Fishbane,
Executive Assistant to the President and Associate Professor of Judaic Studies at Touro College:

How many times after 11 pm at night did I get a phone call from Dr. Lander exclaiming, "I did not hear from my brother; I cannot reach my daughter; please call this or that person to see where they are, drive to Manhattan and look for them." I would try to explain to him that they are grown adults, but he would not take no for an answer. By the time I drove to his home, they usually had called, and everything was fine.

Shortly after Dr. Lander took ill, we were visiting a doctor together. He completed his examination. The natural chain of events would be "So doctor, how am I?" Instead, Dr. Lander turned to the doctor and asked: "Maybe you can help with my daughter. She needs this type of doctor."

Every morning, no matter what, I would be in the house at about 8 AM to pick him up to go to work. My wife daily, until she gave up, would ask me when I was returning home. I only could answer "I don't know!"

Although Dr. Lander had a schedule book with appointments it meant nothing; every day was a new adventure. Suddenly he had to meet this Rav or see some new property or visit a board member or we simply could not leave until an anticipated phone call was received.

The only question in the morning was do we need a black hat or not. He had tremendous respect for the people he would see. If it was a meeting with a rosh yeshiva or an orthodox wedding—then he would go only with a black hat. If we would visit Ohr Hachaim—only a black hat. And when he visited the gedolim and rebbes they would stand up for him and most often kiss him and walk him out after the meeting. "Look," he would say, "look how much they love me." He was a rebbe in his own accord. I would say to him: "Why are you so surprised when they do this to you? You are one of the major Jewish leaders in the world."

"What's new" was a favorite expression of Dr. Lander. That did not mean "How are you?" or what is new in Touro or in the world. It meant: "What is new in Israel?" He called people in Israel to get a report. He needed the newspaper to be read to him just as much as he needed his morning coffee. First and foremost: what was new in Israel? And how he looked forward to his visits to Israel. To see him there was an experience, like a rebbe holding court. From all walks of life they would stream to the hotel and wait in line for his advice. He loved Eretz Yisroel; it was part of his conscious being.

After the attack on 9/11 in New York, Manhattan was closed down. To get out, and especially into Manhattan not by public transportation, was almost impossible. That did not stop Dr. Lander from traveling to his office every day. He would say to me: "Tell them that I am a university president, and we'll get through the blockades!"

"Dr. Lander," I would say, "this will not make a difference to the guards and police." But it did. We did get to Manhattan every single day.

Even during his last days when asked how he was, what became his almost comical answer, was "Better." He suffered tremendously. He could not see, his hearing was poor. He could not stand, could not eat, and most of all could not really speak, yet he did not complain. "How are you?" the doctors would ask and the answer always was "Better!"

by Rabbi Menachem Genack,
Rabbinic Administrator and CEO of the Orthodox Union's Kashrut Division:

Senior Vice President Rabbi Dr. Simcha Katz of the Orthodox Union … tells how he was once with Dr. Lander on a cruise to Alaska. At one point, the ship passed Sitka, an Alaskan city accessible only by air or sea.

Dr. Katz turned to Dr. Lander: "I don't see a Touro College here," he said.

"Not yet," Dr. Lander replied.

by Dr. Mark Hasten,
Chairman, Touro College Board of Trustees:

Once, among many episodes with Dr. Lander on a daily basis, we were together in Israel. He said, "I can make shalom between the Arabs and Israelis." I said, "Reb Berish, how can you make peace?"

"Just introduce me to Arik Sharon," who was, at that time, the Minister of Agriculture. I arranged the meeting that took place in the Knesset, and Dr. Lander made a proposal:

"I will build a school on the border between Jordan and Israel. A school of agriculture." I almost fell off my chair!

Speaking in the 1960s, Dr. Lander proclaimed publicly: "Today's colleges and universities are a crisis area for Jewish survival. They are the crematoria of American Jewish life!" What type of man says such things?

What sort of man wakes up one morning, at age fifty-three, and tells his wife that he is quitting his prestigious position as the Dean of Graduate Jewish Studies at Yeshiva University and going off to found a new college? What manner of man walks along the New Jersey shore with his best friend and has the chutzpah to declare: "Our new school will someday be bigger than Harvard and Yale?" What sort of man, indeed?

The Lander Legacy is one that cannot yet be fully appreciated. It will take the passage of years to fully assess the impact that Dr. Bernard Lander's life had upon the future of our people. This much I can tell you today. He was a one-of-a-kind *tsaddik*. He saw himself, and the school that he built, as something akin to *Havdalah*. The dividing line between the sacred and the mundane. He stood with one foot planted on either side, a clear reminder that without the work week, there can be no Shabbos and vice versa. *Torah* and *Parnassa*. G-d and man. To understand the importance of this distinction, and to place value on both, is to understand Bernard Lander, the man and giant Jewish leader of our age.

by Dr. David Luchins,
Professor of Political Science and Founding Dean
Lander College for Women / The Anna Ruth and Mark Hasten School:

At the 1968 Orthodox Union Convention, Dr. Lander shared with me his dream of building a special kind of college that would provide appropriate education, in separate divisions, for so many segments of the Jewish and general community. He went on and on, and in my most respectful fashion I said, "Sounds great; call me if it ever happens," and beat a hasty retreat. Two years later he called me. It was happening, and would I join him? It was my first full-time job, and almost forty years later I am still enjoying being a small part of Dr. Lander's dream.

One evening in the spring of 1997, I received a phone call from Dr. Lander urging me to call my Rabbi, Rav Ahron Soloveichik, to wish him a happy eightieth birthday. I was delighted to do so and promptly called Rav Ahron, who asked me how I was aware of this occasion. When I told him that Dr. Lander was the source of my "inside information," he began to laugh and declared, "Historians in future generations will have heated arguments over how many people named Bernard Lander were active during the last half of the twentieth century. No one will even consider that it was just one man; rather they will postulate that there was a Rabbi Bernard Lander who founded Yeshivot and Jewish Colleges, a Dr. Bernard Lander who founded law schools and medical schools, and a lay leader named simply Bernard Lander who was deeply involved in communal affairs. But," said Rav Ahron, "I must add a fourth person for them to ponder: Dov Beresh Lander, who remembers his classmates' birthdays sixty years after they sat together in my father's *shiur* ..."

by Rabbi Doniel Lander, son,
Rosh ha-Yeshivah of Yeshivas Ohr Hachaim and Chancellor of Touro College:

This college (the Lander College for Men) was established against all conventional reasoning, against logical thought. Every penny that went into the construction of this campus was borrowed by floating a bond—a $30 million bond. The objective was to create a campus for a nonexistent program and there were those, including myself, who cautioned my father against forging ahead: "perhaps it will not succeed, it will be a terrible embarrassment to you," I counseled. And there were other members of the Board of Trustees of Touro College who echoed my sentiment. But my father, the heroic leader of Klal Yisrael, responded with: "This is what Klal Yisrael needs." My father did not conduct focus groups. There was no marketing analysis. He didn't even construct a business model. But he followed the lead of Mordechai Hayehudi and forged ahead with a broad vision, courage, and heroic leadership.

by Esther Greenfield, daughter:

My father developed a concept that revolutionized the field of education, offering Jewish and secular education to individuals who in the past never would have considered attending college due to standards of *tznius*. My father built schools for men and women so they could attend after their daily studies at yeshivah or seminaries and pursue degrees in fields of education that previously were never an option for them, such as education, accounting, sciences, and medicine. Thanks to those schools and programs, thousands of *frum* students have been able to take advantage of opportunities in higher education and obtain degrees in the most prestigious of educational fields. Now, *frum* households are able to provide *parnassah* and support themselves with dignity. What a *brachah*!

by Hannah Lander, daughter:

My father loved to travel and enjoyed meeting people from different nations and cultures. He was a "people person." However, he loved Israel the most and wanted so much to contribute foremost to his people—the Jewish people. Every day, the first question he would ask was: "What's new in Israel?" He would always want to hear the latest news from Israel, whether from the media or phone conversations with friends in Israel. The highlight of my father's year was to spend Sukkos in Jerusalem, where he would meet with friends from around the world. We could not walk a step without being stopped by his admirers. Even at an advanced age and legally blind, my father was fearless and would eagerly visit archaeological sites.

From my father I learned the lesson of *kibbud av ve-em*. Growing up, I remember him visiting his parents every Sunday and during the week taking the subway to Washington Heights. He also helped them with their business when they were in their nineties. My father started Touro at the age of fifty-four. He was honored to have his mother, in her late nineties, often sit next to him in his office while he conferred with distinguished visitors.

On a personal level, I always appreciated how—despite my father's full schedule—he manifested his love for me daily, always concerned for my welfare, worrying about what I ate for breakfast, lunch, or dinner or different personal and health issues confronting me. He would not go to sleep without knowing that I was home and safe.

by Debbie Waxman, daughter:

On one occasion, a young man visited my parents' home seeking career guidance. My father asked him, "Young man, what do you like to do?" He stated: "I like to take pictures." My father responded, "If you like to take pictures, why don't you become a photographer? If you enjoy what you are doing and you work hard at it, you will succeed." In fact, this individual did become one of the most successful and popular photographers in the metropolitan area.

My father's wisdom and insight were recognized by all who sought his guidance. When one of my children was conflicted over a decision to pursue various graduate professions, my father stated, "Do what you like; do not be concerned with social or economic pressures. You can succeed and excel in any career as long as you work hard and do your best." To me, this was one of the great messages that my father inspired us with, and that is reflected in the philosophy of Touro College. There are so many opportunities waiting for you; pursue that which interests you, do your best, achieve your potential, and you will succeed.

By Dr. Nathan Lander, brother:

My brother was a dreamer, a doer and an accomplisher.

I remember when he was invited to deliver the derashah in his *shul* when he was very young, and he referred to the pasuk in Lech Lecha, Hashem speaking to Avraham and instructing him: "Look now toward heaven, and count the stars, if you are able to count them. ... So shall your seed be." In his lifetime, my brother followed that instruction, always looking upward with a sense of vision and actively involved in trying to fulfill those visions. I say to you today: "Look now to the world and see the results!" His achievements are worldwide and of historic significance.

by Phyllis Lander, daughter-in-law:

The story of Touro College is a story of miracles. That is a fact that cannot be denied. Who else but my father-in-law, such an optimist, would have the audacity to ask the United States government to donate a building in midtown Manhattan when he had no college, no students, no money and no endowment? But he did! And they gave it to him. They gave that first building, on 44th Street, to Touro, over Columbia University and the City University. Go for it, follow the dictates of your heart. He never panicked. He would always laugh and say, "Don't worry, don't worry, don't worry." "But what if?" "Don't worry," he would always say. And you know, this reassured us and calmed us. We believed him. Things would be okay. We would make it over the hurdles. With him we felt safe and secure, and I think that was the feeling not just of his family but of everybody who built Touro College.

by Dr. Rafi Waxman, son-in-law,
Acting Dean and Associate Professor of Psychology
Touro Graduate School of Psychology:

About two years ago, my father-in-law, every so often, would come to our house for Shabbos. By that time he was very weak. He was blind and weak, but he was very proud. I live around the corner from the synagogue in my neighborhood. It takes me less than a minute to walk to *shul*. Walking with my father-in-law, it took us approximately fifteen minutes to get to the synagogue. This particular synagogue has a Shabbos elevator, and I suggested that we take it, because there are steps to get into the *shul*. He said "No, I want you to see who I am." And he struggled up the stairs, walked into the *shul*, and sat there in all his dignity throughout the davening.

Now the really interesting part of that story occurred when I took him home that night. If you remember his house, there were many steps. Huge numbers of steps to get in, to get out, to get down, and I turned to him and I said, "Maybe it's time to get what they call chair lifts," and he replied, "Yes, maybe when I get older." But he didn't say it as a joke; he said it because that's what he believed. He didn't see himself as an old man. He saw himself as a viable, active man who has a mission and has many years in front of him; perhaps at some point, when he gets old and tired, then he would get this chair lift.

by Dr. Stanley Boylan,
Vice-President of Undergraduate Education and Dean of Faculties at
Touro College:

He taught us how to live. I remember when he called me in and said: "The secret to old age is to live an active life." This was at age ninety-four, six months before his death. He taught us not to withdraw from life, but to embrace it, even as life withdrew from him.

by Josh Waxman, grandson:

I fondly remember when my grandfather took me to Israel for the first time, right after my bar mitzvah. He told me that it was a trip to train me for future Jewish leadership. If one would want to learn how to be a true Jewish leader, all one had to do was watch Zeide in action. I saw how my grandfather worked tirelessly and selflessly on behalf of Klal Yisrael. His door was always open to anyone who needed help.

by Dovid Lander, grandson:

Recently, when he was so sick and could no longer speak, I called to wish him a good Shabbos. While on the phone, he pushed himself to ask me how I am learning. Those were the only words he spoke that entire day.

Ruth Schneider,
Dr. Lander's personal secretary:

Working with Dr. Lander and for Touro College in my heart is an adventure. Every day is something new. It's so challenging and rewarding. It's like riding on the New York subway because you never know what's going to happen next.

When I first came to Touro College, Dr. Lander greeted me with a smile and told me, "Welcome to the Touro family." Despite the frenetic pace required to keep up with Bernard Lander and the work to be done around the office, I never considered leaving. Here, you really are part of a family. I confided in Dr. Lander, and he confided in me. If there was ever anything that I really needed, I knew that I could tell Dr. Lander, and he would take care of it. That feeling is not limited to Touro College's executive offices; it is prevalent throughout Touro College.

In 1982, Prof. Lester Eckman was diagnosed with a brain tumor. Dr. Lander told him not to worry about anything but getting better. During an extended leave of absence, Dr. Lander directed Touro staff to continue paying Professor Eckman's salary and to provide whatever help was possible.

by Dr. Alan Kadish,
President and CEO of Touro College:

It will be to my eternal regret that I was able to spend only two months at Touro before Dr. Lander was first hospitalized. In that time, he provided me encouragement, advice, and a detailed series of instructions …. He passed on his dreams for Touro, his advice about the strengths and weaknesses of branches of Touro, and more than once told me, "You have to be tough." He also enumerated those things he had not yet accomplished—but that was a very short list.

by Dr. Moshe Sokol,
Dean and Professor of Jewish Philosophy:

He always, always learned Torah. But I observed another side as well. I recall back on 44th Street there was a small but sophisticated lending library just down the block. I would accompany him from the office sometimes at the end of a long day, and he would invariably stop off at the library, borrow a book or two, then come back the very next day, return those books, and borrow several more. You see, every day he devoured one or two books on the subway ride to Forest Hills: books on history, politics, biography, psychology, and sociology. He could speak knowledgeably, even brilliantly, about almost any topic.

by Martin Oliner,
Member of the Board of Trustees of Touro College

He was gentle and a gentleman. Bernie had a complete sense of decency. He treated rich and poor, powerful and powerless, in the same caring fashion. He would interrupt a meeting with a major donor to make sure that an elderly employee had a ride home. He was loyal and thankful. He never forgot the assistance that he received from early donors and would call them or their widows almost weekly during the last forty years. Bernie never held a grudge. We spoke about his vilification when Touro started; I can remember a lawsuit brought by a former board member. In incident after incident where he was personally wronged, he was immediately forgiving.

by Rabbi Shmuel Menachem Rabinovici,
Rosh Kollel at Yeshivas Ohr Hachaim:

Some people are aware of the help that Dr. Lander gave to Russian Jews. A couple of years ago, I saw Dr. Lander at my niece's wedding celebration. I was a little surprised; the wedding was in Lakewood, quite a distance away. Afterward, I asked the groom's father why Dr. Lander was there, and he told me that his wife runs a school for girls in Russia and that Dr. Lander was involved in the program. He then kept going on and on about how much Dr. Lander did for the Russian girls. He brought them over, took care of schooling and housing, and took a personal interest in them. He went to their wedding receptions. He just cared. Not many people are lining up to take an active interest and be involved day after day with girls coming from Russia trying to get a little background in *Yiddishkeit* (Jewishness). But Dr. Lander was there. He cared.

by Dr. Marian Stoltz-Loike,
Dean and Professor of Psychology
Lander College for Women / The Anna Ruth and Mark Hasten School:

I remember my meeting with Dr. Lander immediately before I was offered the position of Dean of Lander College for Women / The Anna Ruth and Mark Hasten School. I had been invited to meet with Dr.

Lander in his office. I was coming to the position of dean from my tenure in the business world as a corporate consultant. My clients had been Fortune 100 companies, and I was familiar with meeting senior executives. It was always a very formal affair. My meeting with Dr. Lander was vastly different.

When I arrived, there were four other people in Dr. Lander's office, all involved in their own ongoing meetings with Dr. Lander on topics unrelated to our agenda. Dr. Lander was welcoming to me and engaging. We spoke for a short time while the others in the office waited patiently. It was a unique meeting, and it was only some time later that I fully understood how that first meeting truly provided me with a window on Dr. Lander—his generosity and special character.

The only way that Dr. Lander could accommodate all of those who wanted to meet with him and gather their various ideas was to multitask—run multiple meetings simultaneously or engage in other varied activities at the same time. It might be disorienting to someone unfamiliar with Dr. Lander, but the strategy worked well.

by Melvin Ness,
Senior Vice-President and Chief Financial Officer of Touro College:

For the last ten years, I had the *zechus* to walk Dr. Lander to his car at least three times a week at the end of the day. During those brief encounters, we would often recap the day's events, and he would share his upcoming plans for that evening or the next day. Everyone knows I am a night person, and after those walks I was usually left with a few additional assignments before I would go home. Right now Dr. Lander is probably sitting next to G-d, explaining that He needs to expand the heavens. Don't be surprised when scientists suddenly discover new planets or new wonders of the world. We know where the great dreamer is now!

by Dr. Seymour Lachman, former New York State Senator,
Dean at the City University of New York, and
President of the New York City Board of Education:

Almost two years ago, when Dr. Lander had great difficulty seeing and was already in his nineties, I agreed to meet with him at a Manhattan restaurant to discuss Touro's future plans, academic, spiritual, and physical … I was amazed that a man in his nineties could maintain and even enhance his depth of knowledge and vision for Touro's future. He didn't speak of the present, he didn't speak of the past; he spoke of the future and what programs to offer Touro College students in five years, ten years, and beyond that as well.

by Rabbi Moshe Krupka,
Senior Vice President for College Affairs at Touro College:

Dr. Lander was motivated by a compelling desire to treat every person with dignity and respect. A non-Jewish visitor to Touro from a European country complained of severe headaches while visiting with Dr. Lander. Dr. Lander immediately called a leading Manhattan physician who was a member of his vast circle of contacts. Within minutes, the visitor was on the way to the physician's office in Dr. Lander's car and from there to Mount Sinai Hospital, where a life-saving procedure was carried out. The visitor had no American health insurance. Dr. Lander instructed that all medical bills be sent to his attention.

When Yachad, the OU's national support network for individuals with disabilities, needed a home for its vocational training program for special needs young adults, Dr. Lander agreed to house the program at the Lander College of Arts and Sciences on Avenue J in Brooklyn. He graciously housed the program for years free of charge. His one proviso: "Make this an excellent program; give these developmentally challenged members of our community every opportunity to integrate and succeed within the Jewish and general communities." For Dr. Lander, enabling "the individual" was his life's mission.

by William Kaufman, a college classmate who clearly recalled Bernard
Lander as a student seventy years previously:

"He was always smiling. He had the most beautiful teeth I have ever come across. He not only smiled with his teeth, he smiled with his eyes—a very open guy and very sweet."

by George Affsa,
Touro financial director:

Few people in the world were as well read as Bernard Lander. On one occasion, I was walking with him near the 30 West 44th Street building, and we decided to make a detour to the library. I recommended a lengthy book that I had read, and Dr. Lander took it out. The next day, we were walking the same way. Dr. Lander again suggested we stop by the library. I asked, "Why? You didn't like the book I suggested yesterday?" Dr. Lander told me that he liked it but that he had finished it already. I did not believe it was possible. I started testing Dr. Lander with a few questions and was astounded when he accurately described the book, its characters, its style, and its plot, clearly proving that he had read it cover to cover.

by Rabbi Yitzchak Fund,
Chairman of the Board of Machon Lander:

I ask you, how does a Rabbi/sociologist have the audacity to almost single-handedly establish a university? Is there a course one can take in graduate school entitled University Establishment 101? Is there such a thing? Did Dr. Lander have any experience or the skill set necessary to enable him to do this? I can tell you that his closest friends didn't see it. But Dr. Lander had the dream, the inspiration, and—most importantly—the drive and motivation to actualize that dream. The dream was to provide a framework for *bnei* and *bnos* Torah to develop a potential for parnassah in an institution reflecting Torah values. This dream was burning inside of him for years. He believed and knew that he would be granted necessary *siyata di-Shmaya,* and he was right.

by Dr. Reuven Feuerstein,
Founder and Director of the International Center for the Enhancement of Learning Potential:

I remember the moment when Dr. Lander intended to create a master's degree program in education at Touro College. He asked me to recommend a director for the new program, and he didn't let me go until I called the most promising candidate right in front of him. Within five minutes, Professor Carl Haywood of Vanderbilt University's Peabody College of Education and Human Development became the head of the program that Dr. Lander had planned.

by Dr. Yitzchak Handel,
Dean of Touro College in Israel:

I remember when I once came to visit with him, prior to my being involved with Touro. I was sitting in his office, and the time came for me to leave because other people were coming in, and he said: "No, no; stay here." He wanted to provide me with an image of what should be done in one's life and so he brought in the other guests who were international leaders of Jewish communities, and who were coming to him to ask him to help them raise the level of Yiddishkeit in their communities.

by Professor Robert Goldschmidt,
Vice-President of Planning and Assessment and Dean of Students at Touro College:

My first encounter with Dr. Bernard Lander was in 1974. I was a nervous young man going to a job interview with the president of Touro College, then located on West 44th Street in Manhattan. The building had a manual elevator with a rolling gate that had to be opened and closed by an elevator operator. When I arrived that afternoon, the elevator was being operated by Dr. Bernard Lander. College president and elevator operator—Dr. Lander would assume both roles, reflecting a humble and practical personality. He led a simple life. Unlike other college presidents, he traveled to work by subway, until he was past eighty years.

Eulogies traditionally conclude with the *pasuk* (passage) from *Yeshayahu* (Isaiah) that states that G-d will swallow up death forever. As Rabbi Sherer explained, there is only one way for a person to conquer death: he must dedicate his life to that which has eternal meaning and lives on after our bodies have perished.

Rabbi Dr. Bernard Lander dedicated his life to the *nitzchius* of *kevod Shamayim* (eternal honoring of heaven). He devoted all his efforts to spreading *Yiddishkeit* (Jewishness), to the rebuilding of shattered Jewish communities in Europe, to ensure the eternity of the Jewish people, both in America and in *Eretz Yisrael* (the land of Israel).

And thus Dr. Lander conquered death. Although he is no longer with us, his legacy lives on.

by Rabbi Max Rosenblum, biographer:

On a Shabbos afternoon at Moscow's Marina Roscha synagogue in early 1992, two Jews from New York found themselves sitting next to each other waiting for a quorum of ten men to congregate for the afternoon mincha prayers. Bernard Lander was in Moscow visiting Touro's two new schools. The other man, Joseph Zucker, the owner of a wine business, was in Moscow developing a plan to provide kosher wine to Russian Jewry. Zucker recalled how a friendly man, who appeared to be in his mid-sixties, sat down next to him and introduced himself in Yiddish as Berish Lander. They discussed the weekly Torah reading, the history of the synagogue in which they were sitting, Russian politics, and the revival of Jewish life in Eastern Europe. When Zucker explained the complexities of kosher wine making, he understood from Dr. Lander's questions that he grasped everything immediately. He was not surprised to discover that Dr. Lander was the president of a Jewish university. He found Dr. Lander's friendliness and total lack of pretension more surprising.

Some fifteen years later, Joseph Zucker conceived the idea of launching a kosher wine making institute in France. He remembered his "mincha in Moscow" with Bernard Lander and started rehearsing what he would tell the secretaries so he could get through to Touro's president. He had done his homework and was aware that Touro College had grown into a major school with over 20,000 students on campuses all around New York City, in Long Island, Israel, Germany, California, and Nevada.

After rehearsing his words, he picked up the phone, called Touro and asked the operator for Bernard Lander. A deep, male voice answered with a simple "Hello." Zucker again asked for Dr. Bernard Lander. "This is Bernard Lander, who's this?" Zucker started by trying to remind Dr. Lander where they had met fifteen years previously. Dr. Lander cut him off, "Of course I remember you. How can I help?" Caught off guard by having gotten through so easily, Zucker began explaining his idea of a kosher wine institute. Dr. Lander cut him off again, "This sounds like the type of idea we should discuss in person. Can you come to my office this Thursday at three o'clock?"

When they met, Dr. Lander liked what he heard. Though it did not fit in exactly with the academic programs planned in Europe, he thought it might complement other programs that Touro planned to run in its new campus near Rome. Dr. Lander asked Joseph Zucker what he thought about running the program near Rome rather than in France. Zucker was flexible. Dr. Lander made a few phone calls, and the Institute for the Study of Kosher Wine was established as an affiliate program at Touro's Rome campus.

Over a period of five of Touro College's most difficult years in the latter half of the 1970s, Touro's controller embezzled money to support an addiction to gambling. He endorsed and cashed tens of checks that the bank should never have allowed and Touro's auditors would have caught had they properly reconciled accounts. Soon after joining Touro College in a newly created position as Touro's senior fiscal administrator, George Affsa discovered the theft and found a clear paper trail. With Dr. Lander present, Affsa confronted Touro's controller with the evidence.

The controller admitted his theft and described how he had succumbed to his gambling addiction. Dr. Lander had been working closely with his controller for years. He had placed his trust in him and, naturally, had established a warm relationship. At the same time, it was immediately clear to Bernard Lander that Touro College's difficult financial circumstances had been greatly exacerbated by the thief across the table. Countless days had been devoted to cutting costs and watching the bottom line at the same time that this man had swindled Touro. Another man might have been angry. Dr. Lander's reaction was to cry. He knew the controller had a wife and children, and he feared what would happen to the family if the father went to jail. Such was his boundless compassion, even towards those who had wronged him.

At a celebration in honor of his ninetieth birthday, Bernard Lander explained his approach to life. Unlike Aristotle and other Greek thinkers who believed in the eternity of the world, Maimonides and the Jewish thinkers thought of G-d as the Creator who created the world and continues maintaining and forming it. In commanding us to emulate His ways, the Almighty wants mankind to create. In Bernard Lander's words, "Our responsibility is to leave the world a better world than the world we found when we were born and to continue to create and to do. We achieve the purpose of life by doing and creating. As long as one lives and one has the strength, one has that responsibility." At the beginning of his tenth decade, Dr. Lander pledged, "As long as the Almighty gives me the strength and clarity of mind, I shall continue to build, build, and build."

As he had thirty-five years previously, Bernard Lander spoke of his concern for his assimilating brethren. He spoke of the need for a national and international Jewish university that would serve the Jewish people by building religious Jewish life and would also serve the greater society by providing new options in higher education. Touro College would continue to be built on the philosophy that all Jews are responsible for one another, building Jewish life whenever and wherever possible, and serving mankind whenever and wherever possible. The Judaic tradition teaches that Jews have a responsibility to improve the lives of all people.

Success has led to greater success and has given Bernard Lander tremendous strength. Years ago he wrote, "You know full well the mind of a mountain climber. After climbing the top of one mountain, you visualize the challenge of an even higher peak."

Citations and End Notes

Page 23 ["Other (non-Orthodox) students..."]:
Revel letter to Samuel Levy dated May 1, 1926 as quoted in Rakaffet-Rothkoff, page 81. Samuel Levy was a prominent New York attorney who would later serve as borough president of Manhattan.

Page 36 ("At the time, I had been accepted..."):
Monograph by Bernard Lander, "Mentor of Generations-Eleff, A Lifelong Personal Encounter with the Rav." Nov. 8, 2007.

Page 46 ("Behind the delinquent act..."):
Bernard Lander, "The Prevention of Delinquency," Maryland Commission on Juvenile Delinquency, January 1943, page 3.

Page 51 ("The statistical findings in themselves..."):
Ibid, page 7.

Page 77 ("A quiet and unassuming young fellow..."):
The Shofar published by the Queens Jewish Center (QJC). October 1950, page 6.

Page 78 ("In the last two decades we have witnessed..."):
"Greetings from the President," Building Fund Journal, Testimonial Dinner, Belmont Plaza Hotel, Queens Jewish Center and Talmud Torah Inc., May 5, 1951.

Page 99 ("Approximately three years ago..."):
Bernard Lander to Samuel Belkin, March 7, 1957, Yeshiva University Archives (Collection: YU Graduate Schools, Folder: Dr. Samuel Belkin, 1954-1959).

Page 104 ("As a master of the domain…"):
Yeshiva University, Courtesy of Office of Communications and Public Affairs.

Page 117 ("Today's college student…"):
Bernard Lander, "A Challenge of the American College Campus," An untitled, undated and incomplete draft document matches the contents of a study by this name quoted in the New York Times, March 14, 1971. It also matches a description of Dr. Lander's speech at the Orthodox Union Leadership Conference in November, 1969 as described in Irving Spiegel's New York Times article ("Sociologist Links Jewish Youth Alienation to College," NYT , Nov. 29, 1969, page 17). The draft document may be an early version of the study which seems to have been lost.

Page 122 ("The creative aspects…"):
Bernard Lander to Mr. Leon Levy, March 19, 1973.

Page 128 ("The proposed Touro College…"):
"Touro College: A Proposal for the Establishment of a Baccalaureate Level Liberal Arts Institution in Brooklyn, New York to known as Touro College," submitted September, 1969.

Page 130 ("As you may know…"):
Edward F. Carr letter to Stephen L. Simonian, Regional Representative, Office of Surplus Property Utilization, July 20, 1970.

Page 141 ("Here you will find…"):
Bernard Lander interview.

Page 160 ("Touro's Law School…"):
Bernard Lander, "Touro College: An Adventure in Jewish Commitment," The American Mizrachi Woman, Sept./Oct. 1974, page 6.

Page 162 ("Touro's represents a return..."):

"Report to the Faculty, Administration, Trustees of Touro College by An Evaluation Team Representing the Commission on Higher Education of the Middle States Association of Colleges and Secondary Schools," Spring, 1976.

Page 191 ("Our survival in the midst..."):

Bernard Lander letter to Dr. Samuel R. Weiss, January 17, 1978.

Page 191 ("We are going through difficult days..."):

Bernard Lander Internal Memo to Carol DiBari, November 18, 1975.

Page 193 ("Dear Bernie..."):

Richard J. Sawyer letter to Bernard Lander, Nov. 21, 1980.

Page 196 ("Touro College has made substantial..."):

"Report to the Faculty, Administration, Trustees, Students of Touro College by An Evaluation Team Representing the Commission on Higher Education of the Middle States Association of Colleges and Schools Prepared After Study of the Institution's Self-Study Report and A Visit to the Campus on May 2-5, 1982," pages 12-13. A date stamp on the report indicates it was received on June 18, 1982, six weeks after the site visit and one week before accreditation was reaffirmed.

Page 198 ("The first year of college courses..."):

Sally L.B. Sklar, Director of Senior Adults, Hebrew Educational Society letter to Rabbi Abraham Besdin, June 24, 1976.

Page 203 ("There is significant evidence..."):

"Report to the Faculty, Administration, Trustees, Students of Touro College by An Evaluation Team Representing the Commission on Higher Education of the Middle States Association of Colleges and Schools Prepared After Study of the Institution's Self-Study Report and A Visit to the Campus on May 2-5, 1982," page 2.

Page 216 ("Through the years Touro..."):
Prof. Martin Schechter to Bernard Lander, July 27, 1984.

Page 225 ("The reports from Russia..."):
Bernard Lander letter to Mr. Albert Reichmann, December 6, 1988.

Page 225 ("We are currently..."):
Ibid.

Page 230 ("The threat of a world war..."):
"Prospectus," Touro College, International School of Business and Management, Moscow Branch, 1991.

Page 233 ("I witnessed with my own eyes..."):
Daniel Retter letter to Max Karl, April 14, 1993.

Page 246 ("It is abundantly clear..."):
Bernard Lander letter to Mr. Michael Karfunkel, June 28, 2000.

Page 255 ("We seek to move..."):
Minutes of Touro College Board of Trustees Meeting, February 26, 1998.

Glossary

A

Aliya — (Hebrew) Literally, to ascend or go up. The act of immigrating to Israel or going to the Bimah in order to read from the Torah.

Amalek — (Hebrew) The eponymous founder of the Amalekites, mentioned in the Book of Genesis as enemies of the Jewish people.

B

Bachurai Chemed — (Hebrew) Literally, delightful young men. Sometimes used as name for a synagogue.

Beis Medrash or Beth HaMidrash — (Hebrew) Literally, House of Learning. A term for a synagogue or study hall.

Benching — (Yiddish) Grace recited after meals by observant Jews.

Bet Din — (Hebrew) Rabbinic tribunal.

Beth HaT'fillah — (Hebrew) Literally, House of Prayer. A term for a synagogue.

Bimah — (Hebrew) Elevated platform in a synagogue used during the reading of the Torah.

Bocher — (Yiddish) Student

Bund — (German) Alliance or support organization.

C

Chayei Adam — (Hebrew) Literally, The Life of Man. A work of Jewish law by Rabbi Avraham Danzig.

Chazzan — (Hebrew) A Jewish cantor or vocalist who leads the congregation in songful prayer.

Cherem — (Hebrew) Excommunication or expulsion from the Jewish community.

Chesed — (Hebrew) Kindness.

Chidon HaTanach — (Hebrew) An international Bible contest held annually in Jerusalem.

Chol — (Hebrew) Secular, profane.

Chupah — (Hebrew) Wedding canopy under which a bride and groom stand during the ceremony.

Conservative Judaism — (English) A stream or movement of American Jewry positioned between the strict adherence of Orthodoxy and the liberalized practices of Reform Judaism.

D

D'rasha — (Hebrew) Scholarly sermon.

Daven — (Yiddish) To pray.

Derech — (Hebrew) Literally, the way. Refers to a path in serving G-d.

E–F

El Barrio — (Spanish) Neighborhood or community.

Eretz Yisroel — (Hebrew) The Land of Israel as delineated in the book of Genesis.

Frum — (Yiddish) Religiously observant.

G

Gadol B'Torah — (Hebrew) Literally, big in Jewish law. An erudite Torah scholar.

Galicia — A region in east central Europe. A former province of Austria, it now forms part of southeastern Poland and western Ukraine.

Gaon — (Hebrew) Title of the heads of the talmudical academies in Babylonia (late 6th-early 11th centuries); later used to refer to eminent Jewish scholars.

Gedolai Yisroel — (Hebrew) Great leaders of the Jewish people.

Gemara — (Aramaic) The talmudic commentary on the Mishnah.

H–I–J

Halacha / Halachic — (Hebrew) Jewish law and jurisprudence, based on the Talmud.

Hapoel Hamizrachi — (Hebrew) Literally, Mizrachi Workers. A former political party and settlement movement in Israel and one of the predecessors of the National Religious Party.

Haskalah — (Hebrew) The Jewish Enlightenment. A movement among European Jews in the 18th–19th centuries that advocated adopting enlightenment values, pressing for greater integration into European society, and increasing education in secular studies, Hebrew language, and Jewish history.

Hasid — (Hebrew) Literally, pious individual. A person who is an adherent of Hasidism.

Hasidism — A branch of Orthodox Judaism that promotes spirituality through the popularization and internalization of Jewish mysticism as the fundamental aspects of the Jewish faith.

Havdalah — (Hebrew) Literally, separation. A Jewish religious ceremony that marks the symbolic end of Shabbat and holidays, and ushers in the new week.

Hekhsher — (Hebrew) The special certification marking found on the packages of products (usually foods) that have been certified as kosher (meaning ritually fit for consumption).

Hillel — A famous Jewish religious leader of the late first century BCE, one of the most important figures in Jewish history associated with the development of the Mishnah and the Talmud.

Honoris Causa — (Latin) Literally, for the sake of the honor. An academic degree for which a university has waived the usual requirements, such as matriculation, residence, study, and the passing of examinations.

Ivrai — (Russian) Jew.

K

Ketubah — (Hebrew) Marriage contract.

Kiddush — (Hebrew) Literally, sanctification A blessing recited over wine or grape juice to sanctify the Shabbat and Jewish holidays.

Kiddush cup — A vessel, usually decorated, used during the Kiddush ceremony.

Kipa — (Hebrew) Skullcap.

Klal Yisroel — (Hebrew) The entire Jewish nation, people, or civilization.

Kodesh — (Hebrew) Sacred, holy.

Kotel — (Hebrew) The Western Wall surrounding the Temple Mount in Jerusalem. The only portion remaining after the Temple's destruction by the Romans in 70 CE.

L

La Mano Nera — (Italian) Literally, The Black Hand. A form of extortion racket used by Italian criminal organizations in the early twentieth century.

Leshon hora — (Hebrew) Literally, bad tongue. Malicious gossip.

Litvack — (Yiddish) A person from Lithuania or Lithuanian heritage.

Lux et Veritas — (Latin) Light and Truth.

M

Maven — (Hebrew/Yiddish) Expert.

Mazel Tov — (Hebrew) Good Luck or Congratulations.

Mechitsah — (Hebrew) The partition in an Orthodox synagogue separating men and women during prayer.

Merkaz Ruhani — (Hebrew) The spiritual center. The source for the name Mizrachi.

Meshuginah — (Yiddish) Crazy.

Mezuzah — (Hebrew) Parchment inscribed with verses of the Torah, attached to doorposts in a Jewish home.

Midrasha — (Hebrew) An institute of Jewish learning; seminary.

Mishneh Torah — (Hebrew) Literally, Repetition of the Torah. A code of Jewish religious law (Halakha) authored by the twelfth-century Maimonides (Rabbi Moshe ben Maimon, also known as RaMBaM), one of history's foremost rabbis.

Mitnagdim — (Hebrew) Literally, opponents. The plural of misnaged or mitnaged. The term commonly refers to opponents of Hasidism.

Mizrachi — (Hebrew) An acronym for Merkaz Ruhani. Literally, Religious center. The religious Zionist organization founded in 1902 in Vilnius at a world conference of religious Zionists called by Rabbi Yitzchak Yaacov Reines.

Musmach — (Hebrew) A recipient of rabbinical ordination.

N–O–P

Nedarim — (Hebrew) Vows. Title of a talmudic tractate dealing with the laws of vows and oaths.

Nosh — (Yiddish) Snack.

Ohr Hachaim — Chaim ben Moses ibn Attar, known also as the Ohr Hachaim after his popular commentary on the Pentateuch, was a Talmudist and kabbalist; born at Meknes, Morocco, in 1696; died in Jerusalem, 1743. He was one of the most prominent rabbis in Morocco.

Pale of Settlement — The term given to a region of Imperial Russia in which permanent residency by Jews was allowed and beyond which Jewish permanent residency was generally prohibited. It extended from the eastern pale, or demarcation line, to the western Russian border with the Kingdom of Prussia (later the German Empire) and with Austria-Hungary.

Parnassah — (Hebrew) Livelihood.

Parsha — (Hebrew) The weekly portion of the Torah read during the Sabbath service.

Posek — (Hebrew) the term in Jewish law for a decider — a legal scholar who decides the Halakha in cases of law where previous authorities disagree or are inconclusive, or in those situations where no halakhic precedent exists.

R

Rambam — Moshe ben Maimon called Moses Maimonides and also known as RaMBaM (Hebrew acronym for Rabbi Moshe ben Maimon). A preeminent medieval Jewish philosopher and one of the most prolific and influential Torah scholars of the Middle Ages.

Rashi — Shlomo Yitzhaki, generally known by the acronym Rashi (Hebrew:Rabbi Shlomo Yitzhaki) 1040 – 1105. A medieval French rabbi and preeminent commentator on Torah and Talmud.

Rav — (Hebrew) A rabbi who is a person's religious mentor, or one to whom questions are addressed for authoritative decisions.

Rebbe — (Yiddish) A rabbi, especially a religious leader of the Hasidic sect.

Reform Judaism — (English) A liberalized Jewish denomination founded in 19th century Germany as a response to the Enlightenment and modernity and transplanted to the USA.

Rosh Chodesh — (Hebrew) The first day of the month according to the Hebrew calendar.

S

Sochnut — (Hebrew) The Jewish Agency for Israel, involved with the resettlement of Jews in their homeland, representing Jewish communal and secular interests outside of Israel, and building a global Jewish community.

Sarah Emeinu — (Hebrew) Sarah, our mother. The wife of Abraham in the Book of Genesis.

Schnorring — (Yiddish) Fund-raising or begging.

Semicha — (Hebrew) Ordination as a member of the Jewish clergy.

Shabbaton — (Hebrew) Overnight celebration of the Sabbath usually involving Jewish youth groups.

Shabbos — (Hebrew) the Sabbath or day of rest (also, Shabbat).

Shadchon — (Hebrew) A Jewish matchmaker.

Shamash — (Hebrew) Sexton.

Shanda — (Yiddish) A scandal or disgrace.

Sheva Brachos — (Hebrew) The seven blessings administered during a wedding ceremony.

Shiur — (Hebrew) Lesson or lecture.

Shmatteh — (Yiddish) Literally, rag. Article of clothing.

Shochet — (Hebrew) Ritual slaughterer who prepares meat in accordance with Kashruth, or Jewish dietary law.

Shomer Shabbos — (Hebrew) A Jew who adheres to Jewish law in the area of Sabbath observance.

Shtetl — (Yiddish) Small village.

Shtiebel — (Yiddish) A cozy place of Jewish study, prayer, and fellowship, often in a private home.

Shul — (Yiddish) Synagogue.

Shulchan Aruch — (Hebrew) Literally, The Set Table. The code of Jewish law authored by Rabbi Joseph Karo in the 16th century, which—together with its commentaries—is considered to be the most authoritative legal code of Judaism.

Siddur — (Hebrew) Prayer book.

Siman Tov — (Hebrew) A good sign, a good omen. A congratulatory form of wishing for good things.

Simchas Chasan v'Kallah — (Hebrew) Rejoicing with the bride and groom; sometimes refers to the wedding reception or feast.

Sinarquista — (Spanish) A member of The National Synarchist Union, a Mexican political organization. It was historically a movement of the Roman Catholic extreme right, in some ways akin to clerical fascism and falangism, violently opposed to the leftist and secularist policies of the revolutionary (PNR, PRM, and PRI) governments that ruled Mexico from 1929 to 2000.

Sukkah — (Hebrew) A temporary hut constructed for use during the week-long Jewish festival of Sukkot.

T–U–V

Talmud — (Hebrew) The body of Jewish law and lore comprising the Mishnah and the Gemara.

Tanach — (Hebrew) Hebrew Scripture or Bible which consists of three divisions--the Torah, the Prophets and the Writings.

Torah — (Hebrew) The Five Books of Moses; also, the whole body of Jewish sacred writings and tradition including the oral tradition.

Tractate — (English) A book of the Talmud.

Urim v'Tummim — (Hebrew) A means,associated with the hoshen (High Priest's breastplate), by which the High Priest could seek divine counsel.

Y –Z

Yarmulke — (Yiddish) Skullcap

Yeshiva — (Hebrew) An institution of higher Jewish learning.

Yeshivat Sha'alvim — (Hebrew) A yeshiva near Kibbutz Sha'alvim originally affiliated with Poalei Agudat Yisrael (Agudat Israel Workers).

Yiddish — (Yiddish) The German and Hebrew-based language of Ashkenazi Jews living in Europe.

Yiddishkeit — (Yiddish) Jewishness or Jewish way of life.

Yismach Moshe — (Hebrew) A reference to Rabbi Moshe Teitelbaum (1759 - 1841), who wrote the influential book entitled Yismach Moshe, and who served as the Rebbe of Ujhely in Hungary.

Yom Tov — (Hebrew) A Jewish holy day or holiday.

Zionism — (English) A social, religious, and political movement, with many historical antecedents, that sought to return the exiled Jewish people to a national homeland. Founded as a modern, organized movement at the end of the 19th century by Theodore Herzl.

Index